CROWNED

CROWNED

CORONATIONS FROM QUEEN VICTORIA TO KING CHARLES III

YVONNE COVELL

PEN & SWORD
HISTORY
AN IMPRINT OF PEN & SWORD BOOKS LTD
YORKSHIRE – PHILADELPHIA

First published in Great Britain in 2026 by
PEN AND SWORD HISTORY
An imprint of
Pen & Sword Books Ltd
Yorkshire – Philadelphia

Print ISBN 978 1 03612 815 9
ePUB ISBN 978 1 03612 817 3
ePDF ISBN 978 1 03612 819 7

A CIP catalogue record for this book is available from the British Library.

Typeset in Times New Roman 11.5/15 by
SJmagic DESIGN SERVICES, India.
Printed and bound in the UK by CPI Group (UK) Ltd.

The Publisher's authorised representative in the EU for product safety is Authorised Rep Compliance Ltd., Ground Floor, 71 Lower Baggot Street, Dublin D02 P593, Ireland.
www.arccompliance.com

For a complete list of Pen & Sword titles please contact
PEN & SWORD BOOKS LIMITED
George House, Units 12 & 13, Beevor Street, Off Pontefract Road,
Barnsley, South Yorkshire, S71 1HN, England
E-mail: enquiries@pen-and-sword.co.uk
Website: www.pen-and-sword.co.uk

or

PEN AND SWORD BOOKS
1950 Lawrence Rd, Havertown, PA 19083, USA
E-mail: uspen-and-sword@casematepublishers.com
Website: www.penandswordbooks.com

MIX
Paper | Supporting responsible forestry
FSC www.fsc.org FSC® C013604

CONTENTS

Acknowledgements

First and foremost, I would like to thank His Majesty King Charles III for granting permission for me to use material from the Royal Archive.

I would also like to thank Julie Crocker, Senior Archivist at the Royal Archive, for assisting me in my research at Windsor and for painstakingly answering my questions. Thanks also to Colin Parrish and Sarah Mitchell for helping to locate and prepare many trolley-loads of research materials – it was a privilege to read as many as I possibly could during my allocated research slots up in the Round Tower at Windsor Castle.

My thanks also go to the staff of Westminster Abbey library and archive, including Christine Reynolds, Assistant Keeper of the Muniments, for assisting me in my research, providing access to letters and documents and answering my questions.

I have – very happily – spent many hours, days and weeks in libraries and archives while researching this book, and in particular I must recognise the librarians at the British Library and the National Archive at Kew, for always providing a stellar service, and also the librarians at Islington Central Library, whose excellent and supportive service has made a huge difference to me while working on this book and many other projects over the years.

I would like to thank the team from my publishers Pen & Sword Books Ltd for their dedication and professional expertise, including Jon Wright, Olivia Camozzi and Laura Hirst, as well as Cecily Blench for her patience while copy editing; and Jon Wilkinson for the beautiful cover design.

Throughout my career in journalism and editing – from the heady days of the magazine industry in the 1990s, to the digital world of today – I have been fortunate to work with talented and impressive colleagues. Many of those who became friends along the way have kindly discussed this book with me as it slowly took shape, and I am, as ever, grateful for their insights and expertise.

Thank you to the many friends and family members who have been supportive – and provided light relief when needed. Most especially, my daughter Serena, for her enthusiasm for this project, patience with the long hours it took – and for always bringing the joy. My final thanks go to my parents; this book is dedicated to my father, Paul, and the memory of my mother, Gea.

Chapter One

WHAT ARE CORONATIONS FOR?

When Queen Elizabeth II took her last breath on earth at Balmoral Castle in the Scottish Highlands on 8 September 2022, shortly after three in the afternoon, her eldest son immediately became King Charles III.

The statement issued by Buckingham Palace at 6.30pm that day, announcing the death of Britain's longest-reigning monarch, contained just two brief sentences:

> The Queen died peacefully at Balmoral this afternoon. The King and The Queen Consort will remain at Balmoral this evening, and will return to London tomorrow.[1]

It was an understated message that eloquently conveyed a central principle of the British monarchy: continuity is at its very heart. The flag of the British King or Queen, known as the Royal Standard, is flown wherever the monarch is present – which may include royal palaces when the monarch is in residence, and also cars, ships or public buildings graced with a royal visit. The Royal Standard is never flown at half mast, because we are never without a King or Queen. Following the death of a monarch, custom dictates that the flag will be promptly raised above the new monarch's residence. An exception to this deeply symbolic protocol did occur following Edward VII's death at Buckingham Palace in 1910, when the Royal Standard was flown at half mast for several hours before the new King George V discovered the error.

'The Queen is dead, long live the King.' Continuity without pause. Historically, pauses could be high-risk intervals, during which rival claims to the throne may be made. So the thinking presumably went something along the lines of – 'Best get on with it before any regrettable relatives crawl out of the woodwork.' Back in the Middle Ages, coronations also took place rapidly after the accession of a new monarch, and while that tradition has slipped, the alacrity with which a new sovereign is proclaimed has endured. When William IV died in the night, at twelve minutes past two, in June 1837, a delegation including the Archbishop of Canterbury and the Lord Chamberlain immediately left Windsor for London, travelling through the night. They reached Kensington Palace just after dawn and banged on the doors, demanding to be let in, to inform the late King's niece Victoria that she was now Queen. Why couldn't it have waited at least until the household were up and the young princess, now Queen, dressed? The urgency may be partly explained by suspicions that rival claims to the throne might be made if the news of the King's death spread.[2]

So it was that in the late summer sunshine of September 2022, King Charles III, and his consort Camilla, travelled promptly to London the day after Queen Elizabeth died. On the following day, the new King was formally proclaimed monarch at an Accession Council, before embarking on a pre-planned tour of the United Kingdom.

Perhaps the death of a 96-year-old woman, who had only recently been photographed looking frail, shouldn't come as a shock, but it did mark an unsettling shift in the national mood. Most of us had only ever known one Queen. As we came to terms with the passing of our most enduring and much-admired national figurehead, the new King and the royal family offered ceremony, reassurance, shared grieving and, of course, continuity. It was a smoothly executed programme, give or take a malfunctioning pen or two testing the King's patience, that calmed the unsettled emotions that inevitably accompanied the passing of a woman who most British people had only ever known as the Queen.

Eight months later, by the time of the coronation in May 2023, we'd had some time to adjust to our new national normal. We'd watched as Charles assuredly stepped up. People were by and large accustomed to the man they'd always known as 'Prince Charles' being referred to as

'King Charles'; they'd heard the familiar sound of the National Anthem being sung with the unfamiliar words 'God Save the King'. The couple themselves also had to adjust to their new circumstances. Queen Consort Camilla apparently failed to respond on more than one occasion when addressed by courtiers as 'Your Majesty', realising only moments later that they meant her.

So, what then was the coronation for?

Royal coronations, like royal jubilees, royal weddings and royal funerals, are national ceremonies that help to create and strengthen the relationship between a monarch and their people. In modern times, considerable care has been taken to weave these celebrations into the fabric of society with bank holidays, street parties, concerts and televised events to ensure a long weekend of national celebration. Executed well, coronations can deliver a much-needed sense of occasion for a nation to feel pride in its traditions and a sense of belonging.

Those planning such momentous state occasions have at their disposal an impressive tool kit, from the twelfth-century Gothic architecture of Westminster Abbey, a guest list comprised of the great and the good, historic rituals, religious ceremony, priceless jewels and, of course, the crowns themselves. Courtiers will work round the clock to deliver a piece of theatre carefully choreographed to be utterly appropriate for the monarch and the times they are living in.

'I have to be seen to be believed,' Queen Elizabeth II, by all accounts a shrewd judge of the nation's mood and skilled at relating to her people, was fond of saying. During the coronation, the monarch is not only seen, but seen to wear the regalia of monarchy. Resplendent in the crown and the coronation gown, the new monarch swears a sacred oath, before the head of the Anglican Church, before the assembled congregation and the wider nation, *before God.* When the crown is placed on the monarch's head in such surroundings, with such pomp and ceremony, it is almost impossible not to feel moved. The world sees and believes: this is what a King or Queen looks like.

The visual power of coronations – the importance of the key players' costumes and the pageantry surrounding the event – is a relatively recent element of coronations. Queen Victoria's coronation in 1838 was a major state event and the first to capitalise on the power of involving the public in a wider celebration, and this has become ever more important in modern times. Modern media encompasses not just larger television screens, but the internet and social media. Camera and phone lenses are ready to capture every tiny aspect of the day. But while the technology has changed and advanced, and made everything more immediate, cameras and before them artists and writers have always captured the majestic and magnificent details, as well as the comic and the telling. When, at the 1953 coronation, a camera lens caught Princess Margaret flicking a tiny piece of lint from Captain Peter Townsend's jacket, the casual intimacy of the gesture would expose a relationship at the heart of one of the biggest scandals in royal history.

By the time of Queen Victoria's coronation on Thursday, 28 June 1838, the monarch's role as head of state no longer included significant political power. Monarchs in the modern era 'reign' rather than 'rule'. All the more important that a four-foot-eight-inch, 19-year-old woman who few people had ever seen must regally impress at this historic moment. The splendour of the ceremonial processions, the jewels, the gowns, and the somewhat gruelling five-hour ceremony all helped usher in a remarkably long reign during which the Queen would lose further political power, but nevertheless enjoy huge influence and recognition both in Britain and overseas.

Indeed, when Victoria withdrew from public life for many years after the death of her husband Prince Albert in 1861, the people missed seeing her in public processions. It was the absence of the pomp and pageantry and ceremonial side of monarchy that left a void Prime Minister Benjamin Disraeli eventually persuaded the still-mourning Queen to return to fill. By the end of her long reign, successfully executed Jubilee celebrations had helped cement her relationship with her people.

The twentieth century saw monarchies fall across Europe, following the two world wars, which ended royal dynasties in Germany, Russia, Italy, Austria-Hungary, Greece and Romania, among others. Today, there are ten remaining hereditary monarchies in Europe, including Denmark, Norway, Sweden, Belgium, the Netherlands, Spain, Monaco and Liechtenstein. None still have coronations – typically the monarch swears an oath at the country's seat of government. Some, such as Belgium, have never had crowns as symbols of monarchy, whereas others, such as the Netherlands, have a crown and regalia present at a swearing in ceremony, but the monarch does not actually wear the crown.

In Britain, where Kings and Queens have been physically crowned at Westminster Abbey for over 1,000 years, the coronation ceremony has prevailed. Although at times criticised as 'archaic', better suited to medieval times than modern Britain, there have been no significant moves to abolish or radically reform it. Described by the writer Horace Walpole as a 'puppet show',[3] throughout the eighteenth century coronations were seen as curious relics of the past. George IV, with his lavish coronation in 1821, transformed the event into an extravagant pageant, with little religious significance.

The British way has been to tweak the ceremony rather than overhaul it. When Charles III was crowned in 2023, many things had changed, yet the central elements of the ceremony were almost exactly the same as they were in 1838. In the twenty-first century, an age of sometimes uncomfortable post-imperialism, Britain's status in the world is very different. While usually still listed in the top five or six largest global economies, Britain is no longer the head of a vast, disparate Empire, over which its sovereign served as a unifying figurehead. In its place, though, is a quieter affection for the royal family, and for the ceremonies and traditions that endure. At significant royal events, such as the wedding of William and Catherine in 2011, or the funeral of Queen Elizabeth II in 2022, space must be designated for television crews from all over the world, who want to broadcast the occasion to their viewers watching in countries that have long ago become republics. As the horse-drawn carriages travel past London landmarks, accompanied by scarlet-jacketed soldiers marching, there is a sense that Britain delivers such pageantry well.

Over the course of its long history, the monarchy has of course had to adapt to survive. And during its rocky moments, coronations have been a useful way to reinforce the position of the monarch in relation to their people. At the height of the British Empire, the Crown was an important central symbol, holding a collection of realms and dominions together, and the coronations in the early part of the twentieth century were displays of imperial power and might. The grand scale of the 1953 coronation of Elizabeth II was in many ways a farewell to Empire, as the Commonwealth emerged in its place and times moved on. In one of many tweaks and changes to the wording of the service that have been made over the course of the last six coronations, in 2023, Charles III deleted the word 'imperial' from the order of service.[4]

When, in 1936, the unthinkable happened and Edward VIII abdicated the throne, the fact that he hadn't actually been crowned made the bitter pill that bit easier to swallow. The coronation had not yet taken place. This allowed Edward, under pressure from the government, to disentangle himself from the onerous burden of the crown, and flee across the Channel into the arms of the woman he loved – the country he left behind shocked, but not irreparably so. After all, he was never *actually crowned.*

Due to the extraordinary longevity of Queen Elizabeth II, coronations have been rather thin on the ground in living memory. Most of us cannot recall that day in 1953 when a young Queen took her solemn oath. But those who were around always remember exactly where they were. Many were watching on a friend or neighbour's television set – small crowds gathered in living rooms up and down the country, watching grainy black and white images of Britain's first televised coronation.

Our fascination with royalty is perhaps due to its unique combination of lavish, grand-scale events such as coronations, together with the human, relatable family at its centre. While most of us are never invited to such events, perhaps it is easier to live vicariously when we know the characters involved – their life stages, their relationships, their ups and their downs. In the months preceding the coronation of King Charles III, column inches were given over to explaining the importance of the jewels, the crown and sceptre. Tricky questions were raised over everything from the colonial origins of some of the jewels in the Queen Consort's crown, to whether or not Harry and Meghan would show up.

But what makes a coronation memorable? What aspects of coronation make the event live on in the memories of those watching? And how do successful monarchs draw on their coronations throughout their reigns? For King Charles III, crowned in an era where his subjects are fond of talking about 'making memories', can royalty create the memorable moments strong enough to last a reign and beyond? Will the traditional coronation format, with its unique blend of pageantry, religious devotion and national celebration endure to see King William and Queen Catherine being crowned at Westminster Abbey?

Richard Chartres, former bishop of London and friend of King Charles, writing in the coronation edition of *The Spectator*, wrote of the need for abstract universal concepts such as justice and tolerance needing to be bound together with the energy that comes from community experiences, stories and representative figureheads.[5] To infuse our lives with meaning and purpose, it seems we need ritual and ceremony as well as leadership. In the modern era, coronations reached their pinnacle when post-war Britain united to crown a new young Queen in a magnificent, triumphant celebration. Did it teach us anything about what coronations are for? Over seventy years later, making a speech in honour of his father at the coronation concert at Windsor Castle in May 2023, Prince William quoted his grandmother's words from back in 1953: 'Coronations are a declaration of our hopes for the future.'

Chapter Two

THE NEW YOUNG QUEEN

Queen Victoria's accession to the throne came in the early hours of 20 June 1837. The 18-year-old heir to the throne had been asleep in her bed in her mother's room at Kensington Palace when her uncle, King William IV,[1] died in the night. Her journal records the moment when she found out that she was Queen:

> I was awoke at 6 o'clock by Mamma, who told me that the Archbishop of Canterbury and Lord Conyngham were here, and wished to see me. I got out of bed and went into my sitting-room (only in my dressing-gown), and alone, and saw them.

The word 'alone' is underlined for emphasis. Prior to this momentous morning, Victoria has never been allowed to receive visitors alone, to sleep in her own bedroom, or even to walk down the stairs without holding an adult's hand. There were more changes afoot.

> Lord Conyngham (the Lord Chamberlain) then acquainted me that my poor Uncle, the King, was no more, and had expired at 12 minutes p.2 this morning, and consequently that I am Queen.[2]

Much has been written about the young Victoria's hatred of the so-called 'Kensington System', devised by Sir John Conroy, who was once her late father's equerry and became her mother, the Duchess of Kent's, closest advisor. Victoria disliked Conroy, referring to him as 'a monster and demon incarnate'.[3] As the King's health had declined,

Victoria had been put under increasing pressure from Conroy, often supported by the Duchess of Kent, to sign away her powers. Conroy's ambition was to assume a powerful role when Victoria became Queen, becoming the dominant influence in her court. Remarkably for one so young and isolated, Victoria resisted that pressure, and in fighting and winning that battle she herself emerged a stronger-willed personality. 'Alone', she emphasises and 'Queen', and the twin underlinings speak of determination and of confidence: an 18-year-old girl living in a patriarchal society, who has clearly given some thought to her destiny.

While it had undoubtedly been restricted and lacked the freedom Victoria craved, her childhood had been a pleasant, affluent and indulged one. Her journals record news of outings, special occasions and birthday celebrations. For one birthday, Victoria's beloved nanny, Lehzen, makes her a special doll. She is close to her older half-sister, who she refers to as 'her sister' and 'dearest Feodora' who, along with her half-brother, also lived at Kensington Palace, the home of Victoria and her mother since the early death of her father, the Duke of Kent, when Victoria was just a baby. There was a routine, regular holidays and trips to the seaside.[4]

The news of William IV's death was not unexpected. The King's health had been deteriorating for some time; by the spring of 1837, on one of the few occasions he was seen in public, he was described as looking 'small and aged'.[5] Five days earlier, Victoria added a note to her journal, just before 1.00pm:

> I just hear that the Doctors think my poor Uncle the King cannot last more than 48 hours! Poor man! he was always kind to me, and he meant it well I know; I am grateful for it, and shall ever remember his kindness with gratitude. He was odd, very odd and singular, but his intentions were often ill interpreted![6]

For Victoria, this much-anticipated moment marks an extraordinary coming-of-age, and she resolves to meet the challenge head on. 'Since it has pleased Providence to place me in this station, I shall do my utmost to fulfil my duty.'[7]

Next morning, she met with the Privy Council at Kensington Palace, displaying a confidence that could surely not have been attributed either to her years, or the sheltered life that she had led.

The new young Queen was presented on a balcony at St James's Palace. Few people had known about this tradition, so it was only a small crowd that gathered to see their new Queen, among them Harriet Martineau,[8] an influential writer and activist (and coincidentally a distant relative of Kate Middleton; her father Thomas Martineau was the current Princess of Wales's great-great-great-great-great-grandfather on her father's side). 'There stood the young creature, in the simplest mourning, with her sleek bands of brown hair as plain as her dress,' Martineau recalled. 'The tears ran fast down her cheeks, as Lord Melbourne stood by her side.'[9] Martineau finds herself 'agreeably surprised' by Victoria's appearance: 'The upper part of her face is really pretty, and there was an ingenuous and serene air which seemed full of promise.'[10]

Victoria had just over a year to get used to her new role as Queen, before her coronation took place in Westminster Abbey. For the young Queen it was a remarkable time of change and growth. She writes in her journal of her admiration for the bereaved Queen Adelaide, whom she and her mother call upon at Windsor shortly after the death of Adelaide's husband William IV. 'The Queen is really a most estimable and excellent person and she bears the prospect of the great change she must soon go through in leaving Windsor and changing her position in a most admirable, strong and high-minded manner.'[11] Whether or not it was the Dowager Queen's example that she sought to emulate, Victoria herself certainly managed to project capability and self-possession during this extraordinary time.

Indeed, the new Queen appeared to accept the great change in her own position with a youthful energy and inner strength. Frequently seen in London society, at the theatre, and state banquets, her confidence and air of self-possession were noticed and praised. According to Martineau, Victoria appeared to be enjoying herself: 'It so happened that I never saw her when she was not laughing and talking and moving about.'[12] She kept her old governess Lehzen close, but distanced herself from her mother and acted with strength to deny Sir John Conroy the power in her new court that he had plotted for and believed was rightfully his.

At her side at that first Privy Council meeting, and all significant events at this time, was the Whig prime minister Lord Melbourne, who became Victoria's closest ally during this early stage of her long reign. Most known for being a ladies' man, Victoria was not alone in finding William Melbourne's courteous and attentive manner, handsome dark looks and light-hearted laugh very appealing. Melbourne was good company, and seemed happy to spend time almost daily with the young Queen. Never particularly ambitious, nor especially interested in politics, he seemed content with his new role as mentor, guide and friend to Victoria.

Born in 1789, Melbourne was essentially an eighteenth-century man, now navigating the early part of the nineteenth century in the latter stages of a successful political career. What we now term 'the Victorian era' had only just begun, and those of Melbourne's generation had been shaped by the more rigid social hierarchies of the eighteenth century. Born into a titled Whig family, Melbourne's good looks, charm and family connections had made him a welcome guest of the aristocracy; the titled class whose hereditary privileges included political power as well as land ownership. When Melbourne's wife, Lady Caroline, had died in 1828, he had been at her bedside, despite the couple having separated following Lady Caroline's affair with the poet Lord Byron.

Forty years older than Victoria, Melbourne had lived through some rocky history: the young William Lamb had been 10 years old at the start of the French Revolution, and an impressionable 13 in September 1792, when the National Convention of France announced that it had abolished the French monarchy, giving birth to the French First Republic. As an Eton schoolboy, and Cambridge undergraduate, Melbourne had felt great sympathy with the French.[13]

Lord Melbourne became the chief architect of Queen Victoria's coronation, plans for which he brought to his Cabinet from March 1838. Many of the coronation rituals and traditions that featured in the next five coronations were first seen in 1838, resulting from Melbourne's vision that the emphasis for this historic occasion should be on public celebration. From the outset, he understood that Coronation Day had to deliver for the people and he worked to persuade parliament, and win over detractors.

Melbourne believed that celebrating the coronation of a young Queen would deliver a coup on many levels. By the time Victoria acceded to the throne, the popularity of the British monarchy had suffered. The high points of the Regency period, including the final defeat of Napoleon at Waterloo in 1815, were dimming in the public memory. The monarchy had been dealt a bitter blow on 6 November 1817, when Princess Charlotte of Wales, daughter of the then Prince Regent (later George IV), died at the age of 21. Charlotte had been by far the most popular member of the royal family – her father George IV's self-indulgent lifestyle, and her grandfather George III's mental illness having alienated the public.

Surprisingly, given that King George III had fathered six princesses and seven princes, Charlotte had been his only legitimate grandchild. Three of his daughters never married; three married but never had children; his sons, apart from George IV, were unmarried and instead lived with mistresses. Between them, they fathered an estimated twenty children, but none with a legitimate claim on the throne. This reluctance to marry on the part of the royal dukes was linked to the Royal Marriages Act of 1772. The Act, proposed by George III after what he saw as his brothers' unsuitable marriages, prohibited members of the royal family from marrying without the monarch's consent. Since marrying into the English aristocracy was frowned upon, as it would drag the royals into politics, and Roman Catholics were off-limits, the available pool of suitors was small – effectively you were looking at finding a German prince or princess. The troublesome Royal Marriages Act would later pose a problem for Princess Margaret's desired marriage to Captain Peter Townsend. It was not repealed until 2013, when the Succession to the Crown Act replaced male-preference primogeniture as a criteria for succession; allowed anyone who married a Roman Catholic to retain their place in the succession; and established that only the first six people in the line of succession require the monarch's permission to marry.

Charlotte's father, Prince George of Wales, later George IV, had tried to marry the woman he loved – the divorced Roman Catholic Maria Fitzherbert – only to have the marriage voided under the Act. Forced down the German princess route, he married Caroline of Brunswick in 1795, despite the couple having taken an instant dislike to each other at their first meeting. Drinking heavily to get through the wedding ceremony, the groom ended up drunk in the gutter on his wedding night. Things didn't improve and they wasted little time in separating.

Although Charlotte herself had managed to find happiness through marriage to a German prince, it was sadly short-lived and news of her tragic death in childbirth sparked widespread mourning. It was reported that when he heard the sad news, the poet Lord Byron, residing in Venice, opened his windows and let out a piercing scream over the Grand Canal.[14] The news also forced George III's remaining unmarried sons into an unseemly race to produce heirs. Prince Edward, Duke of Kent, heard the news while at home in Brussels, where he lived with his French mistress of twenty-eight years. Seeing an opportunity to secure funds from parliament to pay off his debts in exchange for a respectable marriage, he took decisive action: breaking things off with his mistress and proposing to Victoria, dowager princess of Leiningen. When the couple later had their baby, Alexandrina Victoria, on 24 May 1819, an heir to replace Charlotte had finally been found.

But there was still work to do to boost the monarchy in the public image. After the death of Charlotte's father George IV in 1830, his brother William IV and his wife Queen Adelaide were crowned at Westminster Abbey, in a coronation that lacked much traditional splendour. William IV had hated the idea of public pageantry and abolished many long-standing coronation traditions, including the coronation banquet in Westminster Hall. As a result, the final bill came to just £30,000. But when it comes to their monarchy, the people want a good show – and were less than delighted at the lack of bells and whistles; the cut-price coronation became known as the 'halfcrownation' and proved a flop.

With his eyes on boosting the monarchy in the public image, Melbourne instinctively pulled away from any suggestion that the 1838 event should follow in the footsteps of the low-key 1831 affair. The most expensive coronation to date had been George IV, crowned on 19 July 1821. Aged 57 when he came to the throne, the eldest son of King George III and Queen Charlotte had already lived a luxurious and extravagant life, periodically running up huge debts. On becoming King after his nine-year stint as Regent due to his father's mental incapacity, George planned his coronation to be the most magnificent ever staged, and the event cost an eye-watering £240,000.[15] His lavish arrangements made no provision for his estranged wife Caroline to be crowned, however, and her attempts to gain access to the Abbey on the day were unsuccessful.

However, the public revulsion at George IV's extravagance meant that this was also not a template to copy.

Melbourne rose to the challenge with a middle-way proposal that would put the young Queen in full view of her adoring public with a large public procession, while offering a budget-friendly compromise in the form of not reinstating some of the coronation traditions William IV had abandoned. These included the coronation banquet at Westminster Hall, and other medieval traditions, such as the ritual of the King's champion throwing down the gauntlet. His proposals did face some opposition – there were questions in the House about the timing, cost and even the necessity of a coronation. One eminent peer, Earl Fitzwilliam, told him that the ceremony 'did very well in the twelfth century but in the nineteenth century it was quite useless', and that the exhibition of a youthful princess to a staring populace was not consistent with feminine delicacy.[16] Some high-profile Tories didn't welcome the new emphasis on public celebration, which they argued would detract from the dignity and solemnity of the occasion. And some anti-monarchist left-wing radicals argued that coronations were simply a waste of money.[17]

Overall, though, Melbourne gained broad support, and it was announced on Saturday, 7 April that the coronation would take place at the end of June, as parliament began its summer recess. The organisers sprang into action, with the Lord Chamberlain anticipating the royal household's needs and seeking quotes for the work that needed to be done from jewellers, robemakers, dressmakers and the like. Meanwhile, the Earl Marshal's office drew up the guest list, issued dress codes and sent out invitations, including to overseas monarchs, prime ministers and governors. As it was not customary for reigning monarchs to make the arduous journey for a coronation, they tended to send high-profile ambassadors. The wealthy nobleman Prince Putbus represented the King of Prussia, the Russians sent Count Stroganoff and Prince Anatole Demidoff; the Duke de Palmella represented the Queen of Portugal and the Marquis de Miraflores made the journey on behalf of the Queen of Spain.

Meanwhile, Melbourne and Victoria continued to spend time together almost every day, and their friendship deepened. A diligent and consistent diary writer from the age of 13, Victoria's journalling style is often clipped and factual. The effusive praise, affection and gratitude she clearly feels for her beloved 'Lord M' therefore stands out in her entries: 'He is a very honest, good, and kind-hearted, as well as very clever man.'[18] She no doubt felt her coronation was in good hands. Nevertheless, so much change at once must have had an impact on someone whose sheltered childhood had hardly prepared her for what she now faced, largely alone. Harriet Martineau claimed that the stresses and strains of this 'lonely' period, now distanced from her mother, but yet to meet her husband, were visible: 'At the end of a year, the change was melancholy. The expression of her face was wholly altered. It had become bold and discontented.' The writer Thomas Carlyle also sympathised with Victoria's plight at this time. 'Poor little Queen!' he declared. 'She is at an age at which a girl can hardly be trusted to choose a bonnet for herself, yet a task is laid upon her from which an archangel might shrink.'

Although the aristocracy still very much had its hold on power, privilege and wealth, by 1838, Britain had already started taking the first steps to giving more people a say in how the country was run. While voting rights would not be given to all adults for another ninety years,[19] the 1832 Reform Act had extended the vote to middle-class men and some skilled craftsmen. It created new constituencies in industrial towns such as Manchester and Birmingham and removed 'rotten boroughs' which had only a handful of electors but had been able to send MPs to parliament.

In the early part of the nineteenth century, society was certainly more accepting of established social hierarchies, more deferential and conservative than it is today. But all monarchies need support and a crowned head of state couldn't afford to be complacent. The public procession from the palace to the Abbey planned for the coronation was a politically savvy move to extend what had been a closed, aristocratic affair to a wider group of people. Scaffolding was erected along the route, to enable spectators to get a better view, and efforts were made to plan entertainments for the large numbers of expected visitors to the capital. On Coronation Day, it was planned that there would be a balloon ascent in Green Park, followed by a firework display at night. There was also to be a four-day fair in Hyde Park and illuminations across the city.

Institutions such as hospitals, workhouses and charity schools laid on special coronation meals and theatres planned to open their doors for free performances.

While there were many around at the time who dismissed coronations as little more than tawdry pageants, Anglican ministers sought to root the occasion firmly within the Church, stressing the ceremony's religious significance. Sermons preached throughout the country strove to emphasise the new Queen's devout nature, and the importance of the coronation's religious aspect. Preaching in Godalming Church, Surrey, the Reverend WR Fremantle[20] encouraged his congregation to think of Victoria as 'God's Minister'; comparing the event to the biblical story of the crowning of 18-year-old Solomon as King of Israel, and the public rejoicing that accompanied the event.[21]

He refers to Victoria as 'a girl of nineteen', and argues that, were it not that she had been chosen by and would serve God, such a lot of fuss might seem ridiculous: 'we might blush to think of the vanity of all this show'.

But, interestingly, it is Britain's imperial status that the Reverend points to to justify the opulent scale of the planned coronation. 'Truly it is no vain and empty show,' he insists.

> Look at this mighty Empire, with her possessions, colonies, and foreign dependencies, spread over the Earth, an extent of dominion upon which it may be said, the sun never sets, embracing at least one fifth of the human race – Millions and millions subject to its rule, and intimately connected with every act of its Legislation.

Pride in Britain's imperial status, alongside the huge job of administering the unwieldy Empire, meant that the coronation must be staged as a global event – the monarchy being a much-needed unifying symbol for what was really a disparate collection of countries and territories. At this time, the British Empire was still expanding, despite already covering large parts of the globe, including Canada, Australia, parts of Africa and Asia. Following the defeat of France in the Napoleonic Wars, which ended in 1815, British naval power had emerged as the most dominant in the world.

Whether or not the British people were deeply exercised by imperial status, or religious significance, as the coronation grew closer, the public mood was buoyant. The nation had a new, young Queen, and the feeling was that this was the dawn of a new era and a time to celebrate.

Although tradition dictated that monarchs were crowned with St Edward's Crown, its weight of 5 lbs was thought to be too heavy for the diminutive young Queen and her slender neck. Instead, a new crown was fashioned, known as the Imperial State Crown, whose frame featured a double circlet of gold with silver jewel settings, and a crimson velvet and ermine band. In appearance, it is similar to the St Edward's Crown, but with a flatter top.[22] At the front, the heart-shaped Black Prince's ruby, worn by Henry V at Agincourt, was surrounded by pearls, emeralds, rubies and a striking sapphire.

London was abuzz in the run up to the coronation, with a huge influx of glamorous and wealthy foreign visitors and fashionable society throwing parties and gatherings. At one party, the French Ambassador, Marshal Soult, came face to face with the Duke of Wellington, who he had fought at the Battle of Waterloo some twenty-three years earlier. According to Charles Greville, the two veterans of the Napoleonic wars met 'with great civilities'.[23]

Those lucky enough to have received invitations were thrown into a frenzy of organising. 'The state of bustle & turmoil which we lived in for a week previously to the great day could hardly I think be exceeded by the Earl Marshal's office,' wrote one lady invitee.[24] 'The messages & notes & parcels & preparations innumerable…' There was chaotic congestion in the capital's streets as people tried to get around in horse-drawn carriages. 'Not a fly or cab to be had for love or money. Hackney coaches £8 or £12 each, double to foreigners,' wrote diarist Mary Frampton.[25]

At Buckingham Palace, the court were experiencing similar pre-coronation nerves, with frenetic activity and last-minute arrangements taking place in an atmosphere described by lady-in-waiting Mary Davys as 'a great confusion' where 'everybody seemed in a state of anxiety'.[26]

It was Lord Melbourne who prepared Victoria herself for the coronation, with its ritual ceremonies. On the day before the coronation, he visited her and she confided her fears: 'I was much afraid that the

Archbishop would not put the crown on properly and well.' This is an anxiety shared by the monarchs who followed her, all of whom were aware of how a sovereign with a wobbly, wonky – or worse, dislodged – crown would look at a coronation ceremony. Melbourne, as ever, reassured her: 'I'll tell the Archbishop to put on the crown firmly!'[27] In the late afternoon, Victoria visited the Abbey, on the advice of Lord Melbourne, who made her try out the thrones, 'which was very fortunate as they were both too low!' Otherwise, she was pleased with the scene at the Abbey and enjoyed the drive back to the palace. 'The preparations for Fairs, balloons etc in the parks quite changes all, and the encampments of the Artillery, with all their white tents, has a very pretty effect.' On return to the palace, she had dinner with her household, guests and the ever-present Melbourne, staying up talking about coronation-related issues until quarter past eleven.

Victoria's visit to the Abbey seems to have reassured her that all would be well on the following day. 'I'm very glad I went to the Abbey, as I shall now know exactly where I'm to go and be etc,'[28] she told her journal. Unfortunately, such confidence would prove to be misplaced…

Chapter Three

CORONATION DAY 1838

The Coronation of Her Majesty Queen Victoria of the United Kingdom of Great Britain and Ireland, Defender of the Faith.

Date:	Thursday, 28 June 1838
Weather:	Fine
Guests:	8,500
Cost:	£70,000

Early morning

At Buckingham Palace, Victoria wakes at 4.00am to the sound of guns firing a twenty-one-gun salute in the neighbouring park. It's been a restless night for the young Queen, during which she woke with 'a feeling something awful is going to happen tomorrow'.[1]

As dawn breaks over London at the start of a fine summer's day, the city is already on the move. Around 400,000 people arrive for the coronation, hopeful of catching sight of the procession, seeing their new young Queen, and finding some merriment on the capital's streets. Many have made use of the country's relatively new rail network to make the journey to take part in the occasion personally. Once in the capital, they make their way on foot to line the route of the processions and visit the fair in Hyde Park.

A short distance from the palace, Westminster Abbey bustles with activity, too. Many of those with a coveted invitation to the coronation ceremony will forfeit a night's sleep in order to arrive early. Some have already been up for hours. 'We got up at twelve pm, dressed, had breakfast and set off at 2am in a nice fly,' recalled one lady, who brought with her 'two little baskets full of provisions viz. biscuits, soup lozenges, chocolate and hard eggs'.[2]

At 7.00am, Victoria gets up and looks out at the 'curious spectacle' of crowds, soldiers and bands amassing.[3] She 'takes a little breakfast' before dressing and a little after. By 8.00am, Victoria's attendants are helping her into her white satin dress with gold-embroidered details and her half-sister Feodora comes into her dressing room. Feodora has come over for the coronation from Germany, where she has lived since marrying a German prince. Although Victoria was very young when Feodora left England, she has maintained a close, loving relationship with her via letters and occasional visits and her beloved sister's presence today is a comfort. At 9.30am, she goes into the next room and greets her half-brother Charles and other relatives and members of her household, all in their robes.

Over at the Abbey, the peers and peeresses, summoned by Her Majesty's command to witness the Ceremony of the Coronation, start to arrive. They appear one by one at first then in quick succession. 'Their dress and appearance was splendid in the extreme,' recalls an onlooker, 'with their beautiful crimson robes and dazzling with diamonds... each carrying a coronet.'

They are conducted to their seats in the areas that surround the Abbey's central Theatre: the Lords Spiritual on the North Side of the Area or Sacrarium; the Lords Temporal in the South Transept; and the peeresses in the North Transept.

Many of the men wear military or official dress; the peers wear robes of state, and the peeresses their most beautiful evening gowns and opulent jewellery. Members of the choir wear white surplices and quaintly attired 'Gold Sticks' act as ushers and assistants to the clergy. There's an air of glamour, of excitement, and of tiredness. Writer Harriet Martineau, seated in the Abbey, says of the dazzling scene:

> About nine, the first gleams of the sun slanted into the Abbey and presently travelled down to the peeresses. I had never before seen the full effect of diamonds. As the light travelled each peeress shone like a rainbow. The brightness,

> vastness, and dreamy magnificence of the scene produced a strange effect of exhaustion and sleepiness.[4]

The processions start to leave Buckingham Palace, and the anticipation among the crowds who line the route builds as the carriages approach. Victoria's German relatives, including her half-sister Feodora,[5] take part, along with high-ranking peers and members of the government, squadrons of Life Guards and their bands, the foreign ambassadors, two bands of the Household Brigade, twelve carriages bearing members of the royal family and household, plus a hundred Yeomen of the Guard.[6] Victoria's mother, the Duchess of Kent, is greeted with enthusiastic cheers and waves. The French Marshal Soult also receives a very warm reception, which will be repeated once he enters the Abbey, where he is very moved by the cheering he receives. Later he confesses to having been completely overcome at the English nation's respect for someone who had fought brilliantly against them, declaring 'this is truly a great people'.[7]

The coaches make steady progress, travelling smoothly through streets lined with soldiers and policemen, the carriage wheels pulled over the newly tarmacked road surfaces, that allow them a speed of around 9 miles per hour.

Eventually, the assembled congregation inside the Abbey hear the twenty-one-gun salute that signals that the Queen has left Buckingham Palace, and it creates an air of excited anticipation as those not yet seated hurry to find their places. The Gold Sticks flit about, while the orchestra tune their instruments.

Victoria rides in the Gold State Coach with her Mistress of the Robes, the Duchess of Sutherland and Lord Albemarle. The ornate coach, originally built for the coronation of George III, is so heavy it needs to be pulled by eight cream-coloured horses. Notorious for its lack of suspension, those inside the coach face a jolty ride along the processional route through Westminster, considered the most impressive part of the capital. They take an hour and a half to reach the Abbey.

Poised and waving at the cheering crowds from inside the carriage, Victoria is struck by how many of her subjects have turned out to see her – so many that at times, she worries for their safety. Houses along the route from Hyde Park Corner to the Abbey have scaffolding erected to enable as many people as possible to climb up and watch and wave. Victoria is filled with love for her people and country: 'How proud I feel to be queen of such a nation.'[8]

In the Abbey, distinguished guests in their finery are shown to their seats, including some of the foreign ambassadors and visiting heads of state who have formed part of the procession. 'All were most superbly dressed, especially the Austrians and Hungarians,' notes one commentator. The Princess Schwarzenberg, wife of the Austrian Ambassador, draws admiration for her 'beauty and superior dress'. But it is Prince Esterhazy of Hungary who steals the show in a velvet coat that is covered in diamonds, on his feet diamond-studded boots, and on his head, a cap featuring a long white feather surrounded by five diamond-encrusted feathers. 'I cannot describe the effect they produced, when after arriving in his place we saw the cap placed on the cushion before him, and the sun shone onto diamond feathers,' recalls a dazzled onlooker.

The three royal duchesses: the now-widowed 62-year-old Duchess of Gloucester, daughter of George III; the Duchess of Cambridge, George III's daughter-in-law and maternal grandmother to the future Queen Mary; and the Duchess of Kent, Victoria's mother, have trains of royal purple. They are supported by their ladies who bear the trains. The Duchess of Kent's train bearer is Lady Flora Hastings.

The Gold State Coach comes to a halt outside the West Door of Westminster Abbey. As Victoria steps down, waiting members of the public glimpse for the first time the diminutive figure in her parliamentary robes, over a simple ivory satin dress. Once inside the Abbey, she disappears from view into the robing room, where her eight train bearers are waiting for her. When she reappears, she is cloaked in her royal robe of crimson velvet furred with ermine and bordered with gold lace, and wearing a gold circlet on her head.

The orchestra strike up the anthem, 'I Was Glad',[9] everybody rises to their feet, and Victoria and her entourage prepare for their walk up the Nave.

The Abbey is dressed for the occasion in lavish, regal style. The ancient stone floor of the Nave – the walkway which extends 166 feet from the Great West Door to the Choir – is covered with rich purple and dark red carpet. The galleries erected on each side, crammed with spectators, are hung with crimson cloth edged with gold. The Queen walks slowly, flanked by her supporters: the Bishop of Bath and Wells on one side, and the Bishop of Durham on the other. Following behind are her 'ladies'; the eight daughters of English dukes Victoria has chosen herself who manage the long purple and crimson train of her robes. The ladies are dressed alike in white and silver gowns with pink rose details. The short trains of their dresses become something of a hazard as they try to avoid treading on them while keeping step with the Queen. Like many involved in the day, one of the train bearers, Lady Wilhelmina Stanhope, will later lament the lack of rehearsal, 'for we carried the Queen's train very jerkily and badly'.[10] They are followed by fifty ladies of rank who hold positions in the Queen's household.

The congregation are now rewarded for their long wait, and can enjoy their coveted ringside seats. Many are struck by the young Queen's poise, as one says: 'a royal maiden of nineteen, with a fair pleasant face, a slight figure, rather small in stature, but showing a queenly carriage, especially in the pose of the throat and head.'[11] Only those who know her well sense the calm exterior masks nerves and apprehension.[12] For others, the diminutive Queen doesn't stand out enough in the crowded procession, which bunches up confusingly.[13]

Looking down on the procession are around 1,000 eager spectators crammed into the temporarily erected upper galleries, which are covered in crimson cloth with gold fringe. As they enter the Choir, Victoria and her entourage are forced to make an unscheduled stop: the Turkish Ambassador has found himself overwhelmed at the sight of the dazzling spectacle before him and has fainted, his unconscious body blocking the path of the procession. He is hastily revived and moved back to his seat, and the Queen continues on her way.[14]

The Westminster schoolboys in the gallery shout: 'Vivat Victoria Regina!'

Victoria approaches the altar, which is heaped with gleaming gold plate. In front of the altar, on a platform covered with gold cloth, is her throne. Her breath comes quicker and her cheeks flush a little,[15] before she kneels before the altar and the assembled congregation fall silent to allow her a few moments of private prayer, before she sits in her chair below the throne.

The recognition

The Archbishop of Canterbury William Howley,[16] who had also presided over the coronation of William IV and Queen Adelaide in 1831, begins the recognition. Turning first to the east side of the Theatre, together with the great officers of state – the Lord Chancellor, the Lord Great Chamberlain, the Lord High Constable and the Earl Marshal – with a loud voice he speaks to the people:

> 'Sirs, I here present unto you Queen Victoria, the undoubted Queen of this Realm: Wherefore all you who are come this Day to do your Homage. Are you willing to do the same?'

The people signify their willingness and joy, by loud acclamations:

> 'God save Queen Victoria.'
>
> Next they turn to the south, west and north, and at each side, repeat the same.
>
> Then the trumpets sound and the orchestra blasts 'God Save the Queen'.

The Queen's wardrobe attendants spread throws and cushions on the floor and steps of the altar, where Victoria then kneels to make her first offering – a cloth of gold, and a gold ingot weighing one pound. These offerings are placed on the altar to acknowledge the higher sovereignty of God, and fulfil the commandment 'Thy shall not appear before the Lord thy God empty-handed'.[17]

She returns to her chair, while the bishops begin the litany, a series of lengthy prayers with responses. At one point, the Archbishop turns to the congregation and goes through the Ten Commandments, after each one leading the congregation in asking for God's mercy for their transgressions. This is followed by a sermon.

The oath

Next, the Queen takes the oath to respect the rule of law, the freedoms of the people and the rights and privileges of the Church.

The Archbishop of Canterbury asks her first to 'solemnly promise and swear' to respect the rule of law. Lastly, he asks:

> 'Will you, to the utmost of your power, maintain the Laws of God and the true profession of the Gospel and the Protestant Reformed Religion established by law? And will you maintain and preserve inviolable the settlement of the United Church of England and Ireland, and to the churches there committed to their charge, all such rights and privileges as by law do or shall pertain to them or any of them?'

The Queen, having a printed copy of the service in her hands, responds:

> 'All this I promise to do.'

As the ceremony proceeds, spectators soon notice that the key players don't always seem to know what they should be doing, where they should be standing or who should say what. The scene unfolding now is a curious mix of traditional, opulent and religious ceremony, combined with an air of chaos. At times, the Queen herself appears confused as to where she should be, and receives inadequate guidance from those around her.

Later, she recalls: 'The Bishop of Durham stood on one side near me, but he was, as Lord Melbourne told me, remarkably "maladroit" and never could tell me what was to take place.'

Commentator Charles Greville remarked: 'the different actors in the ceremonial were very imperfect in their parts and had neglected to rehearse them'. Also in the congregation was young MP Benjamin Disraeli, who noted that the key figures 'were always in doubt as to what came next, and you saw the want of rehearsal'.

During lulls in the five-hour service, the key players could pop into the adjacent St Edward's Chapel where the altar was 'covered with plates of sandwiches, bottles of wine, etc'.

The anointing and crowning

After kneeling at her footstool for a private devotion, Victoria goes before the altar and her attendants remove her robe. As the choir sing: 'Zadok the

Priest and Nathan the Prophet anointed King Solomon and all the people rejoiced…' Victoria takes her seat in the ancient King Edward's Chair, as four Knights of the Garter hold a canopy of cloth of gold over her, and the Dalmatic robe, furred with ermine, is clasped around her. The Dean of Westminster brings the ampulla of oil from the altar, pouring a little into the spoon and handing it to the Archbishop. A recent report in *The Times* has described the anointing as 'more recommended by antiquity than delicacy, and will probably be omitted altogether.' But tradition has prevailed and the Archbishop now anoints the Queen, in the form of a cross on the crown of her head and on the palms of both hands: 'so be you anointed, blessed and consecrated Queen over this people…'

The regalia is brought from the altar and presented to the Queen: the Lord Great Chamberlain first kneeling to present the spurs to Her Majesty. As a Queen, when the sword is presented, Victoria is not actually girded with it but rises immediately to offer it to the altar.[18]

A smaller version of the coronation ring has been made especially for Queen Victoria's coronation – but it has been sized for her little finger instead of her ring finger. The unfortunate Archbishop is determined to complete the ceremony however, and as a result rather unceremoniously forces the ring onto Victoria's finger, saying, 'Receive this ring, the ensign of Kingly Dignity.'[19] Victoria says later: 'I had the greatest difficulty to take if off again – which at last I did with great pain.'

The Lord of the Manor of Worksop has his moment as he hands the Queen the Glove, as is his hereditary privilege to do at coronations, for her right hand to hold the Sceptre. His role is also to support the Queen's right arm when needed.

The presentation of the regalia to the sovereign is not straightforward. Individual items must be collected from the altar and presented by different players in a certain order. Not having rehearsed, things get slightly muddled. Confused, she turns to the Dean of Westminster and asks: 'Pray tell me what I am to do, for they don't know.'

The Archbishop says a prayer, and there is a solemn silence while he makes preparations for the crowning, but then, as he places the Imperial State Crown on Victoria's head, the Abbey erupts in noisy acclamation with rousing shouts of 'God save the Queen'; trumpets sound, the choir sing and the organ and the band play. Cannons fire in nearby St James

Park, other cannons are fired in the Tower of London and the City and the noise resounds through the capital.

At the moment of crowning, the peers and peeresses put on their coronets at the same time. 'The effect of the flashing jewels as this act was performed was startling in its brilliancy.'[20] All except the Duchess of Sutherland who, distracted by a sense that Victoria is going to faint, leans forward and forgets to put on her coronet…[21]

One lady notices: 'the queen as if overcome by the overwhelming sensation of the moment put both her hands before her eyes as if to shut out the scene.'[22]

Victoria is thankful for Lord Melbourne's presence: 'My excellent Lord Melbourne who stood very close to me throughout the ceremony was completely over come at this moment and very much affected. He gave me such a kind (and I may say fatherly) look.'

The homage

Next, the Queen is 'enthroned' – ceremonially lifted into the throne chair by the Archbishop, bishops and officers of state, ready for the lengthy homage in which a stream of senior clergy, princes and peers will kneel before her, swear their allegiance, touch the crown and kiss her cheek or hand.

Looking up to the gallery, Victoria catches Lehzen's eye and the two exchange a smile. The Queen is comforted by the presence of this 'most dear Being'.

The Archbishop is first to kneel and pay homage. Next come the 'Princes of the blood' – Victoria's uncles, the Dukes of Sussex and Cambridge – they touch Victoria's crown, utter the oath of homage, kiss her on the left cheek and retire.

Next come a long line of peers in order of rank: seventeen dukes, twenty-two marquesses, ninety-four earls, twenty viscounts and ninety-two barons. The first of each order kneel before the Queen, while all stand around and, removing their coronets, utter the oath:

> 'I, Duke etc do become your liege man of life and limb, and
> of earthly worship, and faith and truth I will bear unto you,
> to live and die against all manner of folks, so help me God.'

At the end, all will approach the Queen in turn and touch her crown, in a gesture that symbolises their willingness to support it, then kneel and kiss her hand.

When the Duke of Wellington, who led the defeat of Napoleon at the Battle of Waterloo in 1815, approaches to pay homage he receives a loud spontaneous cheer from the patriotic congregation: 'It was grand to hear it and it was grand that the foreigners should hear it,' said one. 'It seemed as if it could never cease; it ceased and was begun again – and the Duke himself looked surprised at it.'

A large, elderly peer, Lord Rolle, has insisted on attending the coronation despite being so infirm that he needs to be held up by two supporters. The congregation are transfixed as the 87-year-old totters upwards and shakily approaches close to the royal footstool; then gasp as he suddenly slips through the arms of his supporters, and rolls over and over down the steps, lying at the bottom coiled up in his robes. The unfortunate peer is helped up to try again and again, to shouts of encouragement, but the effort involved proves beyond his capabilities. Victoria, looking concerned, rises from her seat. She is seen to talk to Lord Melbourne at her side, then moves forward and down a step herself and offers the old man her hand. He is not hurt.[23] Everyone claps and cheers and seems moved at this gesture, as one notes: 'the tribute of respect from youth to age was very striking.'

In these early Victorian times, senior Georgian men are still the dominant force in politics, society and at court. Seven of the Lords paying homage have been around since the time of George II, and this is their fifth monarch.[24] Members of the House of Commons, all men, are predominantly older, landed gentry.

Victoria is particularly moved by Lord Melbourne's homage: 'he knelt down and kissed my hand, he pressed my hand, and I grasped his with all my heart, at which he looked up with his eyes filled with tears and seemed much touched.'

While the homage takes place, the Treasurer of the Household, Lord Surrey, throws gold and silver coronation medals among the thousands of people in the Abbey as a symbol of the Queen's largesse. It results in a rowdy scramble as people fight to get at the coins in an atmosphere of chaos. The gesture will not be repeated in 1902, in the interests of decorum.

The homage over, the Queen descends from her throne. Bread and wine are brought from St Edward's Chapel and the Queen offers this and her second oblation – a purse of gold coins, which are placed on the altar.

There are more prayers, and the Queen removes her crown to take communion. She then replaces it and retires to her throne while the service continues.

The Archbishop prays for 'our sovereign Lady Victoria' and also the Dowager Queen Adelaide, who is not present, and the rest of the royal family.

The Queen eventually retires to St Edward's Chapel with her attendants, where she is disrobed of her Imperial Mantle and helped into the royal robe of purple velvet by the Lord Great Chamberlain. Her confidence in those around her does not improve. 'The Archbishop came in and ought to have delivered the Orb to me, but I had already got it, and he (as usual) was so confused and puzzled and knew nothing – and went away.'[25] Melbourne, who looks tired and unwell, helps himself to a glass of wine.

The procession forms up in the Theatre, and when Victoria joins them, wearing her crown and bearing in her right hand the Sceptre with the Cross and in her left the Orb, they process slowly back down the Nave to the West Door and out to the awaiting carriages. From her carriage, the newly crowned Queen waves to the cheering crowds that line the route back to Buckingham Palace.

Artist Robert Leslie is among those who have gone ahead and are waiting at the palace for the Queen's return. He describes how Victoria, on entering the palace, hears her dog barking. 'There's Dash,' she cries and hurries to 'doff her crown and royal robe, and lay down the Sceptre and the Orb which she carried in her hands, and go and give Dash his bath.'

Back at Westminster Abbey, it takes several hours for many of the guests to make their way to the doors and find their carriages. Little effort has been made to ease the departure of thousands of people, and an atmosphere of chaos and confusion once again prevails.

Archbishop Howley writes a note in his copy of the service. It reads: 'We ought to have had a rehearsal'.[26]

Coronation dinner

In the evening, a dinner for around a hundred guests is held at Buckingham Palace. A relatively small affair compared to the large numbers who have taken part in the day, the guest list does not extend much beyond the court, Lord Melbourne, and those staying at Buckingham Palace. The diners, speaking mostly in French and German,[27] mull over the events of the day.[28] The general feeling is one of tiredness and a sense of relief at the end of a long day that had had a fraught build-up, but the guests speak too about how moved they were by the service they had witnessed. The transformative power of the coronation ceremony has worked its magic. For lady-in-waiting Mary Adams, something intangible has changed: 'It seemed so curious to be dining with the Queen who had just been crowned; she looked just the same as usual but I could not help feeling greater respect for her than ever.'

Meanwhile, Victoria chats to Melbourne on more prosaic matters – she complains that the crown hurt her head, and the weight of the robes has left her tired, and the two gossip about the peers and the peeresses' dresses, and they touch on some of the things that went wrong. Victoria is delighted when Melbourne tells her with tears in his eyes: 'And you did it beautifully – every part of it, with so much taste; it's a thing that you can't give a person advice upon; it must be left to a person.'[29]

Later, Victoria watches the fireworks in Green Park from her mother's balcony, 'which were quite beautiful'. Celebrations take place throughout the country and the Empire, and the whole of the capital is lit up with illuminations. Deterred by the huge crowds and confusion in the streets, no one from the court ventures out to the grand ball thrown by the Duke of Wellington[30] and Victoria finally retires to bed at midnight.

Chapter Four

THE VICTORIAN AGE

The day after the coronation, a hazy exhaustion descended on the court. The general verdict is that the coronation has been well received. 'The coronation went off well,' observed the high-profile diarist Charles Greville,[1] 'where as nobody was satisfied before it everybody was after it.' There was appreciation for the way in which this coronation had encouraged ordinary people to celebrate, indeed 'to amuse and interest them seems to have been the principal object'. Such efforts at mass inclusion were still something of a novel idea in the early part of the nineteenth century.

The many mistakes and mishaps of the unrehearsed ceremony were of course mercilessly raked over, but they didn't necessarily detract from the positive impression the young Queen had made. Indeed, some served to enhance her image in the public's eye. The moment when Victoria moved to help the elderly peer Lord Rolle was much talked about and the Queen's actions praised. Charles Greville described it as 'an act of graciousness and kindness which made a great sensation', and would subsequently help endear the Queen to her people's hearts.

In *Mr Barney McGuire's Account of the Coronation*, humourist poet Richard Harris Barham mocks the bungling moment:

> Then the trumpets braying, and the organ playing,
> And the sweet trombones, with their silver tones;
> But Lord Rolle was rolling; – t'was mighty consoling
> To think his Lordship did not break his bones!

The incident also made it into Romantic artist John Martin's magnificent painting *The Coronation of Queen Victoria*, which depicts the Queen, her attendants and the peers and peeresses, richly robed and luxuriously bejewelled, dwarfed against the dominating Gothic structure of the Abbey.

In common with fellow coronation planners in history, poor Lord Melbourne seems to have found the role both as a key organiser and bearer of the heavy Sword of State rather a strain. Laid low with exhaustion following the big day, he missed his regular catch-ups with Victoria, who was characteristically unsympathetic. Enjoying robust good health throughout her life, other people's ailments tended to irritate her. Her journal notes that it was 'most provoking and vexatious' that her beloved Lord M had cancelled his 'agreeable daily visit'.[2]

Although the celebrations around the coronation in 1838 were limited to the day itself, the Queen and key members of the royal family were obliged to sit for commemorative oil paintings to create a visual record of the coronation. We do not have photographs of the royal family until the 1840s. Painting the Queen's portrait at Windsor a few months after the coronation, the artist Charles Robert Leslie said:

> She sat not only for the face, but for as much as is seen of the figure, and for the hands with the Coronation ring on the finger. Her hands, by-the-bye, are very pretty, the backs dimpled, and the fingers delicately shaped. She was particular also in having her hair dressed exactly as she wore it at the ceremony, every time she sat.

The resulting painting, now in the Victoria and Albert Museum, depicts Victoria kneeling, in profile, with the rich gold of her coronation robes flowing out behind her. It is a picture of youthful innocence, cloaked in history.

For wider scenes of the coronation, others had to sit for Leslie, too, including the royal Dukes and the Duke of Wellington. Leslie was not so complimentary about these sitters, accusing the Duke of Cambridge of asking tiresome questions and the Duke of Sussex of wasting his time by failing to show up to appointments. The Duke of Wellington irked him by insisting on talking about matters he knew little about.[3]

Victoria's relationship with Melbourne continued after the coronation. Her journals reveal that during the first three years of her reign, she saw Melbourne almost daily, and that he frequently stayed at Windsor Castle. But the positive energy, mood of celebration and triumph that the coronation created gradually faded.

Following her coronation, Victoria's relationship with her mother deteriorated.[4] The Duchess of Kent, already bristling from being sidelined in her daughter's new court, was further upset by what she saw as the lack of due precedence she received at the coronation. Victoria continued to rely on her former governess Lehzen as a mother figure, and leaned on Lord Melbourne as a father figure. Strained relationships at court fuelled an atmosphere rife with gossip, rumour and backstabbing.[5]

Early in 1839, the Queen behaved badly towards her mother's long-standing lady-in-waiting, Lady Flora Hastings, who had borne the Duchess of Kent's train at the coronation. When the unmarried Lady Flora appeared at court with a swollen abdomen, Victoria spread rumours that she was pregnant and forced the increasingly unwell young woman to undergo an intrusive medical examination, conducted by two male doctors. When they pronounced that Lady Flora was, as she claimed, a virgin, Victoria's actions looked vindictive. Increasingly unwell, five months later Lady Flora died of liver cancer, which had caused the abdominal swelling, and her family sought to clear her name publicly. The press slammed the Queen's behaviour over an affair in which she had shown immaturity and lack of judgement.

Beyond the court, too, during the early years of her reign, Victoria showed little understanding of her subjects' lives. Although her detachment as monarch remained throughout her reign and served the crown to some extent, as time went on she learnt how to connect and relate to her people more, and her political awareness certainly grew. In 1839, her knowledge of the issues of the day, which included overcrowding in the prisons and troubles in the colonies, including Jamaica, where, in the aftermath of the formal Abolition of Slavery Act in 1833, tensions between farmers and former slaves were rife. Melbourne, whose majority in parliament was slim, was forced to resign. Victoria's popularity took another hit over the so-called 'Bedchamber crisis', when Melbourne's prospective successor Robert Peel asked her to make changes to the make-up of the privileged group of 'ladies' who attended her at court, and she refused because she saw her ladies as friends. The problem was that the ladies were mostly the wives or relatives of Whig politicians, and the Tories wanted a more even balance. As a result, Peel refused to form a government, Melbourne hung on to power until he lost the General Election of 1841, and the Queen was the subject of heavy criticism.

Victoria knew of course that her beloved 'Lord M's' days as her treasured companion were always numbered. After he lost the election, she lost touch with Melbourne, who felt terribly rejected. While he was a significant part of her life and her key advisor between 1837 and 1841, overall, his influence was a brief moment in a long reign. There was of course no shortage of powerful men keen to influence Victoria. Her Uncle Leopold, King of the Belgians and widower of Princess Charlotte of Wales, kept up a regular correspondence with his niece, filling his frequent letters with detailed advice on how to manage her affairs.[6]

Sir John Conroy came to realise that the powerful role he had planned for himself as Victoria's private secretary was not going to materialise. The young woman he regarded as 'an ignorant little child' turned out to be capable of excluding him from her court. As prime minister, Melbourne rejected Sir John's demands for a large pension and English peerage, blocking him from entering the House of Lords.[7]

One subject that Victoria did discuss with her advisors soon after her coronation was whether or not she should marry – she was of the view that there were advantages to her remaining unmarried. Since convention of the time meant that if she did marry, it should be to a royal prince, and not a Roman Catholic, the number of potential suitors was quite narrow. The Dutch royal family, her cousin George Cambridge, who she referred to as 'a disagreeable young man',[8] and her Coburg cousins were possibles, but held little appeal for her. When her cousin Albert visited England, in the autumn of 1839, she felt very attracted to him, and the pair began their romance which led to their marriage the following year.

From the time they were married, and Victoria quickly became pregnant with the first of their nine children, Albert's influence grew. Suffering difficult births and debilitating bouts of post-natal depression, Victoria described being almost constantly pregnant as 'the shadow side of marriage'. She may have been Queen – but her own biology was beyond her control, contraceptive options in the nineteenth century being few and unreliable. Albert took over the reins to a large extent – able, intelligent and ambitious, he became the most powerful consort in the history of the British monarchy.

Among the many ways in which Albert shaped the modern monarchy was in his enthusiasm for presenting the royal family's image as a contented, aspirational unit. The public were treated to glimpses of their home life – with Victoria and Albert at the centre, surrounded by their well-behaved, attractively dressed children. Victoria and Albert were quick to adopt photography, as it evolved from the 1840s, and used images and briefings to promote the image of their domestic contentment. Giving the public this wholesome nuclear family model to look to served to distance Victoria further from the rocky Georgian era, when the behaviour of the self-indulgent 'wicked uncles' threatened the stability of the crown.

At the time of Albert's death, Victoria was inconsolable and felt that the deep mourning that she indulged in over the years that followed to be justified in the light of the immeasurable loss she had suffered. However, even though the monarchy's popularity did dip during the long years when Queen Victoria hid from her public, it did eventually bounce back. Towards the end of her reign, Victoria reconnected with her people, and carried out her role conscientiously, effectively deploying the 'soft power' that monarchs could now wield, and keeping her regal distance from politics. While Prince Albert had been capable, energetic, politically engaged and powerful, the survival of the monarchy may owe more to the *laissez-faire* approach of the austere Queen. By remaining aloof from the Westminster fray, she ensured that the Crown did not become too tangled up in politics. [9]

In contrast to much of the rest of the world, Britain enjoyed relative stability and prosperity during the period. Popular pressure throughout the 1840s and 1850s would lead to the second Reform Act of 1867, which increased the number of men eligible to vote from around one million to around two million. Enfranchising women would not start until 1918.[10] By taking these steps to empower more of the population with the right to vote, the Great Reform Act and its subsequent iterations may well have headed off deeper social discontent. Although during Victoria's reign, direct political power moved away from the monarch, and her ability to influence political life declined, her role as a symbol of Empire strengthened. In 1876, following the Disraeli government's Royal Titles Act, she became Empress of India. Although she never travelled to India, she had a strong interest in the country, learning Urdu and collecting Indian artefacts, and employing an Indian assistant, Abdul Karim.

Queen Victoria's Golden Jubilee, in 1887, and her Diamond Jubilee in 1897, to mark the fiftieth and sixtieth years of her reign, were a huge success. Widely celebrated in Britain and across the Empire, with events, services, fireworks and parties, the jubilees helped Victoria reconnect as a figurehead for her people, and also set the tone for future coronations.

Victoria's relationship with her eldest son and heir, who was always known as 'Bertie', was always troubled. Later, grief-stricken and at times hysterical after Albert's death, her anger turned once again on her son, who she blamed for her beloved husband's final illness. Victoria's rejection of the future King Edward VII would have lasting repercussions.

Chapter Five

EDWARD VII AND THE REINVENTION OF MONARCHY

Queen Victoria passed away in the early evening of 22 January 1901 at Osborne, her home on the Isle of Wight, after a series of strokes. The Queen's whole family had been called to Osborne in the days before her death, so Bertie, her eldest son and heir, was also in residence at the time of his mother's death. Next day, he left for the Accession Council in London to take the oaths of sovereignty. Delivering a speech that he had shaped on the journey from the Isle of Wight, he impressed those present by speaking eloquently for eight minutes without notes. He began by paying emotional tribute to his mother, pledging: 'I need hardly say that my constant endeavour will be always to walk in her footsteps.'

It was now that Prince Albert Edward, who had always been known as 'Bertie', declared his wish to reign as 'Edward VII'. The name 'Albert', he believed, should belong solely to his father. 'I am fully determined to be a constitutional sovereign in the strictest sense of the word,' he told his country, in what was perhaps a message to his detractors as much as his supporters. Now aged 59, and with a reputation as a philanderer and *bon viveur*, as Prince of Wales Bertie had made little effort to win over the public or demonstrate aptitude for the top job. In marked contrast to his mother, who became a teenage Queen, Edward VII had served one of the longest apprenticeships in the history of the British monarchy. Only Charles III would wait longer to inherit the crown.

As the first Prince of Wales to be born since 1762, Bertie's arrival at Buckingham Palace on 9 November 1841 was much celebrated.

His father Albert was present at the birth, but had gone against custom in insisting on removing the prime minister and Archbishop of Canterbury to another room. Despite the welcome arrival of a healthy heir, Victoria failed to bond with the baby, and suffered a prolonged period of post-natal depression. She had not wanted to have another child again so soon after the birth of her eldest daughter Vicky in November 1840, resenting the physical suffering she endured as well as the loss of control bearing children brought. Just a few months after her son's arrival, her low mood received another blow when her old friend and ally Lehzen fell foul of Prince Albert, who dismissed her from his children's nursery.

Throughout his childhood and early adulthood, Victoria went to some lengths to ensure that, as heir to the throne, her first-born son wasn't seen as more important than his father, her beloved Albert.[1] Conscious that Albert was still regarded by many with a degree of suspicion, as 'a foreign prince', she insisted that he should officially be given the title 'Prince Consort', in order for him to take precedence over her son. In reality, Victoria's constant pregnancies combined with her husband's abilities and ambition meant that he became an increasingly powerful consort.

During Bertie's early years in the royal nursery, he was overshadowed by his precocious older sister Vicky, who had mastered both reading and speaking French by the age of 3. Fluency in European languages was expected by Victoria, and within the family German was usually spoken. Even as King, Bertie would always keep the traces of a German accent. Vicky was her father's intellectual soulmate, and Albert dedicated himself to teaching her; the two remaining very close until her marriage at 17 to Prince Frederick of Prussia. Bertie, unable to compete, appeared sadly backward by comparison. His parents worried about him and Albert decided that as son and heir, he must be given a strict education and employed a series of tutors. Bertie was separated from his siblings and tutored alone, without the company of children his own age. It was a system that didn't suit his gregarious personality, and his behaviour became difficult: he would throw angry tantrums and frequently refuse to learn at all.

As a boy growing into his teenage years, Bertie loved to play practical jokes, which could make him seem immature. Little in his behaviour or academic achievements would ever please his mother. In her letters, journal and reported remarks about her eldest son, disappointment was often evident – there was certainly little warmth. As Bertie came of age, he only seemed to cause his parents more anxiety.

Edward VII's biographer Jane Ridley[2] describes the experience of reading thousands of letters that survive between Queen Victoria and her children. These include those the Queen wrote to her eldest daughter, Vicky, after her marriage. These letters to Vicky, Ridley claims, reveal Queen Victoria to be one of the best letter writers of the nineteenth century: able to articulate thoughts and events, with vivid descriptions, candid insights and a deeply human voice. In contrast, Victoria's letters to her eldest son Bertie were angry in tone, frequently judgemental and full of instructions and demands.

Although Bertie appears to have been dutiful in the need to reply to his mother's correspondence, his own letters reveal more a talent for dissembling than the full-disclosure type of exchange his mother – who tended always to say what she thought – desired. Padded out with inconsequential remarks, comments on acquaintances' health and small talk; far from baring his soul, Bertie's letters to his mother reveal above all else a determination to shield his inner life from the critical maternal gaze.

Guarding his personal life became a lifelong habit. Later, as King, he would be more accessible and visible than his mother ever was, yet also more private and unknowable. No letters survive between Edward VII and his wife Alexandra, and we know relatively little about their family life, although Bertie appears to have had a good relationship with their children. While Victoria and Albert actively promoted the idea of 'the royal family', sharing photographs and updates of family activities, this wasn't continued by Edward VII. When your parents are morally respectable, family-orientated, constrained types, how do you rebel? As Prince of Wales, Bertie indulged in many affairs, often at the same time, and after his marriage to Alexandra he had a steady stream of significant mistresses. This aspect of Bertie's private life caused Victoria great concern. Having always seen herself, encouraged from an early age by her mother, as representing a complete break from her unpopular, self-indulgent and promiscuous uncles, including George IV and William IV, it caused her considerable distress to see her eldest son apparently following in their footsteps. At one point she declared Bertie to be 'totally totally unfit… for ever becoming King'.[3]

Towards the end of November 1861, Albert went to Cambridge to see his son who was studying there, and try to sort out the latest sex scandal Bertie had become embroiled in. While there, the Prince Consort caught a cold, which on his return to Windsor worsened, developing into deadly typhoid fever. When he died on 14 December, Queen Victoria was plunged into the depths of despair – her grief overwhelming. She immediately departed for Osborne, leaving Bertie to be the chief mourner at Albert's funeral.

Victoria blamed Bertie and the scandals he had been involved in for Albert's early death at just 42. During her prolonged mourning period, her anger towards Bertie seemed to be triggered by everything from his lack of purpose and application to his lifestyle and looks, which did not resemble her late husband's. Of her eldest son, she wrote, 'I never can or shall look at him without a shudder…'[4] Although neglecting public duties at this time, Victoria remained at the helm of the family, and the activities and marriage prospects of all her children continued to occupy her. For his 21st birthday, Queen Victoria bought her son the Sandringham estate in Norfolk, which he rebuilt and refurbished. In 1863, he was also given £100,000 a year and the palatial Marlborough House as his London residence.

Having survived a miserable childhood, lost the father he loved despite their troubled relationship, and been continually rejected by his mother, who didn't allow him to participate in government affairs, Bertie turned to a life of pleasure. Over-indulging in good food and wine, women, fine tailoring, expensive cigars, racing and gambling became a way of life. The Prince of Wales was regularly seen around fashionable and glamorous European cities, including Paris, Monte Carlo and Biarritz. Back in London, he frequented seedy nightclubs with edgy young aristocrats, a group that became known as 'the Marlborough House Set', and were much gossiped about in the popular press.

Determining that Bertie should marry, Victoria and Albert had already been scanning available foreign Protestant princesses to find him a suitable bride. Now, following her husband's death, the Queen followed up on the promising-sounding Princess Alexandra, eldest daughter of Prince Christian IX of Denmark and his wife, Princess Louise of Hesse-Cassel. Alexandra, known as Alix, seems to have had a fairy-tale-like early life: her family were relatively impoverished royals, living in a draughty old castle. Alix shared an attic bedroom with her sister Dagmar,[5] where the two would sew their own clothes. Alix, of course, was beautiful, charming and kind.[6] Her parents were ambitious for her to marry into the British royal family and were open to the marriage negotiations.

Bertie himself was not consulted on the matter, but Victoria did make the effort to meet Alexandra in advance of the wedding. As she explained to her daughter Vicky, she needed to see 'whether she will suit me'.[7] At an arranged meeting in Brussels, Victoria warmed to the young princess, who was beautiful and gentle, though Victoria noted she was 'sadly deaf'.[8] On her return, Bertie was issued with instructions on exactly how and when to propose, which he dutifully followed. Despite the marriage having been arranged by her, Victoria was keen to promote it as a love match, so Bertie was under pressure to fall in love, as well as marry.[9] Bertie and Alix's wedding took place at St George's Chapel, Windsor, on 10 March 1863, disappointing many who had expected a more public event in London. Queen Victoria attended in mourning and sat out of view of the rest of the congregation. The couple went on to have six children together.

A flamboyant figure, in the years after Albert's death when Victoria hid away, the Prince of Wales was often seen in London society. He enjoyed dressing well, and was considered a fashionable trendsetter. Exuberant and not afraid to be seen to enjoy himself, Bertie's love of life was actually very attractive. He became affectionately known as 'Good old Teddie' and people greeted him warmly when they saw him out on the town. Queen Alexandra became known as a great beauty and fashion leader who was much admired for her sense of style. She was also extremely tolerant and long-suffering when it came to her husband's infidelities. During their marriage, Bertie had relationships with, among others, the actress Lillie Langtry, Daisy, Countess of Warwick and, most enduringly of all, Alice Keppel, the great-grandmother of Queen Camilla.

Inevitably, there were uncomfortable scandals. In early 1870, Lady Harriet Mordaunt, wife of Sir Charles Mordaunt MP, told her husband he was not the father of her newborn baby, naming the Prince of Wales and two of his friends as her lovers. In the ensuing coverage, several of Bertie's letters arranging rendezvous were printed in the newspapers. Bertie denied that there had been any improper conduct between himself and Lady Mordaunt.

In the winter of 1871–72, while staying at Sandringham House, Bertie contracted typhoid fever, the illness that had killed his father. Seriously ill for a while, the public and his family prayed for his recovery, but as he gained strength he quickly resumed his old lifestyle, spending a long convalescence yachting in the Mediterranean. At home, Queen Victoria's own public image was suffering. Now spending the majority of her time at Balmoral, often in the company of her Scottish groom John Brown, people were losing patience with a reclusive monarch and starting to ask questions about why no one ever saw her. What use were a reclusive monarch and a philandering, pleasure-seeking Prince of Wales? Some voices in the radical press were even suggesting Britain should follow the example of France and become a republic.

By the time Bertie succeeded to the throne at the turn of the century, the pace of change for both monarchy and country was rapid. People wanted a much more visible monarch, and this suited Edward VII's style. Always a stickler for formality, placing huge importance on matters of protocol, he planned his first State Opening of Parliament in February 1901 to be a grand public spectacle, travelling there with Queen Alexandra in the Gold State Coach, and reading the speech himself. It was an immediate and marked change of tone from his mother's later years. Queen Victoria hadn't attended a State Opening of Parliament in person for fifteen years. She had attended the ceremony in person just seven times in the forty years since Albert's death, and even then refused the public state procession and didn't read the speech herself.[10]

Although Edward VII's reign was much shorter than Victoria's, as King he contributed many things to the way in which monarchy has since evolved. While a different character may have taken Queen Victoria's low-key sovereignty in the latter part of her reign as a cue to deliver a more ordinary sort of monarchy with the royal family living lives more similar to those of their subjects, Bertie made a deliberate choice to reinvent the idea of monarchy as spectacle. Pomp, ceremony, pageantry and all their trimmings were moved firmly centre stage.

Edward VII, in common with his great-granddaughter Elizabeth II, instinctively understood that the monarch needed to be seen to be believed. Having witnessed how well the jubilees of 1887 and 1897 had been received and also visited the courts of European monarchies, he had clear ambitions about how to do things. He was also passionate about theatrical formality, and could be obsessive about the most minor details of dress, uniforms and protocol. Anything inappropriate or out of place – a decoration, or the wrong hat – were noticed immediately. Punctual himself, he expected everyone else to be on time, and frequently argued with his wife over her tardiness.

His wife may have been long-suffering when it came to her husband's women friends, but as Queen, she projected a similarly majestic, glamorous image. It helped that she was beautiful, well dressed and often showed her light-hearted side. She was a popular figure as Princess of Wales, then Queen and later Queen Mother, when she moved back to Marlborough House after her husband's death. Alix was undoubtedly an asset to Bertie: dignified and charming in public; affectionate and high-spirited at home with her family. She was also confident in her own opinions: she would not entertain the notion of being known as 'Queen Consort' and insisted on being styled as 'Queen'.

The ambition took shape to make the 1902 coronation an event of such unparalleled majesty and splendour it would thrill the British people and overawe the rest of the world. Such ambition for a grand, theatrical occasion would need a strong team of organisers if it was to be realised. The Privy Council duly set up a Coronation Committee, out of which came the Coronation Executive Committee, convened in December 1901. Chaired by the Earl Marshal (the Duke of Norfolk), the executive committee also included the Archbishop of Canterbury Frederick Temple, and Viscount Esher, who had organised the Diamond Jubilee in 1897 and became a driving force behind setting the agenda for the coronation. The organist and choirmaster at Westminster Abbey, Sir Frederick Bridge, was given the position of Director of Music.

The Dukes of Norfolk have the hereditary right to organise coronations and in 1902 this responsibility fell to Henry Fitzalan-Howard, the 15th Duke of Norfolk. As Earl Marshal, Fitzalan-Howard had organised Queen Victoria's funeral, and had taken an active role in organising notable Diamond Jubilee celebrations in the city of Sheffield in 1897. At age 53, he had volunteered for active service in the Second Boer War, and was wounded while fighting near Pretoria. Unfortunately, in 1902, Edward VII appears to have had little confidence in the Duke's organising ability, at one point trying unsuccessfully to have him replaced.

The Abbey itself had undergone much restoration and refurbishment since 1838, and there was a greater reverence for its historical and architectural features, and its role in important public ceremonies. Electricity was installed in Westminster Abbey for the first time in advance of the 1902 coronation. In another key change, it was decided to significantly reduce the number of people in the Abbey, to improve safety and make the event more visually spectacular. There were to be no rows of seats above the High Altar, as seen in 1838. An annexe was once again erected outside the Abbey, to serve as a robing room and for marshalling processions. The 'annexe' was actually quite a grand affair, built in the Gothic-inspired Perpendicular style and adorned with the figures of the six previous 'King Edwards'. Designed to appear as though it was an extension of the Jerusalem Chamber across the Abbey's west front, it was accessed via an octagonal entrance hall, hung with tapestries borrowed from Blenheim Palace, and armoured figures from the Tower of London.

Victoria's long reign meant that by the time her son succeeded to the throne, there were few people alive who remembered the coronation of 1838. One of the few who did have a longer memory was the Princess of Wales's Aunt Augusta, the Grand Duchess of Mecklenburg-Strelitz. Princess Augusta was the daughter of George III's seventh son, and the sister of Princess May's mother. Born in 1822, three years after Queen Victoria, she had married at age 21, to her first cousin Frederick William Mecklenburg-Strelitz, in a ceremony at the private chapel at Buckingham Palace. Although she then moved to Germany, she always retained close ties with the British royal family and was particularly close to her niece, May, now Princess of Wales. Her knowledge and experience, as someone who had both attended and taken a close interest in the coronations of William IV and Queen Adelaide in 1832 and Queen Victoria in 1838, was called upon by the Duke of Norfolk in planning the 1902 coronation.

Aunt Augusta had taken notes. She shared her handwritten record of the coronation of William IV and Adelaide with Queen Alexandra – with instructions as to what the Queen Consort had to do, where she should stand and how she had to move around the Abbey. A traditionalist, Aunt Augusta was not always impressed by some of the changes proposed, and what she saw as a downgrading of the Queen Consort's role, and a failure to stick to the script as she had faithfully recorded it. 'It is extraordinary,' she wrote to her niece, 'that nobody knows anything more about the last Reign but one!'[11]

One area that required a lot of discussion were the proposed routes of the processions, with Bertie eventually deciding on a longer procession through the streets after the coronation, rather than before. As early as January 1902, the route for the coronation procession the following June was published, together with plans for an additional royal drive through London. The information confused Princess May's Aunt Augusta, who wrote to her niece: 'Do tell me when you have time, what the route of the Procession means … are these 14 miles to be passed with the *Crown on the head* … or is it to take place next day? It is impossible to understand what is meant.'

Her niece replied: 'Well, as far as I can make out we only drive to the Abbey & back that day, the following day we drive round the town in open carriages & bonnets … no question of robes and coronets which is an invention of the fertile press … there are limits to one's endurance.'[12]

Coronation dresses for queens had traditionally been very simple – a plain white or cream-coloured dress, reminiscent of ecclesiastical robes, that allowed the coronation robes to take centre stage. However, portraits of Queen Adelaide, the last Queen Consort to be crowned in 1831, show her in her coronation robe over an elaborate tulle gown, with large sleeves, gold embroidery and a stiff collar. In 1902, as excitement grew around a magnificent celebration that not only crowned a King and Queen, but ushered in a new more glamorous age, Queen Alexandra took things a step further. She would not take advice about how to dress for the event, telling courtiers: 'I shall wear exactly what I like, and so shall all my ladies.'[13] Known around the world for her style, the fashion-conscious Queen commissioned a dramatic, show-stopping dress, with fabrics sourced in India. Alix specifically wanted something not 'too conventional or stiff', preferring a gown in the 'flowing style'.[14]

Work began on the Queen's coronation gown in October 1901, but the final design of the dress was kept secret. Queen Alexandra suggested that the dress should be embroidered with the English Tudor rose, the Scottish thistle and the Irish shamrock. Her husband's coronation mantle also featured these national emblems of Britain, embroidered by seamstresses at the Royal School of Needlework, and it's a tradition that has been followed at coronations ever since. Much of the work on the dress was done in India: for five months, forty needleworkers in Delhi painstakingly embroidered the gown's gold net, before it was sent to Paris to be laid over cloth of gold by the female-led Parisian couturier Morin Blossier. The final gown was made of dazzling cloth of gold, with a tulle overlay onto which was sewn thousands of tiny gold spangles. It featured long lace over-sleeves and a wired collar, embroidered with gemstones and pearls in a style reminiscent of sixteenth-century fashions in both Denmark and England.

Meanwhile, the Coronation Committee continued to plot, plan and assign roles and responsibilities: at a meeting in December 1901,[15] they divvied up some of the key jobs to prominent peers: the Duke of Somerset to carry the Orb; the Duke of Richmond to carry the Sceptre; the Duke of Roxburgh to bear the staff of St Edward… One hurdle they faced was how to create a less cumbersome, overly long service. Records that the organisers were able to look at revealed the many mistakes and errors of sixty-five years earlier – though there was no one still around at the Abbey who remembered it.[16] Canon of Westminster Dr Armitage Robinson worked hard to make himself something of an expert on coronations and did much to raise awareness of the spiritual significance of the service.

It was announced in June 1901 that the coronation would take place on 26 June 1902, and in due course invitations went out to over 6,000 guests. As the date drew nearer, London was decked out with stands, barricades, flagpoles and decorations. Foreign representatives began to arrive from all over the world, with large deputations from the countries of the Empire.

Since becoming King, Bertie had thrown himself into the job and become something of a changed man. The idle, philandering Prince of Wales transformed into a workaholic. Reluctant to delegate even routine tasks, Bertie put in long hours, both at his desk in his office at Buckingham Palace, and out on many public engagements. He visited wounded Boer War veterans, personally handing out thousands of medals while insisting on overseeing every detail of his new court himself. The King insisted on rigid order and formality in everything around him, which may have shown a need for control, but he didn't always appear in control of himself. His failure to delegate left him with a never-ending work schedule; he routinely smoked around twelve large cigars a day, as well as twenty cigarettes. He was also eating and drinking more and more, and his girth dramatically expanded.

On 15 June, the King had a bad attack of lumbago and was unable to get up. Next day, Queen Alexandra reviewed 31,000 troops on the King's behalf.[17] On the 17th, Bertie was at Windsor, and due to attend the racing at Ascot. When he failed to appear, word went round that the King had been taken ill. In fact, his belly had become swollen and very painful, but although he saw a doctor at Windsor, he then returned to London to prepare for the coronation, despite his physician Dr Laking's warning that he needed an immediate operation. 'I will go to the Abbey on Thursday if I die there,' protested a devastated Bertie, who knew the effect that postponing the coronation would have on the people. But Dr Laking's reply was unequivocal: 'If your Majesty did go on Thursday to the Abbey, then in all human probability you would die there.' Bertie finally conceded that he was too weak to take part in a lengthy coronation ceremony.[18]

Like most people who were around at the time, the writer J. B. Priestly would always remember the exact moment when he heard the news that the coronation was to be postponed. He recalls being driven at dusk by a farmer in his trap to the railway station, following a visit to his parents in the country, when 'a man shouted the news at us'.[19]

At Westminster Abbey, a final rehearsal for the coronation was about to begin, when proceedings were abruptly halted by the announcement that the coronation was to be postponed, due to the King's grave illness. The announcement was greeted with a shocked silence. Dr Edmund Fellowes, minor canon of St George's Chapel, Windsor, was present and recalls: 'The profound sensation created by this announcement is difficult to describe.' After a short service in which those present prayed for the recovery of the King, the assembly dispersed.

Fellowes made his way to Windsor, sharing the news with several people he met on the way, but found their reaction to be one of disbelief. On arriving at Windsor Castle, he discovered that the news had not even reached courtiers there yet.

Doctors performed abdominal surgery on the King while he lay on a makeshift table erected in his dressing room at Buckingham Palace. After he was anaesthetised, the surgeon cut deep into his abdomen, rupturing and draining a large abscess. This type of surgery was quite risky at the time, and when the news got out, rumours swiftly escalated and people started to gather outside the palace, in anticipation of the King's death being announced. Fortunately, the operation was a success and Bertie made a good recovery. On the following day he was able to write a note to Alice Keppel, asking her to visit, and he also saw his children. He later recuperated for a spell aboard the royal yacht, the *Victoria and Albert* and, although weakened by the whole ordeal, felt ready to fix a new date for the coronation.

The Prince and Princess of Wales had only recently returned from a seven-month tour of British dominions and protectorates, including Gibraltar, Malta, Aden, Ceylon and Singapore, Australia, New Zealand, South Africa and Canada. When the coronation was cancelled, they were called upon to entertain the European royalties gathered in London for the now-postponed coronation. Many distinguished guests, including ambassadors and foreign royals, began to drift back home.

It was announced that the coronation of Edward VII would now take place on Saturday, 9 August. The implications of this delay were many and varied: while the six extra weeks allowed more time for rehearsals and probably resulted in a more coherent event, there were fewer foreign dignitaries than had been expected in June. Those who had made the journey in June had gone back home by August and did not return to London. The service itself was also altered – being shortened further to allow for the King's weakened state.

The postponement of the coronation, as well as the planned naval review, affected thousands of individuals and businesses up and down the country. In London, stands erected along the coronation route were taken down. Many people with houses and businesses along the route had already rented out rooms for the date to those who wanted to secure a good view. The cancellation led to a string of 'coronation cases' in which those who had paid for a spot tried to get their money back. It led to an important common-law precedent that established 'frustration of purpose', where due to unforeseen events, the purpose of the contract is no longer valid. In the high-profile case of Krell versus Henry, a Mr Krell had rented a room to Mr Henry, for the original coronation date, but the contract in place did not actually mention the coronation. Krell therefore argued that he should still be paid. The courts ruled that, since the purpose of the contract had been frustrated, the contract was discharged and Mr Henry was not obliged to pay. This legal principle, first established in 1902, has been used since where exceptional circumstances have arisen, including during the COVID-19 pandemic of 2020 to 2023.[20]

Small town councils arranged emergency meetings to discuss what to do about the coronation celebrations, activities and decorations that had been months in the planning. Some, like the Isle of Man, went ahead with their processions on 26 June, as they had already put up lights and made arrangements – but it resulted in an odd mood as people partied in the streets, while half anticipating that any minute they might hear news of the King's death.

In London, planned coronation dinners for the poor went ahead on 5 July, with around 500,000 people being served a celebratory meal, funded by the King and wealthy donors. These events took place at 800 different locations across the city and surrounds, requiring considerable organising, and it was Bertie's wish that they went ahead.

Asked to compose a piece of music to mark the coronation, Edward Elgar had written the Coronation Ode, 'Pomp and Circumstance', the melody for which became known as 'Land of Hope and Glory' and an important English anthem. On the suggestion of Edward VII, Arthur Benson wrote the words:

> Land of Hope and Glory, Mother of the Free,
> How shall we extol thee, who are born of thee?
> Wider still and wider shall thy bounds be set
> God who made thee mighty, make thee mightier yet.

Due to the postponement of the coronation, the full Coronation Ode was not performed publicly until the Sheffield Festival in the autumn. It was a rousing anthem for an imperial power, though less kind commentators suggested the lyrics referred to the King's expanding girth.

Mortified at having had to postpone the coronation, Bertie was determined that the new August date should see the magnificent celebration he had planned. But, in the corridors of power, anxious aides were whispering to each other about the precarious state of the King's health. Would Edward VII really have the stamina to make it through his own coronation?

Chapter Six

CORONATION DAY 1902

The Coronation of His Majesty King Edward VII of the United Kingdom and the British Dominions, Emperor of India, Defender of the Faith, and of Her Majesty Queen Alexandra, His Consort.

Date: Saturday, 9 August 1902
Guests: 6,600
Cost: £193,000[1]
Weather: Cool, mostly cloudy

Early morning

Across London, people are on the move early as guests make their way to the Abbey and ordinary members of the public try to secure good spots along the processional routes.

Peers and peeresses start to arrive, wearing their robes, over 'full court dress', as instructed by the Earl Marshal. For peeresses, this means white or lightly cream-coloured dresses, with lace, embroidery, or brocade, and feathers and veils, with opulent jewellery completing the look.[2] As the Gold Sticks escort them to their seats, some of the peeresses find their heels getting stuck in the thick pile of the new carpet that covers the old stone floor of the Abbey.

Coronations are still very much the aristocracy's show, and the hereditaries bring their full ancestral tool kits, including horse-drawn carriages, hand-me-down robes, coronets in hand, and accompanying pages – boys aged between 12 and 14, usually sons or other relatives.

But this time, members of the new professional middle classes have been invited, too. The guests who troop into the Abbey include representatives from newly formed professional societies, county councils, the mayors of the London boroughs, and representatives from non-Anglican religious bodies.

In what is quickly dubbed 'the King's look-box', Bertie's women friends have been given prime seats in an upper gallery. Alice Keppel, an important mistress of Edward VII from 1898, is front and centre. In her early 30s, with thick dark hair, alabaster skin, wide shoulders and an ample bust, in common with Bertie's other favourite mistresses, she cuts a powerful, dynamic figure. Red-head Sarah Bernhardt, an actress and skilled self-promoter, stands out in white.

The British Empire, at the height of its power, is well-represented, with three hundred seats given to premiers and governors from different realms and territories. The India Office have been given 183 seats,[3] and India's maharajas, governors and other officers enjoy particular prominence.

The processions

Because of the postponement, many of the foreign royal guests who travelled to London in June have not returned. As a result, the coronation procession is made up almost entirely of representatives from different corners of the Empire, therefore taking on 'something of the character of a family festival', as one peer remarks.[4] There are over 30,000 soldiers marching or lining the route. The procession also includes prominent aides-de-camp and high-ranking officers, including Lord Kitchener.

The King and Queen make their way from Buckingham Palace to Westminster Abbey, riding in the Gold State Coach, pulled by eight cream-coloured horses. On arrival, they retire into the robing room. The King is attended to by the Lord Great Chamberlain, and emerges in his crimson velvet robe, furred with ermine, over a crimson satin tunic, breeches and crimson satin stockings. On his head, the Cap of Estate, also of crimson velvet.

In the royal box, overlooking the High Altar, two young boys – Prince Edward and Prince Albert of Wales, aged 7 and 6 – chat animatedly about the scene they see in front of them, waiting for their older family members to emerge from the Choir after their walk up the Nave. Soon, the daughters of the King appear: Princess Louise, Princess Victoria and Princess Maud – none of whom are very well known to the public. They are followed by the King's sisters – Princess Helena, Princess Louise and Princess Beatrice, Queen Victoria's youngest daughter. Unlike her sister Louise, Beatrice is not particularly close to her brother, the King. The sibling relationship isn't improved today when, during the ceremony, she accidentally drops her prayer book from where she is sitting in the royal gallery and it crashes down onto a table below laden with gold plate. The Grand Duchess of Mecklenburg-Strelitz, Princess May's Aunt Augusta, is one of the few attending who were also at the previous coronation sixty-five years earlier.

Next come the ruling families of the Continent, who process up the Nave and take their seats in the Choir. They are followed by the Prince and Princess of Wales, wearing their robes of estate, accompanied by their entourage. Princess May attracts admiring glances, with her heavy purple velvet and ermine train being borne by her two ladies wearing white satin dresses, with feathers and diamanté embellishments.

The Queen and her attendants bearing her regalia – the Rod with Dove, the Queen's crown and the Sceptre with the Cross – begin their walk up the Nave. Queen Alexandra cuts a dazzling figure: the beads on her gold dress shimmering in the light as she moves, framed by the richly heavy robe of purple velvet and ermine.[5] Her layers of stunning jewellery include her diamond necklace and earrings, given to her by her husband as a wedding present, and the ornate Dagmar necklace, a wedding gift from the King of Denmark. Heavily made up, on her head is a cap of purple velvet, rimmed with ermine and with a circlet of gold adorned with precious stones. She is wearing a wig to cover her baldness, but at the age of 56 she is still beautiful – and appears to the watching eyes as a 'fairy-tale queen'.[6] Breaking with tradition, her train is borne by page boys rather than maids of honour.

Behind her follows her husband and his attendants, bearing the coronation regalia, including the Sceptre, Orb and crown. Attending to the train of his robe are six eldest sons of peers. The King walks briskly up the Nave – and has to be urged to slow down a little. With his portly stature, full beard and dressed in his robes and cap of maintenance, the watching Westminster schoolboys think he looks exactly like Henry VIII.[7]

Hubert Parry's spine-tingling arrangement for the traditional coronation anthem 'I Was Glad' is having its first outing, but musical director Sir Frederick Bridge misjudges the timing and the anthem is finished too early. Quick-thinking organist Walter Alcock improvises until Bridge directs the choir to repeat the anthem, which is based on Psalm 122, 'I was glad when they said unto me, Let us go into the house the Lord.' Parry's arrangement incorporates the traditional Westminster boys' 'Vivats' to thrilling effect.

'Vivat Regina Alexandra! Vivat! Vivat!'

'Vivat Rex Edwardus!' shout the Westminster schoolboys, then realising they have shouted too early, they repeat the cry.

By now the congregation is still and a hushed silence has descended in the Abbey. The King and Queen enter the Theatre and kneel on their faldstools in private prayer before sitting in their Chairs of State.

Music takes a more prominent role in this coronation, with several new pieces composed for the ceremony performed by the 400-strong choir and orchestra of eighty to great effect.

The recognition

The Archbishop of Canterbury presents the King to each side of the Abbey's theatre, repeating the traditional words of the recognition, and the people respond with loud acclamation: 'God Save King Edward.'

The altar is majestically adorned with gold plate, some of which has been secured from the Tower of London for the occasion. The striking opulence sparks pride in country: 'there was a brilliance of colour,' one of the official artists present recalls, 'a facet of a rich and mighty country's character is exposed on such an occasion.'[8]

Just as in 1838, the altar is prepared with throws and cushions for the King to kneel and make offerings of a pall of cloth of gold, and a pound-weight ingot of gold.

The service begins with a series of prayers and responses.

The oath

The King uncovers his head and the Archbishop asks him:

> 'Sir, are you willing to take the oath usually taken by your predecessors?'

The King replies: 'I am willing.' He is then sworn in, taking the same oaths his mother did as a 19-year-old. The congregation is silent, and some of those watching are moved to tears. Afterwards, he kisses the bible and signs the oath.

The anointing and crowning

After more prayers and responses, the choir begin the anthem 'Zadok the Priest', which is the signal for the King to rise and approach the altar. The Lord Great Chamberlain removes the King's robe before he takes his seat in St Edward's Chair, and a gold canopy is held over his head by four Knights of the Garter. The ampulla, containing the consecrated oil from the altar is handed to the Archbishop who proceeds to anoint the King with the oil, in the form of a cross, on the palms of his hands, on the breast, on both shoulders, and between them and on both arms. The Dean of Westminster then dries with cotton wool all anointed parts, except the head, and closes the King's garments. Afterwards a silk cap is put on the King's head and linen gloves on his hands.

The investing

The Dean of Westminster brings symbols of royalty for the King to wear, including the Colobium Sindonis – a simple white sleeveless coat, and the coronation girdle, into which the sword is fastened. The Sword of Offering is then presented to the King, who delivers it to the Lord Great Chamberlain.

Next, the King, now sitting again in St Edward's Chair, is approached by the Archbishop of Canterbury, Frederick Temple who, at the age of

81 has insisted on retaining his prominent role in the service, despite his obvious frailty and the toll it appears to be taking. The Archbishop is nearly blind, so his words are written out in large letters and held up before him by one of the bishops.

Due to his recent illness, Bertie, to his disappointment, is too weak to support the weight of the traditional St Edward's Crown – and it is with the lighter Imperial State Crown that Temple crowns him now. It is the Dean of Westminster, the Archbishop's principal assistant at coronations, whose job it is to fetch the crown from its place on the High Altar. But when the Archbishop turns hopefully to receive it, he finds the Dean, who is almost the same age as him and equally doddery, has wandered away with it. When he does manage to retrieve the crown, the congregation watch for an agonising moment as the frail Archbishop appears to fumble and nearly drop it. Finally, with trembling hands he holds it above the King's head before, to everyone's relief, he manages to lower it into position. Unfortunately, it's been placed back to front, and now the Archbishop has to be assisted by supporting bishops to correct it. Reassurance comes from Bertie himself: 'It is very difficult to put it on rightly,' says the King kindly.[9]

A loud cheer breaks out, with shouts of 'God Save the King!'

At the moment of crowning, the newly installed electric lights are turned on for the very first time to spectacular effect. At times, Queen Alexandra appears in an extraordinary blaze of golden light, as her dress with its metallic thread and gold spangles glows in the electric light.[10]

The Abbey and its surroundings erupt in theatrical acclamation as trumpets sound, the bells ring and gun salutes are fired.

The King removes his linen gloves before the Archbishop of Canterbury blesses the coronation ring, a symbol of kingly dignity, and places it on the King's finger.

The glove is presented by the Lord of the Manor of Worksop for the King's right hand – this time the white leather is embroidered in red, white, blue and gold, depicting a crown, with floral details. It also displays the arms of the Duke of Newcastle, who had bought the Manor of Worksop in 1839, shortly after Victoria's coronation. With the glove in place, the King accepts the Sceptre.

The ceremony of the swords takes place, and the choir sing the 'Te Deum', the traditional hymn of gratitude and praise.

The homage

The King is enthroned in the traditional way and, now elevated and wearing the crown, he is ready to receive the homage. Attempting to fulfil his role as the first to pay homage to the newly crowned sovereign, the frail Archbishop gamely approaches the throne and attempts to kneel but is clearly finding it a struggle. Eventually, on his third attempt, he succeeds, but finds he cannot get up again and has to be lifted. Throughout the ceremony, the bishops find themselves quite literally in supporting roles: on a number of occasions preventing the Archbishop from falling. Several times they go to his aid at the request of the King himself, who is heard to say: 'I am very anxious about the Archbishop.'[11]

When the Prince of Wales does his homage, and approaches to touch his father's crown, the King unexpectedly reaches out to hug him, and kisses him twice. Despite their very different lifestyles, father and son are close and Bertie has worked hard to ensure their relationship is an improvement on his relationship with his own parents.

The peers pay homage in their hierarchical order, ending with the barons. To shorten proceedings, they say their homage together with others of their order, then each one approaches the King to touch the crown and kiss his hand.

During an interval in the service, the King is seen drinking some soup.[12]

The Queen Consort's coronation

Now it is Queen Alexandra's turn to approach the altar, where she kneels beneath her gold canopy which is carried by the Duchesses of Marlborough, Sutherland, Portland and Montrose. The Duchess of Sutherland is the sister of Daisy, Countess of Warwick, who as one of Edward VII's long-term mistresses sits watching in the upper gallery.

The Queen's circlet is removed. In a scene captured by the painter Laurits Tuxen, the four tall duchesses stand very straight: all are wearing the same long white dresses with gold embellishments, crimson robes, with ermine mantles, long white gloves, strings of pearls at their necks and tiaras perched atop upswept curls. Alexandra's six pageboys kneel behind her, still holding the long train of her robes.

At her husband's insistence, Alix is crowned by the Archbishop of York, William Maclagan, in an attempt to limit the duties of the frail Archbishop of Canterbury. There has been some opposition to this move, with its lack of historical precedent, but the King's views have prevailed. Alexandra has asked the Archbishop of York to anoint her with the holy oil on her forehead, rather than her hair – since she is wearing a wig, and her religious beliefs decree that the anointing oil must touch her skin. Maclagan rather inelegantly performs the task, and trickles of oil run down the Queen's nose. Her ladies undo the Queen's robes for the Archbishop to anoint her breast.

The canopy is removed and the Archbishop places the ring on the fourth finger of her right hand. He then takes the crown from the altar and holds it with both hands above the Queen. This is a new crown, made especially for Queen Alexandra, and is set with a selection of her own jewels as well as a stunning centrepiece – a jewelled cross into which is set the spectacular Koh-i-Noor diamond. As the Archbishop brings the crown slowly down onto the Queen's head, lightning flashes from the diamond shoot across the Abbey's theatre.

At the moment of the Queen's crowning, the 400 peeresses put on their coronets – a rather tricky manoeuvre for those who have chosen to wear tiaras. As in 1838, this is a dazzling moment, likened to a dance of swans as the ladies raise their white-gloved hands at the same time. The King will remember this as the most impressive part of the ceremony.[13]

The newly crowned Queen is handed her Sceptre and Ivory Rod and, carrying them back to her seat, she bows when she passes the King.

The choir sing as the newly crowned King and Queen descend from their thrones to receive communion, after which they move to St Edward's shrine, where their crowns are placed upon the altar by the Archbishop. Afterwards, the King and Queen withdraw and the King is helped out of his sacred vestments and arrayed in the robe of purple velvet, furred with ermine, while out in the Theatre the procession forms up.

The procession

Their Majesties and attendants process back down the Nave to the West Door, where carriages await. Around one million people are now gathered on London's streets, expectantly waiting to witness the promised spectacular procession and maybe even get a glimpse of the King and Queen.

The longer route back to the palace passes under triumphal arches, erected by members of the Empire along the route, which goes from Parliament Square, along Whitehall to Trafalgar Square, along Pall Mall, St James's Street and Piccadilly to Hyde Park Corner, and then down Constitution Hill to the palace. Originally intended to include contingents from Germany, Austria-Hungary, Denmark, Russia and Portugal, these representatives had to return home after the coronation was postponed. But the procession is still impressive, with large military contingents from across the British forces, plus around 2,000 members of the Indian military and other colonial and dominion forces.

Those left in the Abbey face a long and uncomfortable struggle to get home. Arrangements to facilitate the huge numbers leaving at the same time are hopelessly inadequate. Some exhausted guests whose carriages have gone astray are invited into the houses within the Westminster precinct, occupied by Abbey staff, for refreshment.

Balcony appearance

On their return from the Abbey, King Edward VII and Queen Alexandra appear on the Buckingham Palace balcony, to greet the waiting crowds, who cheer, sing and wave flags.

It's the first time that the monarch has appeared on the balcony following their coronation, but is another feature of the day that will be copied by all future monarchs.

Chapter Seven

A Popular King

The 1902 coronation was pronounced a success, with broad acknowledgement that it achieved what it set out to do. Critics, including those who had questioned the relevance of having a coronation, calling it an anachronism, had been answered. Thanks to the mix of splendour, solemnity and traditional rites, the effective staging of the event had re-established its central importance in the lives of the Church, the state and its people. Commentators remarked on the solemnity of the service, the moving rituals and, above all, the regal bearing and apparent reverence of the King himself.

Those at the heart of the coronation undoubtedly felt the transformational effects of the ceremony. 'Nothing in the world comes up to it,' wrote Queen Alexandra, in a letter to her daughter-in-law, Princess May. 'How beautiful & solemn it was & quite ineffaceable from one's mind for ever – & the heavenly music – adding to it all.'[1]

Those involved in staging the coronation have many loose ends to tie up. Sir Arthur Ellis was kept busy for many months in the coronation planning office, dealing with queries, upsets and unpaid bills. Much of his correspondence during this time now sits in the Royal Archive[2] and makes for fascinating and varied reading. Alongside settling accounts from councils, who are entitled to their share of the King's Dinner Fund and chasing down missing coronation robes, he is obliged to correct a claim from Bovril, who have tried to gain a bit of unofficial royal endorsement for their popular hot drink by claiming that the refreshment the King enjoyed in the Abbey was in fact their very own product. 'It might interest you to learn that we have been informed that in the interval of the coronation in Westminster Abbey, his majesty took a cup of Bovril, and handed one to the Archbishop of Canterbury,' they wrote to their suppliers.[3] In response, Sir Arthur explains that the King in fact drank a specially prepared soup from the palace kitchens.

Bertie used the coronation as a moment to generously bestow honours on many of his subjects – in total handing out 1,540 awards including peerages, baronetcies, privy councillorships and knighthoods. He also formally gave the Osborne estate on the Isle of Wight to the nation. Already financing the running of the private estates at Balmoral and Sandringham, Bertie decided that he didn't want to hold on to the house that his father Albert had energetically restored. Parts of Osborne were subsequently used as a training college for naval cadets,[4] as Britain further built up its already mighty navy in response to Germany's ambitions to build up its own navy and become a world power.

Continuing the imperial theme of the celebrations, British naval power was on display at a naval review at Spithead on 16 August. Although many naval reviews took place during Queen Victoria's reign, including to celebrate the Golden and Diamond jubilees, this is the first time such an event had been staged to mark a coronation. British maritime dominance was evident in the huge fleet of warships that stretched for miles between Portsmouth and the Isle of Wight.

Sandringham in Norfolk continued to be a favourite retreat for Alix and Bertie and their family after the coronation. While he had never been particularly fond of Osborne, Edward VII and Queen Alexandra both enjoyed Balmoral, where they would spend a month each autumn. The King and Queen liked to immerse themselves in Scottish traditions during their Highland stays, when Bertie would wear a kilt and invite bagpipers to play while they dined.

Early in his reign, Edward VII created the Order of Merit, as distinct from the many titles and honours that were bestowed on politicians and patrons, it was awarded solely on merit in recognition of distinctive service towards the advancement of the Arts, Learning, Literature or Science. Regarded as Britain's highest honour, the Order is restricted to twenty-four members and is still going today – current members of the Order include Sir David Attenborough.

Bertie insisted that Alix was made Lady of the Order of the Garter, overruling objections that women were not admitted into the Order. Queen Alexandra continued to be a popular figure who undertook much charity work, but her deafness, her husband's reluctance to delegate or share duties, and his close friendships with other women inevitably left her rather isolated and she spent increasing amounts of time at Sandringham.

The invention of royalty as spectacle at the 1902 coronation mirrored what was happening elsewhere in Europe. In the run up to the outbreak of war in 1914, imperial pageantry was the order of the day in Europe's most prominent cities.[5] In reality, the British Empire was already in decline by the early years of the twentieth century. Across the Atlantic, America's burgeoning economic strength was becoming apparent, and Italy, Germany, Portugal and Spain were rival colonial powers in Africa.

However, the renewed emphasis on ceremonial also helped Edward VII position the monarchy as an institution that served all of the people – rather than simply the pinnacle of a small aristocratic class. Dubbed 'King Teddy', his visibility helped him to become a popular monarch and he enjoyed support from all classes. People warmed to the new King's ebullience and enthusiasm after Queen Victoria's drab and austere persona in her later years.

At the time Edward VII came to the throne, Britain's international popularity was low. The ongoing Boer War in South Africa had seen General Kitchener oversee a strategy that had resulted in Boer farms being burnt to the ground and women and children moved into poor conditions in concentration camps where many died.[6] Extremely divisive, the British government's imperialist agenda failed to gain widespread support, even at home where 'Pro-Boers' sympathised with the South African farmers whose skill in defending their homes prolonged what the British military leaders had assumed would be a short conflict.

Edward VII, through his own frequent travels in Europe, and through his family connections, was very European in outlook. In France he was known as 'the Uncle of Europe', due to his being related to so many foreign royals. In the decade before the First World War, he saw himself as a diplomat – able to speak to European ministers, royals and influential figures with his characteristic bonhomie. This did cause some tension with the British government, who wanted to control the agenda, and their King more closely at times, though it was widely acknowledged that the King's support and courting of the French assisted in better relations between Britain and France, that would lead to the Entente Cordiale in 1904.

The Edwardian era in Britain was one of remarkable stability, relative to the rest of the world. The monarchy appeared to benefit from Edward VII's visible enjoyment of prosperity, and indeed life itself. The court expanded during his time; based firmly in London at the lavishly redecorated Buckingham Palace, those fortunate to receive an invitation to one of the glittering evening receptions enjoyed champagne and dancing to a live band. While Bertie was dedicated and conscientious in carrying out his constitutional duties, he didn't forgo a life of pleasure to do so. He continued his relationships with women, visited Biarritz in the spring, and enjoyed racing, yachting and good food and wine. With the austere, often dreaded Victoria gone, he seemed to relish life all the more, and he enjoyed being King.

Of course, the King's reputation went before him and reports in the expanding press weren't always favourable. While Queen Victoria had been able to direct journalists as to what to say, Bertie did not have that luxury as the press started to run more royal stories, and became less interested in being flattering. He was called 'Edward the Caresser' due to his very public affairs, and mocked for his overindulgence in food and drink. The American writer Henry James, who took British citizenship, denounced Edward as 'an arch-vulgarian' and foresaw that his reign would be 'all vulgarity and frivolity'.

But, as King, Edward VII surprised people. Although he remained obsessive when it came to adherence to the formalities of court and dress, in other areas he was more relaxed and indulgent of the people around him. The writer J. B. Priestly, author of *The Edwardians*, remembers being a child when Edward VII succeeded and says, 'I can testify to his extraordinary popularity. He was in fact the most popular king England had known since the earlier 1660s, the first years of Charles II's Restoration.' Priestly argues that his extrovert, anti-intellectual approach to life actually made Bertie connect well with his subjects – if the King 'could not read books, he could read people'.[7] He paints a picture of a liberal-minded man who 'changed the whole look and feel of the monarchy' and even facilitated social reform.

The term Edwardian still conjures golden-age images of high-society parties during an era that has been dubbed a 'long summer afternoon'. This is a myth, of course: the vast majority of the British population never attended a country house tennis party, sipped cocktails at glamorous evening soirées, or were served eight-course dinners by attentive butlers and footmen, *Downton Abbey* style. But it was undeniably a period of growing prosperity and relative peace, with a King who clearly enjoyed life. Those who lived through the horrors of the First World War understandably often felt nostalgic about the Edwardian era, contributing to its enduring image.

Edward VII's years of high living took their toll, and he succumbed to chronic bronchitis, dying at Buckingham Palace on 6 May 1910 at the age of 68. When Bertie was dying, it was Alix who sent for Mrs Keppel, her husband's favourite mistress for some years, in order that she could say goodbye. A quarter of a million people filed past Edward VII's coffin to pay their respects as it lay in state at Westminster Hall.

This theme of imperial might reflected through the pomp and pageantry of coronation was to continue throughout the twentieth century.

Chapter Eight

STEPPING UP

Queen Victoria had reigned for twenty-eight years, four as a widow, when she welcomed a new grandson into her large extended family. The future George V was born unexpectedly early on Friday, 3 June 1865. As the second son of the Prince and Princess of Wales, the new baby was greeted by his family and the country as a welcome 'spare'. The baby's father, Bertie, the future Edward VII, was present at the birth, which happened at the family home of Marlborough House in London.

Though still deep in her prolonged mourning for Albert at this time, Queen Victoria was still very much head of the family and took a detailed and often critical interest in her children and grandchildren's lives. The new baby's christening was postponed due to Victoria's dislike of the name 'George' with its associations with her disreputable Hanoverian relatives, from whom she had always tried to distance herself and her family. But Bertie stood firm, though he did add 'Albert' to the new prince's names as a concession.[1]

George's mother Alexandra, the woman he would always call 'Motherdear', was a gentle, beloved influence in George's childhood. Unusually for her time and class, Alexandra was an affectionate mother, happy to look after her own children, and keen for them to experience the freedoms of her own Danish childhood. His father Bertie, on the other hand, had no interest in repeating formats from his own unhappy early years, and was content to leave the nursery to his wife.

George and his brother Eddy, who was just seventeen months older, grew up together. The boys were first schooled at home by a tutor, the Reverend John Neale Dalton, to whom George was close and remained so – he would go on to write affectionate letters to Dalton for over fifty years. Dalton instilled a love of routine, tidiness and order – the attributes George would be associated with as King, and no doubt helped him to feel safe and in control.[2]

At the age of 11, George was sent, together with Eddy and Dalton, away from home to continue his education aboard the *Britannia* naval training ship, which was moored in the river Dart. Their father had made the decision due to his frustration at the boys' lack of academic progress at home – Eddy in particularly seemed to learn little – and reluctance to send them to a school. The navy was the traditional career route for a second son, so combining private lessons with Dalton, while learning the ropes as a naval cadet, seemed to make sense. Life on board the old wooden sailing ship was regimented, and often harsh, with the princes becoming the targets for bullies. Lessons were practical and designed to create good sailors – navigation, seamanship and maths were taught, but creative subjects such as music and art were not. George coped well with the curriculum, passing the final exams in April 1879; Eddy, on the other hand, had shown no interest in the lessons, was accused of 'feebleness' by his tutor, and failed the exams.

Next came a spell aboard the navy warship HMS *Bacchante* on which George would travel the world and pass his midshipman's exams. The boys shared a cabin, but were allowed only very limited contact with the other cadets – George had few friends as a child, but he did have the constant presence of Eddy, a close attachment to his valet, Fuller, as well as his tutor, Dalton. He clearly loved his mother, Queen Alexandra, dearly – writing affectionate letters to 'My Darling Motherdear' and once describing her as 'the most beautiful woman I have ever seen'.

Continuing his naval career, George joined HMS *Canada* in June 1883, for the first time without the brother with whom he had shared a bedroom all his life. He found himself homesick and missed Eddy, to whom he writes: 'I can't tell you *how* strange it seems to be without you and *how* I miss you in everything all day long.'[3]

George's relationship with his father, the high-living, self-indulgent Bertie, who would serve his long apprenticeship as Prince of Wales until George was 36, was affectionate but more distant. In comparison with Eddy, who was more sensitive and less physically able, George's robust, more sociable personality made him easier for his parents to deal with. As George grew up, it became apparent that he had inherited few of his father's tastes and personality traits, in many ways seeming to actively choose a polar-opposite lifestyle for himself. How do you rebel against a flamboyant, high-living, philandering father? George disliked dining out, ate and drank moderately, enjoyed home life, did not enjoy travel, struggled to learn French and German, despite Queen Victoria's insistence that he should do so, and was famously quoted as saying, 'I'm not interested in any wife except my own.'

Although friendships outside the family were discouraged – Queen Victoria was suspicious of them – the practice of royals marrying European royalty meant that George had a wide, cosmopolitan network of relations to connect with across the continent. While on leave from the navy, George would visit his mother's Danish family in Denmark, and enjoy the company of his Russian cousins. Since childhood, he and his cousin Nicky, the Tsarevich of Russia, whose mother was Queen Alexandra's sister, had formed a strong bond. Sharing many common interests as well as looking almost identical, they always enjoyed each other's company and became firm friends.

In January 1892, George was at Sandringham, still recovering from a nasty bout of typhoid fever that had laid him low for weeks, but well enough to enjoy time with his family to see in the New Year and celebrate his brother Eddy's 28th birthday. But during the break, Eddy started to feel unwell and soon afterwards he took to his bed. The doctors were summoned and, after examining the stricken Eddy, diagnosed pneumonia and influenza. A recent flu pandemic had killed around one million people worldwide and, although the worst was over, it had not disappeared yet. The illness ravaged Eddy's body and mind, leaving him weak and delirious. While his distraught family were at first hopeful of a recovery, as the days passed, it became clear that Eddy was dying. In the early hours of 14 January 1892, George was woken by his father and he gathered with his parents and sisters around Eddy's bed for a sad vigil. 'Oh!, how shall I ever forget that dreadful scene all of us sobbing round him as if our hearts would break,'[4] George's diary entry reads.

The shock and sadness that George felt on the death of a beloved brother was only compounded by the sudden change in his own position.

Like his son King George VI and granddaughter Queen Elizabeth II, George V was not born to be crowned. Raised as a second son, and anticipating a naval career combined with a peripheral public profile as a relatively minor royal, aged 26, he found himself catapulted directly into the line of succession. Everything changed for him at this point.

While still trying to come to terms with the painful reality that he would never see his beloved Eddy again, George did what was expected of him and stepped into his dead brother's shoes. Queen Victoria, on her 73rd birthday in May 1872, made George Duke of York, Earl of Inverness and Baron Kilarney. The old Queen, with her dynastic antennae fully intact, turned her attentions more fully to George's future. His first household staff were appointed and arrangements were made for him to move into Eddy's apartment at St James's Palace. She continued to push him, largely unsuccessfully, to learn French and German – it was her belief that senior royals should be fluent in both, in order to network effectively with their relations in the courts of Europe. Of course, Victoria was not slow to remind her new second-in-line-to-the-throne that he needed a wife. George had a couple of romances with suitably well-connected young women, including the charming, high-spirited Xenia, the sister of his Russian cousin, Nicky. But Queen Victoria had other plans, and summoned him to Osborne, where she talked to him at length about 'May of Teck', the woman to whom Eddy had been engaged when he died. The daughter of an Austrian-born nobleman, Prince Francis, Duke of Teck, and Princess Mary Adelaide of Cambridge, a granddaughter of George III, May had been hand-selected by Queen Victoria, from what was a very small pool of potential brides. Having suddenly lost her future when her fiancé Eddy died, the 25-year-old May managed to maintain warm relationships with the royal family, which led to another arranged courtship with her dead fiancé's brother. It may have helped that, as those who knew her suggested, she was always poised and ambitious, but not passionate enough to truly fall 'in love' with either prince.[5]

The couple married on 6 July 1893 in the Chapel Royal, St James's Palace. Among the 300 or so guests crammed into the small space was cousin Nicky, who was also staying at Marlborough House with George and his family. At this time, the two bearded cousins looked almost identical and were often mistaken for one another.

Having left the navy, and dutifully married May, George was given York Cottage, in Sandringham, also once Eddy's, as a country residence. Small by royal standards, and described as 'ugly' and 'dark', George nevertheless seemed pleased to have his own home and spent many hours furnishing and decorating it. The couple spent their honeymoon here, in the intensely hot summer of 1893, negotiating a relationship in which they barely knew each other, in a house where they were rarely alone due to the presence of servants and often May's mother. Three months after the wedding, George wrote a letter to his wife, which suggests that his feelings for May grew steadily, despite a rocky start.

> I have said lots of nasty, stupid & rude things to you I know … but I didn't mean them really, & I ask you to forgive me for having said them … I also want to tell you how happy how very happy I am with you now my own darling…[6]

George and May, who became known as 'Mary' on George's accession to the throne, went on to have a long and successful marriage. Their first son, christened Edward Albert Christian George Andrew Patrick David – a long list of names, the last four of which after the patron saints of England, Scotland, Ireland and Wales – was born in June 1894, within a year of the wedding. Always known as 'David', the baby's godparents included his father's favoured cousin Nicky, who later the same year became Tsar of Russia. He was joined in December of the following year, on the anniversary of the death of the Prince Consort, by his brother Albert, known as 'Bertie'. In April 1897, the couple welcomed a baby girl, Mary, and she was followed by two brothers, Henry, born in March 1900, and John, born in July 1905. Sadly, John suffered from epilepsy and died at the age of 13 after a severe seizure.

George V has most often been characterised as a distant, cold father. His naval habits, almost fanatical obsession with punctuality, a strict routine and stern sense of duty were the things he was most keen to pass on to his children, frequently lecturing them on the subject of good manners. One of his favourite themes was the importance of his children never imagining they were different to or better than other people. Such statements were both delivered and received within the prism of the family's social stratum: 'To be sure, by *other people*, he meant children of the well-born,' clarifies his oldest son.[7]

Back in the closing decade of the nineteenth century, though, George, having left the navy, receiving a generous allowance and required to perform few public duties, enjoyed domesticity and country life at Sandringham. In the scathing words of his biographer Harold Nicolson: 'For seventeen years ... he did nothing at all but kill animals and stick in stamps.' Nicolson was not alone in criticising the future King during these 'idle' years for failing to improve upon his rudimentary education and accomplishments and prepare himself for his future role. Always of a perfunctory nature, his diary entries during the grouse shooting season from August until the end of January, which he spent at Sandringham, Balmoral and staying at other grand country houses, including Chatsworth and Holkham, for shooting parties, relay the – quite astonishing – tally of birds he shot each day. During the shooting season of 1896–97, he calculated that he shot a total of 11,006 birds, including 2,509 partridges and 5,993 pheasants.[8]

For his intelligent, cultured wife, now the Duchess of York, this period wasn't the 'idyll' that George enjoyed. Enduring difficult, painful pregnancies, with little distraction or stimulation at York Cottage, life was quite restricted. Her mother-in-law, occupying the Big House across the lake, had a high profile in the local community, leaving no room for May, and her sisters-in-law could be hostile towards her. May found it difficult to bond with her babies, and for the early years of her eldest children's lives the nursery at York House was run by a tyrannical nanny who conspired to keep May away from her children, even when she did want to spend time with them.

As Prince and Princess of Wales, George and May played a prominent role at the 1902 coronation of Edward VII. When, in 1911, George succeeded to the throne himself, they had the unusual advantage of having experienced a coronation as adults, relatively recently. At the age of 44, the new King was neither the teenage ingenue his grandmother had been, nor the 60-year-old elder statesmen his father was when crowned. Soon after his accession to the throne, coronation planning got underway and plans were set in place for a great imperial show. But the mood was very different this time. In 1902, at beginning of a new century and the end of a very long reign, the coronation of Edward VII had signalled the beginning of a new era, with the promise of something quite different to what went before. In 1911, the emphasis was more on continuity and consolidation, both of monarchy and Empire.

Having been somewhat sidelined in 1902, Earl Marshal Henry Fitzalan-Howard was keen to exercise his hereditary right to organise the coronation. The 15th Duke of Norfolk wasn't a natural in the role, having poor organisational skills and no particular interest in state ceremonial. As both George V and Prime Minister Asquith lacked confidence in his management skills, he was given the role of Chair of the Coronation Executive Committee, backed up by staff from the Office of Works (the government department with responsibility for maintaining royal properties, which later became the Department for the Environment).

George V's eldest son David, having completed almost four years of naval training, and about to go to sea for his final training cruise and graduation, was bitterly disappointed at being ordered back to London by his father, to prepare for the coronation.[9] He joined his family at Buckingham Palace and was given a room on the third floor overlooking the Mall. But he failed to warm to his new home, later recalling the 'musty' smell of the building and the fact that he never felt happy there. Next morning after breakfast, he was summoned to his father's study and told that he must now focus on taking a leading role at the coronation.

The coronation had by now extended well beyond the day or even week of the ceremony itself and in 1911, there were months of associated tours, dinners, services, galas, parties and the like. The Festival of Empire, which opened in May at London's Crystal Palace, a huge display of imperial culture, was a part of the coronation year celebrations.

On Tuesday, 1 November 1910, a supplement to the *London Gazette* included a notice from the Earl Marshal's office requesting that all peers who believed that they were entitled to assist in the coronation write to him at his office, stating their claim. He also asks dowager peeresses and peeresses 'who may claim to attend at the said Coronation, will be also pleased to transmit their respective Christian names and addresses to me, in order that their letters of summons may be prepared without delay'.

The Earl Marshal also issued a strict dress code:

> These are to give notice to all Peers who attend at the Coronation of Their Majesties, that the robe or mantel of the Peers be of crimson velvet, edged with miner, the cape fur with miniver pure and powdered with bars or rows of ermine [i.e. narrow pieces of black fur], according to their degree, viz:
>
> Barons, two rows
> Viscounts, two rows and a half
> Earls, three rows
> Marquesses, three rows and a half
> Dukes, four rows
> The said mantles or robes to be worn over full Court dress, uniform or regimentals.
> The coronets to be of silver gilt; the caps of crimson velvet turned up with ermine, with a gold tassel on the top; and no jewels or precious stones are to beset or used in the coronets, or counterfeit pearls instead of silver balls.

But this wasn't to be exclusively an upper-class affair. When it came to the guest list, the 1911 committee were more proactive about including new sections of what was a fast-changing society on the guest list. By this time, the Labour Party had emerged as a significant force in politics, articulating issues of the working class. There was also a growing professional middle class, and a corresponding curbing of the hereditary rights and powers of the aristocracy. In particular, the Parliament Act of 1911 removed the House of Lords' power to veto a bill, allowing the Liberal government to push through their 'People's Budget', which imposed taxes on land ownership to fund welfare provision.

To ensure a range of professions and leading figures from the arts and sciences were included, invitations were sent to representatives from the Royal Societies. At the time, these included: the Royal Geographical Society, the British Academy, the Royal Astronomical Society, the Royal College of Physicians, the Royal College of Surgeons, the Institute of

Mechanical Engineers, the Royal College of Veterinary Surgeons, the Royal Academy of Arts and the Royal College of Music.

Invitations were also extended to representatives of many religious communities, including the Church of Ireland, the United Free Church of Scotland, the Episcopal Church of Scotland, the Roman Catholic Church and the Chief Rabbi.

But invitations did not go out to many who might have considered it their hereditary right to receive one. Peers' sons and daughters, and widows had been dropped off the guest list to make way for more democratic representation from organisations such as the Trades Congress Parliamentary Committee, the Central Board of the Co-operative Union and the National Conference of Friendly Societies.[10]

One of the largest contingents of guests – and most time-consuming to manage – were the foreign representatives. The convention was that crowned heads didn't attend coronations, as that would give them seniority, by virtue of length of time served as monarch, over the King or Queen whose coronation it was. For the most part therefore, heads of state sent their heirs or another suitable representative. This rule meant that George's cousin Nicky was not at the coronation. Now Tsar Nicholas II of Russia, his own magnificent coronation in 1896, which would turn out to be the last one held in Russia, took place at the Kremlin's Dormition Cathedral and was a lavish, glittering affair.

In addition to issuing the invitation to foreign representatives, the organisers had to put their guests up, and hotel rooms all over London were requisitioned for the purpose. A working document with a list of countries, with their intended attendees, plus where they would stay, was kept by the Earl Marshal's office.

The A–Z starts 'Abyssinia, Austria-Hungary, Baden, Bavaria, Belgium, Brazil…'

As countries responded with details of who they were going to send, notes were added:

> China – Prince Tsai Chen [son of Prince Ching, who had attended Edward VII's Coronation]
> Denmark – HRH the Crown Prince of Denmark

Foreign representatives from Britain's closest allies and/or royal relations were put up at Buckingham Palace. This involved finding suites for the royals, as well as accommodation for their valets, maids and aides-de-camp. They were also assigned 'Gentlemen attached' – a suitable member of the British nobility who would act as host. Those staying at Buckingham Palace in 1911 included many foreign royals from monarchies in the final stages of their existence.

The map of Europe looked quite different in this pre-First World War era, with the German Empire being made up of many grand duchies, kingdoms and principalities, each with their own ruling families. The Earl Marshal's A–Z became populated with the names of many of Queen Victoria's descendants:

> Austria-Hungary – His Imperial Highness The Archduke Charles Francis Joseph (Representing His Majesty The Emperor of Austria, King of Hungary)
>
> Baden – His Grand Ducal Highness Prince Maximilian and Her Royal Highness Princess Maximilian of Baden – Representing His Royal Highness the Grand Duke of Baden [whose mother was related to Queen Victoria's daughter by marriage]
>
> Germany – Their Imperial and Royal Highnesses The Crown Prince and Crown Princess – Representing His Majesty The German Emperor, King of Prussia [Queen Victoria's eldest grandchild]
>
> Greece – Their Royal Highnesses The Crown Prince and Crown Princess of Greece, representing his Majesty The King of the Hellenes [brother of Queen Alexandra]
>
> Hesse – Their Royal Highnesses The Grand Duke [a grandson of Queen Victoria, whose sister Alix married King George V's cousin Nicky, and became the last Empress of Russia; another sister, Victoria, was the grandmother of Prince Philip, the Duke of Edinburgh] and Grand Duchess of Hesse

> Saxe-Coburg – Their Royal Highnesses The Duke [a grandson of Queen Victoria] and Duchess of Saxe-Coburg
>
> Saxony – Their Royal Highnesses The Prince and Princess Johann George of Saxony (representing his majesty the King of Saxony)
>
> Württemberg – His Royal Highness The Duke Albrecht of Württemberg (Representing His Majesty The King of Württemberg)

To Queen Mary's disappointment, her beloved Aunt Augusta, the 89-year-old Grand Duchess of Mecklenburg-Strelitz, said that she could not face the journey to attend what would have been her fourth coronation. She did, however, keep up a regular correspondence with her niece, sharing her experiences of coronations, going back to William IV and Queen Adelaide in 1831. With her keen eye for detail, she sent her niece a stream of specific enquiries, as to the dress and movements of the key players, all of which were patiently answered.

Finding space to accommodate all those who were intending to come was a considerable challenge. Queen Mary wrote to her aunt: 'The amount of Guests of all kinds, who have announced themselves is quite overwhelming, *all* of George's first cousins of all nationalities have asked to come.'[11]

Queen Mary, a meticulous record keeper, wrote a detailed list of all the new clothes she ordered for the coronation celebrations. She spent many hours with dressmakers. In a letter to her aunt, she describes her boredom with the process, referring to her 'tiresome trousseau of clothes which has meant endless trying on'.[12] The Queen spent over £2,000 on a selection of dresses in her signature pale colour palette – including 'gold and white', 'grey and silver', 'white broché with roses', 'mauve cut velvet', 'yellow satin', and 'muslin with large roses'.[13]

Queen Mary had an established signature style which consisted of long, pale-coloured gowns, upswept hair, elaborate layered jewellery and often a parasol. Her statuesque figure and consistent style projected a regal image that remained unchanged throughout her life. Her own innate conservatism and her husband's dislike of the changing women's fashions meant that she was never a fashion leader like Queen Alexandra was. But her distinctive, immediately recognisable look was a lesson in regal style that her granddaughter Elizabeth II appears to have learnt – during her long reign relying on single block-colour outfits, rarely varying the style that ensured she was easily seen and recognised.

The London couture house Reville and Rossiter were commissioned to make Queen Mary's coronation gown: a hand-stitched, full-skirted dress of cream-coloured silk satin cut in the 'princess line', with an extended train at the back. The dress had a boned inner bodice made of cream silk taffeta, trimmed at the neck with handmade Irish needlepoint lace. Three-quarter-length sleeves had an inner sleeve of handmade gilt metal bobbin lace, visible around the bottom of the sleeve. The measurements for the dress were: 104.2 cm (bust); 68.5 cm (waist); 132.2 cm (length); 218.5 cm (length: whole object).[14]

The Princess Louise Needlework School in Sloane Street were responsible for the elaborate and detailed embroidery on Queen Mary's coronation dress. Working with gold thread and tiny gilt metal beads, they embroidered the national emblems: the Tudor rose, the thistle and the shamrock into the design. They also embroidered a border of waves at the hem, to represent the oceans connecting the Empire, as well as the national flower of India – the lotus – and the Star of India. Reville and Rossiter, who had gained the royal warrant in 1910, as dressmaker to Queen Mary, also designed the Queen's coronation robe. The silk velvet robe and train were woven in Sudbury, an established centre for silk weaving. The King's coronation robe, made of purple silk velvet, also featured gold-embroidered national emblems, and would be reused by George V's great-grandson, Charles III.

Queen Mary was kept very busy with coronation preparations. Her knowledge and reverence for the history of the royal family and conscientious approach to planning meant she worked very hard. Whereas her mother-in-law Queen Alexandra had been struck by the dazzling visual aspects of the ceremony, for Queen Mary, its historical and religious significance had the greatest impact on her.[15] The King and Queen faced an exhausting workload in coronation year, with all the related functions, events, dinners, visits and tours arranged for them. Although, as Prince and Princess of Wales, George and Mary were used to being involved in public events, they found suddenly being centre stage very daunting. In a letter to her daughter-in-law, Queen Alexandra, speaking from experience, begs the couple not to take on too much: 'Do please both of you not pledge yr selves at first to undertake more than any human people can stand … I speak like an old woman from sad experience – so please both of you remember my words & act accordingly.'[16]

Amid the flurry of preparations, the new King looked forward to Coronation Day with more dread than excitement. Lacking confidence when speaking and appearing in public, and still getting used to his new role, he can hardly have relished the prospect of taking the starring role in a great imperial show. After attending his first State Opening of Parliament on 6 February, he described the event as 'the most terrible ordeal I have ever gone through'.[17] It didn't bode well…

Chapter Nine

CORONATION DAY 1911

The Coronation of His Majesty King George V of the United Kingdom of Great Britain and Ireland, and of the British Dominions beyond the Seas, Defender of the Faith, Emperor of India; and of Her Majesty Queen Mary, His Consort.

Date:	Thursday, 22 June 1911
Congregation:	7,139[1]
Cost:	£185,000
Weather:	Overcast, breezy, with some showers

Early morning

At 6.30am, the entrance of Westminster Abbey and the gates of Hyde Park are opened, and one hour later guests start entering the Abbey.

In a nod to technological progress, the photographer and MP Sir Benjamin Stone is the first official photographer to attend a coronation. He has been granted permission to take photographs of the ceremony, though – at Archbishop of Canterbury Randall Davidson's insistence – he must sit in a hidden spot, and not take photographs of the most holy parts of the service.

The procession

The first procession of fourteen carriages carrying members of foreign royal families and governments leaves Buckingham Palace at 9.30am.

They are followed by carriages containing members of the royal family, including a carriage containing the King and Queen's children. More carriages containing officers of state follow.

Queen Victoria's legacy lives on in the generous numbers of 'minor royals' taking part in the procession of princes and princesses. Colourful figures include Princess Louise, the Duchess of Argyll, the late Queen's sixth child and one of the royal family's most unconventional members. Now in her early 60s, Louise has defied tradition by refusing to marry a foreign prince, and instead choosing a husband from the English aristocracy – the first time such a marriage by a member of the royal family had been approved since 1515, in the reign of Henry VIII.[2] She went on to be a prominent supporter of women's equality and the suffragette movement.

Queen Victoria's youngest child, Beatrice, is also in the procession. Now aged 54 and widowed, she is listed under her married title 'Prince Henry of Battenburg', which she will go on to drop during the First World War when the royals distance themselves from German titles, reverting to 'Princess Beatrice'.

With the previous coronation having taken place just nine years earlier, some recycling has been possible. The princesses wear violet mantles, instead of the traditional blue – because Queen Alexandra had chosen violet for her coronation, and although Queen Mary's instincts are more traditional, she has also been keen to avoid unnecessary expenditure.

Queen Alexandra is missing: she does not attend the coronation and spends the day at Sandringham with one of her daughters. She declined to attend on the grounds of tradition – Queen Adelaide had not attended her niece Queen Victoria's coronation – but it seems the event has also triggered a wave of grief and melancholy for her dead son Eddy. The Dowager Queen is continually heard saying: 'Eddy should be King, not Georgie.'[3]

At 10.30am, the King and Queen leave Buckingham Palace, riding in the Gold State Coach, pulled by eight cream-coloured horses with red and blue trappings. Theirs is the twenty-fifth carriage to leave, and they are surrounded by mounted officers, aides-de-camp, the Horse Guards, the Yeoman of the Guard and colonial and Indian cavalry. Unlike for their wedding procession in 1893, when the carriages simply headed straight out of the Buckingham Palace gates and down the Mall, they now have to wind around the newly built island in front of the palace with its huge Victoria Memorial, unveiled the previous year. They proceed in state down the Mall, passing through newly built Admiralty Arch, which like the Victoria Memorial was commissioned by Edward VII as a tribute to his mother and designed by architect Sir Aston Webb. These new London landmarks will form the backdrop to royal processions from now on. The carriages continue along Whitehall, Parliament Street and Broad Sanctuary to the Abbey. Onlookers describe His Majesty as 'looking a little pale'.[4]

Arrival at the Abbey

Once again, a temporary annexe has been built at the west front of the Abbey which acts as a robing room. Designed by the architect Alfred Young Nutt, its Gothic style complements the Abbey itself.

The Queen's procession is first to begin their walk up the Nave. With her eye for historical precedent, she has chosen six earls' daughters to bear her train. She has checked the records and found no explanation for why Queen Alexandra had chosen six pages, since all previous Queen consorts had six earls' daughters.

The King and his procession follow behind, accompanied by the sound of the choir singing Parry's coronation anthem 'I Was Glad', based on Psalm 122 in the bible. 'I was glad when they said unto me, we will go into the House of the Lord.'

They make their way slowly up the body of the Church and through the Choir, where foreign dignitaries sit. The Westminster schoolboys in the upper galleries shout out in Latin the traditional greeting that symbolises the spontaneous recognition of the monarch by the people.

'Vivat Regina Maria!'

'Vivat Rex Georgius!'

Their Majesties kneel on the faldstools set for them before their Chairs of Estate, on the south side of the altar. They spend a few moments in private prayer, before sitting in their chairs.

The recognition

The first stage of the service takes place in the same way it always has, with the Archbishop of Canterbury, together with the Lord Chancellor, the Lord Great Chamberlain, the Lord High Constable and the Earl Marshal, turning to each side of the Theatre – first the east, followed by south, west and north. The only difference is that, rather than remain standing by his Chair of Estate, King George V moves forward to stand by the Coronation Chair during the recognition, therefore being more visible.[5] It's a small departure from tradition and one that will be repeated at future coronations.

Unlike in 1902, the Archbishop's voice can be heard clearly, even without amplification as he declares at each turn: 'Sirs, I here present unto you King George, the undoubted King of this Realm. Wherefore all you who are come this day to do your homage and service, are you willing to do the same?'

There are loud shouts of 'God Save King George' in reply and the trumpets sound.

The bible and regalia are presented by their carriers and placed on the altar. They join the ampulla, filled with oil, and the spoon, which have been placed there earlier in the morning by Abbey clergy.

Two bishops sing the litany, with the Choir singing the responses, beginning: 'O God, the Father of heaven, have mercy upon us miserable sinners.'

After which the communion service begins. The Archbishop prays: 'Grant unto this thy servant, George, our King, the Spirit of wisdom and government…'

A sermon is delivered by the Archbishop of York. He has ruffled feathers among Abbey clergy by letting it be known that he intends to carry his own primatial cross on his walk to the pulpit in the north-east corner of the Theatre, rather than the Abbey cross, as is traditional. As he makes his way to the pulpit, a member of the Abbey clergy quietly steps out in front of him, seizing the Abbey cross and carrying it ahead of the Archbishop. Ancient custom preserved, the sermon, taken from the Book of Samuel, begins; meanwhile, the King puts on his cap of crimson velvet, turned up with ermine.

The oath

As the sermon concludes, the Archbishop stands in front of the King and asks: 'Sir, is Your Majesty willing to take the oath?'

And the King answers: 'I am willing'

Archbishop: 'Will you solemnly promise and swear to govern the people of this United Kingdom of Great Britain and Ireland, and the dominions thereto belonging, according to the Statutes in Parliament agreed on, and the respective Laws and Customs of the same?'

King: 'I solemnly promise to do.'

The King is called upon to maintain the Protestant Reformed Religion established in law.

The King arises out of his chair and, the Sword of State being carried before him, approaches the altar and there his cap is removed, he lays his right hand on the bible and makes his solemn oath.

'The things which I have here before promised, I will perform, and keep. So help me God.'

Then the King kisses the bible, signs the oath and prepares for the anointing and crowning.

The anointing

The King and Queen kneel at their faldstools as the choir sing the medieval hymn 'Veni Creator Spiritus', in praise of the Holy Spirit.

The Archbishop prays, while laying his hand upon the ampulla. To the sound of the opening bars of 'Zadok the Priest', the King rises and is helped out of his crimson robe and cap by the Lord Great Chamberlain and moves to the altar, taking his seat in St Edward's Chair. Four Knights of the Garter hold over him the canopy of cloth of gold.

The Dean of Westminster hands the Archbishop the ampulla and spoon ready with a little oil in it, which the Archbishop uses to anoint the King's head in the form of a cross.

He then anoints the King's breast, followed by his hands, and says another prayer.

Now King George is helped into the traditional Colobium Sindonis, and girdle. He is presented with the spurs and another sword in a scabbard of purple velvet, which is girded to him 'for the terror and punishment of evildoers, and for the protection and encouragement of those that do well...'

After another prayer, the King rises, detaches the sword and places it on the altar. The peer who carried in the sword is now required to offer 100 shillings for it; having made the offering, he receives back the sword, which he removes from the scabbard and carries it before His Majesty for the remainder of the ceremony.

More regalia is presented to the King, including the ring, which the Archbishop places on the fourth finger of his right hand. The King's Glove is presented by the Lord of the Manor of Worksop, whose family have always been proactive in claiming their historic right to perform this task. The glove on, the Archbishop hands the King the Sceptre 'the ensign of Kingly power and justice'.

The crowning

Unlike his two predecessors, George V is crowned with the traditional St Edward's Crown – in robust health, he can handle its five-pound weight. Seated in the Coronation Chair, he looks solemn as the Archbishop raises the crown and reverently places it on his head.

At the moment of crowning, there are shouts of 'God Save the King!', the peers crown themselves with their coronets, trumpets sound and the great guns at the Tower of London roar into action.

Now the King has been anointed and crowned, and been presented with the regalia, he receives the Archbishop's blessing including the words: 'The Lord give you a fruitful Country and healthful seasons; victorious fleets and armies, and a quiet Empire...'

The homage

The formal 'enthronement' takes place as the King is helped into his throne, which has been upholstered with crimson silk damask designed by William Morris.[6] There is movement in the galleries and around the Theatre itself, as those taking part in the homage prepare themselves.

The Archbishop is the first to kneel in front of the King, as the bishops kneel in their places and they pay homage together before the Archbishop kisses the King's left cheek.

All eyes are now on the golden-haired Prince of Wales, who cuts a dashing figure on the eve of his 17th birthday, as he approaches his father's throne, removing his own coronet. In one of the many minor crises relating to rank, precedence and correct style, and their sometimes conflicting requirements, that afflict those organising coronations, David, as Prince of Wales, takes precedence over the peers present, yet cannot wear the appropriate robes as he is not of age. To solve the problem – described as 'a very real one'[7] – the King has hastily arranged for him to be invested with the Order of the Garter, one of the most ancient orders of chivalry, in a ceremony at Windsor Castle.

The young heir to the throne and his sister Mary have found the build-up and festivities around the coronation and their central roles in it exciting and fascinating, but the young prince understands the poignancy of this moment and he is nervous.[8]

He kneels down before his father and recites his lines in a clear voice: 'I, Edward, Prince of Wales do become your liege man of life and limb, and of earthly worship; and faith and truth I will bear unto you, to live and die, against all manner of folks. So help me God…'

Those witnessing this touching tribute of son to father, including Queen Mary who is seated nearby, admire the presence of such a handsome and dutiful heir to the throne. The shimmering scene is captured in a painting by Laurits Tuxen, one of two artists who have been invited to record the day. None present in the Abbey now can surely imagine the events that will unfold during the short-lived reign of the future Edward VIII.

As the prince touches his father's crown and kisses his cheek, the deep current of feeling that travels between the two is palpable: 'when my father kissed my cheeks, his emotion was great, as was mine,' recalled David.

For King George, the whole day is tinged with poignant memories of his parents' coronation just nine years earlier, and at times his feelings are almost overwhelming: 'I nearly broke down when dear David came to do homage, to me, as it reminded me so much when I did the same thing to beloved Papa, he did so well.'[9]

All of the royal princes do their homage, kneeling in their places, at the same time as the Prince of Wales, after which all arise and touch His Majesty's crown, and kiss his left cheek.

Next it's the turn of the peers, efficiently batched according to their rank: starting with the dukes, followed by the marquesses, the earls, the viscounts, the relatively lowly barons bringing up the rear. The first of each group kneel before the King, while the others kneel in their places as they all recite their homage together.

The homage complete, the drums beat, trumpets sound and the Abbey is filled with cries of:

> God Save the King
> Long live King George
> May the King live forever

Queen Mary's coronation

The shorter Queen Consort's coronation follows that of the monarch and, although the task was delegated to the Archbishop of York in 1902, the Archbishop of Canterbury reclaims this role in 1911. Queen Mary approaches the steps of the altar, while the Archbishop prays for her. She kneels on her faldstool, which has been positioned between the steps of the altar and St Edward's Chair. Four peeresses hold the canopy of cloth of gold over her, and the Archbishop anoints her with the holy oil.

'Let the anointing with this oil increase your honour, and the Grace of the Holy Spirit establish you…'

He takes the coronation ring and places it on the fourth finger of Queen Mary's right hand: 'Receive this ring, the symbol of a sincere faith…'

The Archbishop takes the crown from the altar and places it on the Queen's head: 'Receive the crown of glory, honour and joy…'

Queen Mary's crown has been made especially for her and features the spectacular Koh-i-Noor diamond as well as the Cullinan III and

Cullinan IV diamonds, with hundreds of small diamond clusters set on elegant silver arches.[10] The peeresses are ready for their moment, and just as the Archbishop brings down the crown on the Queen's head, they crown themselves with the coronets in one dazzling move.

The Archbishop places the Sceptre into the Queen's right hand and the Ivory Rod into her left hand, praying fluently all the while.

Then the Queen rises, turns towards the royal box and circles round the Theatre on the way to her throne. With her crown on her head, a Sceptre held upright in each hand, and her splendid train extended at full length behind her, held by her maids, she appears to glide, 'moving as only Queen Mary knew how to move',[11] and makes her way to her throne, bowing reverently, and cautiously so as not to dislodge her crown, as she passes the King. An onlooker believes they have witnessed 'the very perfection of movement and grace'.[12]

Following the end of the service, the processions form up and the King and Queen leave the Abbey at around 2.15pm, wearing their crowns and holding their sceptres.

Queen Mary, in her crown, is majesty itself. 'As if she has undergone some marvellous transformation,' remarks one onlooker.[13] Her husband is thankful for her presence throughout the day, recalling later in his diary: 'May looked lovely and it was indeed a comfort to me to have her by my side, as she has been ever to me during these last 18 years.'[14]

The procession

The carriages return to Buckingham Palace in reverse order. The route back goes via the Mall, St James Street and Piccadilly, and the King and Queen do their best to wave to and acknowledge the huge, cheering crowds, without dislodging their heavy crowns. Queen Mary draws comfort from the goodwill of the people, later reflecting: 'Magnificent reception both going and coming back.'[15]

The royal children have a coach to themselves. Princess Mary, age 14, is seen struggling to control two of her younger brothers, as a full-on fight breaks out. Meanwhile, David finds it hard to bear even the weight of a coronet: 'My coronet felt very heavy, as we had to bow to the people as we went along.'[16]

Back at Buckingham Palace, the King and Queen appear on the balcony, to show themselves to the people, in their coronation robes and crowns. After the photographs are taken, they have a late lunch with some of their guests, before the King spends the rest of the afternoon working with his private secretary to answer telegrams and deal with correspondence.

In the evening, King George and Queen Mary make another balcony appearance to greet their adoring crowds; lit up with beautiful illuminations and packed with exuberant well-wishers, the mood in the capital is buoyant. They dine with their guests at 8.30pm.

The day has left the King 'rather tired'[17] and he retires to bed at 11.45pm.

Chapter Ten

GEORGE AND MARY

The day after the Coronation is the Prince of Wales's 17th birthday, and he receives presents from his family around the breakfast table at Buckingham Palace.[1] At 10.00am, members of the extended royal family arrive for a post-Coronation Day catch up – although they were all present at the previous day's proceedings, this is their chance to actually talk to the King and Queen.

At 11.00am, the King and Queen embark on a post-coronation carriage procession around London. The route, which is over seven miles in total, takes them through some of the capital's most prominent streets. The showers of earlier in the day clear, and the couple are moved by the huge turnout and show of love and support from their subjects, who have come to see them. The King is impressed by the beautifully decorated streets, lined with around 64,000 troops, and especially the warmth of their reception by the people: '…who cheered in a way I have never heard before and shall never forget. The enthusiasm and loyalty thus expressed indeed touched my heart deeply.'[2]

On their return to Buckingham Palace, the King and Queen once more appear on the balcony, to more cheering from the crowds, 'a sight which I'm sure could never be seen in any other country in the world',[3] remarks the grateful, patriotic King.

On the following day, Saturday, 24 June, coronation-related duties continue apace at Buckingham Palace; after breakfast the King receives all the pages who carried his train in the Abbey and presents the excited boys with coronation medals. The royal couple then travel by train to Portsmouth, for the inspection of the fleet at Spithead. The King and Queen are steamed past the assembled thirty-two battleships, thirty-six cruisers, twelve scouts, sixty-seven destroyers, twelve torpedo boats and eight submarines manned by almost 60,000 navy personnel. In addition, there are 'Foreign men of war representing every nation'. It's an impressive display of British naval power, the largest in the world, and a cornerstone of the British Empire.

The transformational magic of the coronation ceremony has not been lost on Queen Mary, who writes to her aunt:

> It was an awful ordeal for us both especially as we felt it all so deeply and taking so great a responsibility on our shoulders. To me who love tradition & the past, & who am English from tip to toe, the service was a very real solemn thing & appealed to my feelings more than I can express…[4]

Mostly, the feeling is one of relief that the day is over. The run up to the coronation had been an anxious time for Queen Mary, and the day itself placed many demands on her. But, as a deeply religious woman, she also draws strength from the coronation ceremony, feeling that she will be aided by God in her new role.

For David and his sister Princess Mary, seeing such splendid ceremonies at close range has been a thrill, and like many who witnessed the spectacle, they are fascinated with the magnificence of the show: from the uniformed foreign dignitaries, to the military parades, gilt coaches and glittering guests.

Critical voices were not altogether silenced, of course. Among them, the Socialist Keir Hardie, who described the lavish coronation spectacle as 'an orgy of wealth and senseless spending'. On the whole though, the coronation only appeared to buoy the widespread support the monarchy enjoyed among all classes. There was more pomp and pageantry to come in July, with the elaborate investiture of David as Prince of Wales that took place in Caernarfon in Wales.

In December, George V and Queen Mary travelled to India for the great Delhi Durbar, where they received the homage of the Indian princes in their roles as Emperor and Empress of India. It was a grand colonial affair – the first and last that a British monarch would attend in person.

The twenty-five years of George V's reign would see great change, a world war, the overthrow of European monarchies, the Anglo-Irish war, the rise of Fascism, the Great Depression, the emergence of the Labour movement in Britain, and the beginning of the end of colonialism.

In 1915, while on a low-key visit to France to visit the troops, George had a serious accident when he was thrown from and then crushed by a horse. His recovery was slow and he was left physically weaker, with lingering pain that affected him for the rest of his life. George and Mary were visible during the First World War, visiting hospitals, handing out medals and trying to keep spirits up in the country. They led a relatively austere life during this time, living on rations and banning alcohol from being served at their residences, even when guests were present. The King had a difficult relationship with the Liberal wartime prime minister David Lloyd George, who was openly contemptuous about the monarchy and ceremonial, and tried to exclude George V as much as possible.

Fearful of losing public sympathy, George V changed the royal family's name in 1917, from the German-sounding Saxe-Coburg to the much more British 'Windsor'. His deep anxiety over the 1917 Russian revolution, and the fear of anti-monarchist sentiments taking hold in Britain, led him to refuse to allow his cousin Nicky, the now deposed Tsar, and his family from living in exile in England. Nicky, his wife Alicky, a favourite grandchild of Queen Victoria, and their five children were later all murdered by the Bolsheviks. In 1919, King George did agree to send a warship to rescue his former Russian flame, Xenia, and her mother the Dowager Empress Maria Feodorovna, George V's aunt, from the Black Sea. Maria lived with her sister Queen Alexandra at Sandringham, while Xenia later lived at Frogmore Cottage on the Windsor Estate[5] (briefly home to Harry and Meghan). The German and Austro-Hungarian monarchies, as well as the Ottoman Empire, were also deposed, with republics being established after the war. Many of the foreign royalties who had attended the 1911 coronation found themselves living in exile from the countries they once ruled.

George V continued to fear the anti-monarchist sentiments in Europe, viewing all republican movements as an indirect threat to his own position. Unsettled by events on the continent, for a man known for his conservatism, the changes in British society after the First World War were not always welcome either. According to his eldest son, the King was not just firmly of the Victorian era, but quite content to stay there. 'His habits, tastes and views reflected the era when his grandmother ruled over the British Empire and the British aristocracy stood admired and envied throughout the world.'[6]

Known for his hearty manner, naval ways, and for his fixed prejudices, George V had a preference for simplicity. His private life revolved around his family, his hobbies – shooting, sailing and his world-class stamp collection – and a small, unchanging circle of friends. But simple did not mean spartan. The Duke of Windsor's memoir recalls his father's love of comfort and luxury which meant that everything he owned was always of the finest quality – from his guns, to his food, his stationary and his Fabergé cigarette case. A huge Edwardian household staff kept everything around the King running like clockwork. George V's lifestyle has been described as a masterpiece in the art of well-ordered, unostentatious, elegant living, with an upper-class Edwardian attention to detail that expected and delivered nothing short of perfection.

When the Conservative government lost the General Election in January 1924, it fell to George V to appoint Ramsay MacDonald, Britain's first Labour prime minister, with whom he talked for an hour before concluding: 'He impressed me very much, he wishes to do the right thing.'[7] Privately, the King worried about how his new government ministers might behave towards him. Many of them had been openly scornful of the monarchy, and there were fears that they may refuse to participate in state ceremonies, or decline to wear the 'correct' dress. In the event, Mr MacDonald, the illegitimate son of a farm labourer and housemaid, was courteous towards the King and obligingly donned the gold-braided tailcoat and white knee breeches worn by Ministers of the Crown for ceremonial occasions.[8]

It wasn't just in politics and the upending of the old societal hierarchies where change was afoot. The Duke of Windsor recalls the aspects of the modern world his father struggled with. He was appalled by the 'emancipated flappers' – women who had taken to wearing shorter skirts, and cutting their hair into bobs. And more… 'He disapproved of Soviet Russia, painted fingernails, women who smoked in public, cocktails, frivolous hats, American jazz, and the growing habit of going away for week-ends.'[9]

Even as King and Queen, George and Mary and their family continued to live at York House when they didn't need to be in London. The main house at Sandringham had been left by Edward VII to his wife Queen Alexandra, who continued to live there with her daughter, until her death in 1925, at the age of 80. It was an awkward arrangement for the King and Queen, their large family and their extended court – but despite Queen Mary and many others pointing out that it was ridiculous for one old lady to reside in such a large mansion, while the King and Queen could not put up guests in their cramped cottage, George V could not bring himself to ask his mother to move. 'It is my mother's home. My father built it for her,' was his view.[10]

George V became known as the founder of the modern monarchy. As well as creating the House of Windsor, he oversaw the transition to a crown that represented continuity and stability, its values symbolised during ceremonial state occasions that became opportunities for national celebration. George and Mary worked hard throughout their reign to promote a positive public image, doing good works, keeping up morale, setting an example, recognising the achievements and sufferings of their subjects. It was a far cry from the days when Queen Victoria saw no reason why she should emerge from her long years of mourning, shut up at Balmoral. When their daughter, Princess Mary, married Harry Lascelles, the heir to the Earl of Harewood, at Westminster Abbey in 1924, it was the first major royal celebration since the coronation. It set the tone for future royal weddings, with public celebrations and much accompanying media coverage.

George V and Queen Mary celebrated their Silver Jubilee in 1935. The accompanying events, including a carriage procession through London, a bank holiday and many celebratory parties, were considered a triumph, and the King and Queen were moved by the gestures of love and respect they received from the British people. The Jubilee celebrations would mark the closing of the reign of George V. Spending Christmas at Sandringham with his family as usual, the King developed a bronchial infection and rapidly became seriously ill. He died on 20 January 1936, aged 70. While the body of George V lay in state at Westminster Hall, in the 'vigil of the princes' his four surviving sons stood watch over it. This gesture was to be repeated in 2022 when Queen Elizabeth II died, with her children and then grandchildren standing vigil in Westminster Hall.

During his lifetime, the four surviving sons of George V had all had troubled relationships with their father. As eldest son and heir, David in particular repeatedly clashed with his father over his very different lifestyle and approach to royal duties. George V, the man who had worked so hard to put the continuity of the monarchy above all else, had not managed to produce an heir he and the country could have confidence in. For the institution of monarchy, it was a ticking time bomb.

Chapter Eleven

THE UNCROWNED KING

Following on from his father's coronation, at which he had so movingly paid homage, the young Prince Edward (David) faced the prospect of his own investiture as Prince of Wales. Scheduled to take place at Caernarfon in July, the occasion promised yet more royal pageantry, with 12,000 guests invited to watch the ceremony. Ironically, it was the vocal critic of the monarchy and inherited privilege, Welsh MP and Chancellor of the Exchequer David Lloyd George, who proposed the revival of this ancient ceremony, which hadn't been used for centuries. Keen to rally support among the Welsh people, he was convinced that a spectacular pageant in Wales would be a welcome source of national pride. David submitted to being coached for his starring role in the ceremony, even learning some Welsh to use in his speech. But, when a tailor arrived to measure him for his costume – white satin breeches and a mantle, and a coat of purple velvet edged with ermine – the youth whose fashion sense came to be much admired decided things had gone too far. When he protests to his parents that he doesn't want his Navy friends seeing him in such a 'preposterous rig', his mother tries to soothe him. Queen Mary assures him that his friends will understand that, as prince, he is sometimes obliged to do things that seem a little 'silly', but it will be 'only for this once'.

Indeed it was. Against the dramatic backdrop of a medieval castle, Prince Edward was invested with a robe, a coronet, a sword that symbolised justice, a golden ring to represent duty and a golden rod as a symbol of government. His elaborate investiture as Prince of Wales was the closest he came to his own coronation.

Following his birth on 23 June 1894, Prince Edward was named after his father's brother who had always been known as 'Eddy', but as is common in the royal family he was known by one of his other Christian names – 'David'. At birth he was in the unique position of being the third male heir in direct line to the throne. This situation wasn't repeated for over one hundred years, on the birth of Prince George in 2013. During his early childhood, David's family were still very much dominated by the overarching presence of his great-grandmother Queen Victoria, who took a close interest in most things and was forthright in voicing her opinions. As a boy, David was present at both the funeral of Queen Victoria, and the coronations of his grandfather and father. After the accession of his father in 1910, David became heir apparent and moved with his family to Buckingham Palace.

After being educated privately at home by tutors, David studied at the Royal Naval College, Osborne, followed by the Royal Naval College at Dartmouth. During the First World War he served in the British army, though was not allowed to fight on the frontline. As he got older, his fondness for ceremonial and royal duties did not appear to grow. Although he undertook gruelling royal tours of the dominions on behalf of his father, and was a popular figure, he found the role of Prince of Wales onerous. On one visit to Nottinghamshire in the summer of 1923, he was greeted by 3,000 flag-waving schoolchildren, singing 'God Bless the Prince of Wales', and toured local mining towns. At the end of the day, when one of the hosts expressed relief that the event was over, the prince replied, 'It may be over for you, but it's never, ever over for me. Most of my days are like this, and there seems to be no end to it.'[1]

As Prince of Wales, David brought star power to the monarchy, in a way that wasn't seen again until the days of Diana, Princess of Wales. He had a charisma and popularity that even his father envied. But by age 38, the still unmarried Prince of Wales's lifestyle was a cause for concern, to his parents and the government. He had many relationships with married women, including a passionate affair with a French courtesan, who later shot her husband at the Savoy hotel in Paris. His father George V talked to him about the need to marry – telling him that the days of the British public accepting royal princes having mistresses were long gone.

In response, the reason David gave that he hadn't married was that he didn't care to marry a foreign princess and he understood that the

King would not want him to marry a commoner. His father assured him that times had changed and he would be prepared to accept 'a suitable well-born English girl'. David replied that the only woman he had ever felt that he might want to marry was Freda Dudley-Ward, his long-term mistress, but since she was already married this was not quite what his father had in mind.

George V tried to talk to his son about his future destiny, and for the dutiful monarch who had always striven to do what was expected of him, it must have been painful not to be able to exert greater influence over his son. In a series of conversations between father and son, he tried to be understanding as well as frank. He asked David if he was happy, because 'he never looked very happy', and wondered if David did not sometimes long to have someone he could turn to for sympathy and true affection, apart from mere physical satisfaction. To which David admitted that no, he wasn't particularly happy.[2]

At stake was more than just personal happiness, but the future of the Crown itself. George V impressed upon his son that England had never had an unmarried King, and how would that work? Life at court would be difficult without a Queen. He also spoke of David's lifestyle, which was public knowledge and considered immoral. On one occasion he said he had met with the Archbishops of Canterbury and York that week, and how could David, once King, undertake such meetings when they knew all about his immoral lifestyle? From the records we have of these conversations it seems that, while obviously difficult for both parties, they were amicable and frank, with David admitting many of his father's concerns were fair criticism.[3]

But they did not appear to have much effect. By the early 1930s, it became obvious among the Prince of Wales's friends that he had settled into a relationship with one woman in particular – the married American Wallis Simpson. Wallis and her husband were frequent guests at David's house, Fort Belvedere, where Wallis would act as his hostess during glamorous house parties.

In Whitehall and at Buckingham Palace, managing the fallout from the affair caused many diplomatic headaches. Files labelled 'Concerns over the PoW' grew ever thicker. David's frequent trips abroad with Wallis threatened to damage the international reputation of the monarchy. In

1935, the Austrian government tried to pre-empt a rumoured arrival of Edward and Mrs Simpson in Venice, which they thought would create a 'deplorable impression'.[4]

When he became King, on the death of George V, in 1936, David saw no reason to change his lifestyle or give up Wallis. It was his view that once she had secured her divorce, the country would accept their marriage.

Still wary of royal ceremonial, Edward VIII did not really want a coronation, and questioned the need for having one at all. Like William IV, he seemed to have no personal appetite for the ceremony, and failed to understand its importance. Just a few months into his reign, when Archbishop of Canterbury Cosmo Lang spoke to him about the historical and religious significance of the coronation, he was shocked when the King expressed the wish that the service could be shortened or perhaps dropped altogether. Eventually, he was persuaded as to its necessity, but insisted on cutting out the litany and sermon to make it shorter. He also wanted cutbacks to the pageantry element, believing there was no need for a royal procession on the day after the coronation. We might never have seen the huge, celebratory pageants that characterise modern coronations had the abdication never happened.

A Coronation Committee was duly formed, and planning got underway for the event, which was to take place in May of the following year. While they pondered over logistics, guest lists and carriage processions, the government, the country and the media were more concerned with the developing scandal surrounding the King's relationship with Mrs Simpson. As Wallis's divorce was finalised, and David appeared to distance himself from his family, fears grew over how the situation could be resolved. When Prime Minister Stanley Baldwin eventually made clear to the King that marriage to Wallis and remaining on the throne was not a viable option, David chose to abdicate, announcing that he couldn't continue in his role without the woman he loved. The shock waves of this decision reverberated through the country, being felt most strongly by his family. Queen Mary found it very hard to comprehend how, understanding the sacrifices people had made coming through the war, the King was not prepared to make what seemed a much smaller sacrifice, to fulfil his duty. Never before had a monarch voluntarily given up their position, and the abdication posed difficult questions for the institution of monarchy. If being King was a job you could resign from, then how could that be squared with the notion that sovereigns are chosen by God? The presence of the Duke and Duchess of York, Bertie and Elizabeth, who could step up in the place of Edward VIII helped ease the pain, as did the fact that David had not yet had a coronation. Although not legally binding, the very public crowning of a monarch during a coronation, along with the religious rites and ancient traditions, not to mention the cost, implies an unbreakable commitment. Edward VIII's timely decision may have saved the monarchy: had he abdicated following a coronation, it might have been far more difficult to row back. Even if the monarchy had survived, it's difficult to see how coronations could have carried on in the traditional way. How could a monarch take a sacred oath if that oath had been shown to be not binding?

Following the abdication announcement on 11 December 1936, material that had been prepared for Edward VIII's coronation had to be hastily buried. Such items included a 'Coronation Issue' of the *Illustrated London News* that featured portraits of Edward VIII in coronation scenes including his crowning and homage, by well-known artists of the time, including Fortunino Matania and Albert H. Cowlings, who had painted the front cover portrait of Edward VIII in his coronation robes. The *Illustrated London News* had been planning the issue for months, and was expecting huge sales for its special edition to be published immediately after the coronation. The news of the abdication came as a blow, but editor Bruce Ingram was determined not to let all the work and expense go to waste: in an early 'royal photoshop', he called Cowlings back and asked him to replace Edward VIII's head with George VI; a task for which Cowling was paid £21 (around £1,800 in today's money).[5]

Coins featuring Edward VIII's image, scheduled for release in January 1937, had to be melted down, and many retailers were left with unwanted stock of coronation mugs, plates and other mementoes. In the years since the abdication, Edward VIII coronation memorabilia has gained favour with collectors precisely for its rarity value. An Edward VIII coronation mug may fetch £50 to £80 at auction, while you can pick up a more common George VI coronation mug for a few pounds.

For David's loyal friends and supporters, the news that they would never see their glamorous celebrity-King take the starring role at his own magnificent coronation was a bitter pill to swallow. 'The operetta reign is over, ten months of fun and splendour and indiscretion,' lamented Henry 'Chips' Channon. 'What would the coronation season have been like had only he remained? Something too splendid to dwell upon: it had been hoped for a fantastic summer; but now – convention will triumph, and gaiety will lie dead.'[6]

A few weeks later, on 3 June, David married Wallis at the Château de Candé, her divorce having been finalised. The wedding was a small, 'sad little service',[7] with no members of David's family attending and only a handful of his English friends. Guests who did attend included the Château's owner Charles Bedaux and his wife Fern, who had generously hosted the wedding. Bedaux's contacts with the Nazi party in Germany would later lead the Duke and Duchess of Windsor to create stronger links with Hitler's Germany. Indebted to Bedaux, whose business interests motivated him to create good relationships with Nazi Germany, and embittered by his treatment from the British royals, David agreed that he and Wallis would tour Germany in the autumn of 1937. The resulting pictures were a propaganda coup for Hitler, and another blow for the Duke of Windsor's reputation and by extension the British monarchy. Bedaux himself was imprisoned by the FBI during the war for his close links with the enemy, eventually committing suicide before he could stand trial.[8]

The subject of what to do with the Duke of Windsor was frequently discussed back home: at one point Churchill came up with an idea for him to settle in America, taking on a diplomatic position, but there was concern around him having a high profile in Washington.[9] The King was concerned about his brother's tendency to get too involved in political affairs, even giving unwanted advice to government officials. Visits to London were fraught with tension, the mood in Buckingham Palace when the Duke of Windsor departed again was invariably one of relief. 'Anyhow, he has come and gone, without a breach of the peace. I feel rather as one did on hearing the all clear after a prolonged air-raid,' reads the King's Private Secretary Tommy Lascelles's diary entry after one such visit.[10]

David visited London in September 1951 to promote his memoir, *A King's Story*. Written with the help of an American ghostwriter, the book alienated the Duke of Windsor further from his family, who saw it as yet another betrayal and didn't welcome the attention it would bring once again on the abdication.

But, in the immediate aftermath of the abdication, life went on. Throughout the summer and autumn of 1936, amid a backdrop of the developing abdication crisis, the Coronation Committee had stoically continued to meet regularly. Now that Edward VIII had gone, there was still a coronation to organise, albeit for a different King.

Chapter Twelve

THE CROWN LANDS ON THE SECOND SON'S HEAD

On Saturday, 12 December 1936, the nation woke up in the new reign of George VI, the third King that year. When, twelve days later, the Coronation Executive Committee gathered for their scheduled meeting, no reference was made to the abdication or change of King. In sublime 'Keep Calm and Carry On' mode, everything was seamlessly transferred to the new monarch.[1]

During his ten-month reign as King, Edward VIII had been preoccupied with Wallis, and continued to enjoy long cruising holidays with her, so he had been absent for much of the coronation planning. In his absence his younger brother Bertie, now George VI, had taken his place on the Coronation Committee, so fortuitously he was already well briefed. Items on the agenda at their regular meetings, which had taken place since July, had included how to include the dominions in the service, what routes the processions should take, and how to accommodate the vast numbers of dignitaries and troops who would descend on London for the occasion. It was immediately accepted that the coronation would go ahead on the originally scheduled date of 12 May 1937; the most significant alteration to the plans was the need to accommodate a Queen Consort in the ceremony.

His father George V, as a royal second son, had been required to step into his older brother's shoes, yet Bertie, second son of George V, could never have imagined that a similar fate would befall him. But, just three days before his 41st birthday, having said goodbye to his brother and lifelong companion, who sailed away into exile in the night, Bertie ascended the throne. Christened Albert Frederick Arthur George, but always known as Bertie, he declared his wish to be known as George VI as a tribute to his father. Suddenly having Kingship thrust upon him must have come as an unwelcome shock both for himself and his wife, who was 'quite overcome with horror and emotion'[2] when Bertie first told her what his brother planned to do.

Until now, Bertie had followed a fairly traditional path for a second son. Having grown up somewhat in the shadow of his able, articulate older brother, he had struggled all his life with a speech impediment, and didn't seek the limelight. As a child, he had to wear leg braces, considered a cure for 'knock knees', and he was often ill. His tutors forced him to write with his right hand, even though he was naturally left-handed. At 8, he developed the stammer that would plague him for the rest of his life. Joining the Royal Navy in 1913, Bertie, as a dispensable 'spare' had, unlike his older brother, been allowed to see active service during the First World War and was mentioned in despatches for his role in the Battle of Jutland in 1916. A gentler, more conventional character than his brother, he married Elizabeth Bowes-Lyon, who was from an aristocratic Scottish family, at Westminster Abbey in 1923. As Duke and Duchess of York, they created a happy family life together with their two daughters, Elizabeth (known as Lilibet) and Margaret Rose, undertaking charity work, attending royal events and making Commonwealth tours. Although Bertie considered himself to be unfit to be King, when he was required to step up, his strong sense of duty meant he didn't shy away from the task ahead. He also benefitted from the loyal support of his wife, now Queen Elizabeth, and mother, the dowager Queen Mary.

The Coronation Executive Committee was chaired by the Duke of Norfolk and included the Archbishop of Canterbury Cosmo Lang, who took a prominent role in the planning of the service. Although the Earl Marshal has overall responsibility for organising coronations, it is the Lord Chamberlain who is responsible for the provision of the regalia, robes and arranging their transportation safely to the Abbey. Records now held in the Royal Archive at Windsor Castle detail the efforts of the Lord Chamberlain's office in tracking down the relevant crowns, robes and regalia, last used in 1911. It was decided that a new crown would be commissioned for Queen Elizabeth, at a cost of £6,820. A new columbium sindonis (white surplice) is provided at each coronation, and in 1937 cost five pounds and five shillings.

Some items proved easier to track down than others. A new canopy and poles were purchased at a cost of £410, after those used at the 1902 and 1911 coronations 'could not be found anywhere'.[3]

It also falls to the Lord Chamberlain, as the most senior member of the King's household staff, to supply the Earl Marshal with a list of names associated with the royal household, who will need coronation invitations. In 1937, the numbers looked like this:

> Royal Family in Royal Box – 49
> The King's Box – 52
> The Queen's Box – 30
> Queen Mary's Box – 30
> Seats at disposal of Royal Family – 60
> Royal Households (with wives) – 230
> Officers of the Royal Yachts – 11

Just one week after Edward VIII delivered his abdication speech to a shocked nation, the new King and Queen were holding their first meeting with the crown jewellers to discuss their coronation crowns. The jewellers explained that the Imperial State Crown was in fact in poor condition, and the King asked for an estimate for remaking it, at the same time reducing its weight. At a further meeting in January, the crown jewellers were instructed to prepare designs for a new crown for the Queen Consort, incorporating the Koh-i-Noor diamond. The design finally selected, at a meeting in Sandringham on 20 January, was for a conventional crown of four arches set with over 2,800 diamonds, including jewels that had belonged to Queen Victoria.

The St Edward's Crown was also in need of some sprucing up and was brought, under police escort, from the Tower of London, to Messrs Garrards' premises in Albemarle Street on 26 April. The royal jewellers then set about restoring the crown, including fitting a new internal cap. The jewellers also had to re-size the coronation rings and polish up the rest of the regalia.

Meanwhile, the India Office and Colonial Office were busy preparing lists of representatives from the Empire who would be invited. These included twenty-nine Indian princes and, for the first time, African royalty. Monarchies from around the world mostly signalled their intention to send their crown princes and princesses, observing the convention that crowned heads themselves do not attend coronations. Among royal guests were the Count of Flanders, the Crown Prince and Princess of Denmark, Princess Juliana and Prince Bernhard of the Netherlands, Crown Prince Michael of Romania, Crown Prince Olaf of Norway, the Crown Prince and Princess of Sweden, and Prince Chichibu, brother of the Emperor of Japan.

Many monarchies, of course, had disappeared in the twenty-five years since the previous coronation.

There were significant changes in the guest list since 1911. Following Germany's defeat in the First World War, King Wilhelm II had abdicated, leading to the establishment of the Weimar Republic, which mandated an end to legal privileges and titles of German nobility, including their royals. The long list of grand dukes and duchesses associated with the former German Empire had vanished, along with several other European monarchies. Sweeping changes across the continent in the aftermath of the war meant that the Russian Empire had gone, as had the Austro-Hungarian Empire and the Ottoman Empire. The Kingdoms of Prussia and Hungary were no more, and the Spanish monarchy was abolished in 1931 when the second Spanish republic was established. By 1937, Hitler was in power in Germany, Mussolini in Italy and Stalin in Russia, though none of these dictators attended the coronation in person.

The aristocracy had to be accommodated, of course, along with the upper echelons of the church. The Norroy King of Arms suggested seats needed were:

Archbishops – 2
Bishops – 41
Dukes – 4
Earls – 77
Barons – 138

The peers and other guests received their summons from the Earl Marshal which, as tradition dictated, were written in antiquated language.

> Right Trusty and Well-beloved – We greet you well.
>
> Whereas the twelfth day of May next is appointed for the Solemnity of our Royal Coronation.
>
> These are to Will and Command you and the Lady your wife (all excuses set apart) to make your personal attendance on Us at the times above-mentioned, furnished and appointed as to your Rank and Quality appertaineth, there to do and perform all such Services as shall be required and belong unto you respectively.
>
> Whereof you and she are not to fail. And so We bid you most heartily farewell.
>
> Given at our Court of St James's this twelfth day of April in the first year of Our Reign.[4]

The use of language that wouldn't have seemed out of place in fifteenth-century England on the invitations was also seen elsewhere in printed materials relating to the coronation. In the same way, even though motorised transport was now the norm, horse-drawn carriages continued to be used. In many ways, the coronation, far from being 'modernised', was very deliberately kept in the past, with archaisms employed to drive home the weight of centuries of tradition that gave it gravitas.

While accepting that the coronation was a matter for the Earl Marshal's office to organise, staff at the Abbey remained diligent in their efforts to safeguard their traditional responsibilities. In 1937, there was much deliberation and concern over who should be in charge of the music. Whereas in 1911 and 1902, the Abbey's Sir Frederick Bridge had been in charge, there were questions over whether the current organist Dr Ernest Bullock had sufficient experience, and it was mooted that the role should go to Master of the King's Music, Sir Walford Davis. Although the Coronation Committee had the right to appoint whom they pleased, a memo from the Abbey was sent, emphasising precedents that showed the Abbey was almost always in charge. Dr Bullock was duly appointed with the proviso that he would consult with the Master of the King's Music on all matters.[5]

Beneath all this activity and planning and the 'Don't mention the abdication' stiff upper lip that prevailed in the corridors of power, there was a very real determination to double down on coronation preparations. The need was not just to crown a new King and Queen, but to steady a ship that had been severely rocked. How do you sail the monarchy and the country into calmer waters, after it has just been dealt a painfully destabilising blow? Through pageantry, of course. The coronation just got bigger. From a whole month's worth of official celebration and events, to a more extensive parade, and larger guest list, scaling up was the order of the day. The historian Roy Strong has described how in 1937, the monarchy went into overdrive, escalating the coronation celebration in order to regain the confidence of a nation. What had begun as a liturgical ceremony centuries earlier was now a vehicle to secure the survival of the monarchy itself.[6]

Constitutional changes since the coronation of George V in 1911 meant that certain sections of the coronation service had to be reworded, and subsequent alterations were reported in *The Times* on 20 February, following discussions with the Governments of the dominions. In 1931, a landmark piece of legislation known as the Statute of Westminster had formally recognised the legal equality of the dominions, including Canada, Australia, New Zealand, South Africa and the Irish Free State, with the United Kingdom sitting within the Commonwealth of countries. This gave the dominions full legislative authority – the power to make their own laws, including on foreign policy. Rather than issuing a general commitment to uphold the laws of the British Empire, George VI would govern the peoples of the various realms 'according to their respective laws and customs'.

Several of the Commonwealth prime ministers were Roman Catholic, and the Coronation Committee also had to negotiate a change to the wording when it came to maintaining the Protestant faith, limiting this responsibility to the United Kingdom. So, the King would now swear to maintain the true profession of the Gospel and to maintain the 'Protestant Reformed Religion' only as established by law in the United Kingdom.

The decision wasn't a universally popular one, and there's a distinct whiff of understatement when Australian Prime Minister Joseph Lyons alluded to 'minor difficulties' in getting various dominions to agree on a new wording, but said that the discussions had been 'most valuable in clarifying the existing constitutional relationship between the members of the British Commonwealth'. Mr Lyons also supported the change to the wording around the maintenance of the Protestant religion, arguing that this part of the oath concerned only the United Kingdom, and had no relation to Australia, as there was no established Church in Australia.[7]

As coronation fever took hold, the costs mounted up: the total bill for the 1937 coronation would be almost three times that of 1911. The annexe at the entrance to the Abbey was once again constructed, this time in an Art Deco design, decorated with tapestries and heraldic beasts.

On 8 August, the King's private secretary Alec Hardinge wrote to Sir John Reith, director-general of the BBC, giving an 'early intimation to the effect that the King has expressed a wish to broadcast to the Empire on the evening of Coronation day'. It was the start of months of correspondence between Buckingham Palace and the BBC to make arrangements for an evening broadcast, which included secret rehearsals and even an advance recording, which the BBC wanted to have to broadcast throughout the night of 12/13 May to the Empire.[8]

Reith's earlier suggestion that the coronation service itself should be televised had been dismissed by Archbishop Cosmo Lang, who regarded the idea as incompatible with the religious ceremony, and might possibly risk exposing the King's physical twitches.[9] It was agreed, however, that the service would be broadcast on the radio – the first coronation that the public could listen in on.

For King George VI, the coronation loomed like a trial date. Would he be able to demonstrate to the country and the watching world that he was the man to lead Britain? There were some who voiced doubts as to his fitness for the job, and there were even unfounded rumours that he suffered from epilepsy.[10] The news that the King and Queen did not plan to travel to India for a 'Delhi Durbar' style celebration, as George V and Queen Mary had done, provoked more questions about the never-robust health of the King. In a role where communicating with the people was essential, a King who often quite literally couldn't get his words out was at a disadvantage.

Such negative perceptions only worsened after the Archbishop of Canterbury, Cosmo Lang, during an interview with the BBC, alongside praise for the new King's abilities and strengths, rather unhelpfully started to talk about the 'hesitation in his speech', adding that the King had 'brought it into full control' and stressing that it need not be a source of embarrassment. The King's speech therapist Lionel Logue was annoyed by the remarks, which seemed unnecessary and untrue: they would only bring attention to the King's stammer, which in fact he still struggled with on a daily basis. Logue was closely involved in putting in place arrangements for the evening broadcast, as well as continuing to work hard with Bertie in the weeks leading up to the coronation, as has since been dramatised in the film *The King's Speech*. The King practised broadcasting standing up, which allowed him to breathe more easily. An earlier traumatising experience when he had attempted to give a speech at Wembley in 1925 had left him ever more anxious around microphones. With Logue, he really put in the work ahead of the coronation, with hours and hours of voice drills, breathing exercises, word practice and more… But would it be enough?

The King's performance when addressing a lunch arranged for the dominion prime ministers at Westminster Hall on 7 May, just five days before the coronation, did not bode well. After lunch, the Lord Chancellor made a short speech and toast to the King's health, after which His Majesty rose to speak. The amplifier was put in front of him, and 'for a few terrible seconds, minutes even, there was a dead silence, as he could not get his words out'.[11] The King recovered and managed to give the short speech, but it was painful for the audience to listen to, although recalling the lunch to Queen Mary, Bertie himself noted that the event was 'very moving' and 'struck just the right note'.[12]

On Tuesday, 11 May, at 7.30am, all the regalia, including the crowns, were transported from 24 Albemarle Street to the Jerusalem Chamber at Westminster Abbey, in a police van with an escort. Once inside the Jerusalem Chamber, Mr A. C. Mann of Garrard and Company, who had escorted the regalia, carefully unpacked each item and showed it to the Dean of Westminster, Dr Foxley Norris, who examined and signed for it.

A guard of Yeoman Warders of the Tower was on duty at the Jerusalem Chamber during the whole period the regalia were kept there.[13]

Later on Tuesday, Dr Foxley Norris gave a tea party for a small, fortunate group, who worked and lived at the Abbey, to enable them to view the regalia. The Garrard's jeweller took each object out of its case in turn and carried it around the room, so everyone was able to see it close up. Abbey staff member Lawrence Tanner vividly remembers the experience: 'It was a very wonderful sight and I remember especially the flawless beauty of the Cullinan Diamond in the King's Sceptre and the Black Prince's Ruby in the Crown.'[14] In the midst of this most rarefied of tea parties, Tanner also noticed that the guard standing behind him was holding a poorly concealed loaded revolver under his tunic and, on glancing around, saw several other similarly armed guards in close proximity. Afterwards Tanner joked to the Governor of the Tower about the security, pointing out that the tea party was supposed to be for the Dean's personal friends, and received the reply: 'Yes, but it was the Regalia of England and I wasn't going to take any chances!'[15]

In the evening, the King and Queen met with the Archbishop of Canterbury to run through the service and pray together. Lang recalled the meeting: 'I was much moved and so were they. Indeed, there were tears in their eyes when we rose from our knees.' Bertie's sincere religious faith was to help him get through the ordeal he faced on the following day. Every monarch is under pressure to perform well at their coronation, but for George VI, in the wake of the abdication scandal, the stakes were higher than ever. On the eve of his coronation, he knew that he must convince in the role of King Emperor – but would he even be able to utter his five brief responses to the Archbishop during the ceremony, let alone broadcast to the Empire?

Chapter Thirteen

CORONATION DAY 1937

The Coronation of His Majesty George VI of the United Kingdom of Great Britain and Northern Ireland and of the British Dominions beyond the Seas, King, Defender of the Faith, Emperor of India, and of Her Majesty Queen Elizabeth, His Consort.

Date:	Wednesday, 12 May 1937
Guests:	8,000
Cost:	£454,000
Weather:	Overcast with rain showers and a few sunny spells.

Early morning

At Buckingham Palace, the King and Queen are woken at 3.00am by the sound of loudspeakers being tested on nearby Constitution Hill.[1] 'One of them might have been in our room,' recalled the King, who was unable to return to sleep due to the noise.

In her bedroom down the corridor, 11-year-old Lilibet is woken at 5.00am by the band of the Royal Marines striking up just below her window. Running to the window, Lilibet and her nanny Bobo, who slept in the bed next to her, look out onto a misty morning and see people already arriving to take to the stands that have been erected outside Buckingham Palace. There is a chill in the air and Bobo drapes an eiderdown around her young charge's shoulders. Lilibet returns to bed but does not get much more sleep, hopping up every now and then to watch the scene unfolding outside the palace.

By 7.00am, crowds have also assembled along the route to the Abbey – trains on the London underground have been running all through the night – and they cheer as a steady stream of cars carrying guests drive past. Some people have been in place all night to secure a good view.

Excited guests meet in the streets around the Abbey, while inside, Gold Sticks conduct the guests to their blue-velvet-covered seats. The seating plan is conscious of social hierarchies; diarist and MP Chips Channon is seated in the gallery of the South Transept, immediately behind the viscounts and barons. Some government ministers have also been placed behind the barons, to the indignation of some.

At Buckingham Palace, the royal family get ready for the day. The King is too nervous to eat breakfast, and has 'a sinking feeling inside'. He finds this part of the day, waiting to make the journey to Westminster Abbey, the most nerve-racking.[2] His valet helps him dress in white knee breeches and stockings, a red satin surcoat, an ermine cape and a red velvet cap of maintenance.[3]

Guests continue to arrive at the Abbey. The King, through his connections with the Industrial Welfare Society, has personally invited four 'working people' to be present at the coronation: a Scottish woman weaver, a South Wales steelworks foreman, a young woman employed at the Birmingham Electrical works, and a young pit worker from Chesterfield.[4]

They are far outnumbered by the peers, dowager peeresses and peeresses, in their robes of estate, and others invited by His Majesty's command to be present at the coronation. All are conducted to their places in the Abbey before 8.30am at which time the doors of the Abbey are closed.

Complying with the dress code orders from the Earl Marshal, gentlemen are wearing full dress uniform or full velvet court dress. Ladies are wearing court dress, with feathers and veils and as much jewellery as possible – whether their own or borrowed – which creates a sparkly and sometimes dazzling atmosphere in the dim light of the Abbey.

The peeresses sit together, jewels blazing, in hierarchical rows. The four duchesses who have been chosen to hold the Queen's canopy have pride of place at the front. Sitting opposite, Channon gazes on 'a vitrine of bosoms and jewels and bobbing tiaras';[5] while another spectator describes how the peeresses' flashing jewels gave the illusion of a waterfall as they moved: 'through them seemed to trickle streams of clearest water'.

The Lords Spiritual are seated on the north side of the central Theatre or Sacrarium, the Lords Temporal in the South Transept and the dowager peeresses and peeresses in the North Transept. In the traditional setup, between the two transepts is the Theatre itself, with the thrones. The ancient St Edward's Chair faces the altar.

Even the lavatory arrangements are rank-conscious, with facilities set aside for the exclusive use of 'peers' and 'peeresses'.

At around 8.30am, the Dean of Westminster, 78-year-old William Foxley Norris, is in the Jerusalem Chamber, handing out the various objects of regalia to members of the clergy, who will carry them, via a side route through the Cloisters, to the altar. The Dean, to his 'horror and consternation',[6] suddenly realises the Imperial State Crown, which he had intended to hand to the Sub-dean to carry, is missing. In what he later describes as 'the worst 10 minutes of my life', the Dean instead hands the Sub-dean the St Edward's Crown and is forced to join the outwardly calm and dignified clergy procession empty handed, having no idea as to the whereabouts of the priceless Imperial Crown entrusted to his care. When he finally reaches the altar, he discovers to his immense relief that someone has already placed the crown there.[7]

The regalia is then borne through the Abbey to the West Door, to await the arrival of their Majesties. The congregation pause their chatter to watch the regalia being carried.

Foreign representatives arrive at the Abbey and are shown to their seats. The delegation from the United States includes World War I Commander General Pershing, and Mr James Gerard, former US Ambassador to Berlin.

Germany was one of the last countries to confirm who they would send to the coronation, which led to a good deal of anxiety over the possibility that Hitler himself might attend.[8] In the end, the German delegation is exclusively a military one, made up of Field Marshal Werner von Blomberg, the War Minister, naval officer Admiral Otto Schulze, and Major General Hans Juergen Stumpff of the air force.

The Soviet Union have sent their foreign secretary, and King Victor Emmanuel III and Queen Elena attend from Italy.

The two young princesses ride from the palace with their aunt, Princess Mary, in the glass coach. Lilibet finds the carriage ride down the Mall, through Admiralty Arch and along Whitehall 'quite jolty', but can be seen waving and smiling from the windows.

All eyes are now on members of the royal family as they enter the Abbey and begin the walk down the Nave. The two royal duchesses draw admiring comments from the watching Channon: the Duchess of Kent ('surpassingly beautiful'); and the Duchess of Gloucester ('looked so lovely that for a moment I thought she was Princess Marina!').

Those who catch a glimpse of the two young princesses, Lilibet and 7-year-old Margaret-Rose, are enchanted by their fairy-tale appearance. Identically dressed in white silk puff-sleeve dresses, decorated with cream lace and gold bows down the middle, they too are wearing robes made of rich purple velvet with gold edging. Their impeccable behaviour does not quite mask their excitement as they walk up the Nave, to the gentle strains of Grieg, and climb up to their seats in the royal box on the south side of the Sacrarium, accessible via a curved staircase.

At 10.35am Queen Mary arrives – she is breaking with tradition in being the first Dowager Queen to attend a coronation. She has seen it as her duty to support her son, and has been very involved in preparations for the day, attending rehearsals, giving advice for what will be her third coronation, and visiting foreign royals arriving in London. She is accompanied by her sister-in-law, Princess Maud, the Queen of Norway, and an entourage of senior members of her household, and they are met by the Earl Marshal.

The orchestra switch to the more demonstrative melody of Edward German's 'Coronation March', and the congregation are moved by the sight of the dignified and revered 70-year-old Queen Mary moving slowly up the Nave, statuesque and regal as ever, for what is a poignant moment for her. She wears a long gold dress, hand embroidered with flowers, layered diamond necklaces and a diamond circlet on her silver hair. 'Granny looked too beautiful,' approves Lilibet.

The King and Queen leave Buckingham Palace at 10.34am. They are accompanied by officers and cavalry of several regiments, including mounted Life Guards in red coats with black plumed helmets, the

Royal Horse Artillery, mounted and marching bands, and the King's Indian Orderly Officers. The King and Queen are in the huge Gold State Coach, drawn by eight grey horses. They are followed on horseback by high-ranking officials and aides-de-camp, including the Gold Stick in waiting and the King's brothers, the Dukes of Kent and Gloucester, and Lord Louis Mountbatten, in his role as personal aide-de-camp to the King.

The Route to Westminster goes by the Mall, Admiralty Arch, Trafalgar Square, Whitehall, Parliament Street, the east side of Parliament Square, St Margaret's Street, and Broad Sanctuary to the west entrance of Westminster Abbey.

A guard of honour has formed at the vestibule for the King and Queen's arrival and as they enter the West Door, they are greeted by the Archbishops, the Earl Marshal and other great officers of state, as well as the peers carrying their regalia.

A fanfare of trumpets sound and all rise.

The anthem 'I Was Glad' strikes up as the Queen's procession starts up the Nave. She is flanked by two bishops and attended by six maids of honour wearing identical white gowns and diamond tiaras. The Queen is dignified in her beautiful silk satin gown, with gold-embroidered emblems of the national symbols, but the characteristic charm is there as she smiles in acknowledgement of those she passes. Soon the procession comes to an abrupt halt – it seems that one of the chaplains has fainted, causing an obstruction. A mini-drama now plays out as aides and fellow clergy wonder what to do with him, and the King waits with his own procession, 'it seemed for hours'.[9] Finally, the unfortunate chaplain is removed, and the procession restarts.

As she passes through the Choir, which is packed with dignitaries, the traditional shouts from the Westminster schoolboys in the seats above ring out:

> 'Vivat Regina Elizabetha!'
> 'Vivat Rex Georgius!'

The Queen and her entourage bow to the altar, before the Queen smiles at her young daughters in the royal box, and takes her seat in her Chair of Estate.

The King's Procession follows the Queen's; he is also flanked by two bishops and surrounded by his officers bearing the regalia. The King's crimson great robes of state, with an ermine-bordered train, are borne by nine pages of honour; on his head he wears the Cap of Estate. The King bows to his mother, Queen Mary, and his family in the gallery, before taking his seat.

The recognition

The King now doffs his cap of maintenance and stands in the Sacrarium for his 'Recognition' as 'King George your undoubted King'.[10] He turns to show himself to each of the four corners. There are shouts of 'Long Live King George!' and the sound of trumpets and beating drums.

The oath

The oath has been moved up in the service since 1911, restoring it to its 'logical medieval positioning'[11] at the beginning of the service. Seated in his Chair of Estate, the King is asked by the Archbishop: 'Sir, is Your Majesty willing to take the oath?' Many in the congregation hold their breath, willing the King to be able to respond fluently.

'I am willing,' comes the reply, without hesitation.

The King kneels before the altar and swears on the bible.

In the first amendment to the coronation oath since 1689, the wording now reflects the legislative independence of the dominions.

Archbishop:	Will you solemnly promise and swear to govern the Peoples of Great Britain, Ireland, Canada, Australia, New Zealand and the Union of South Africa, of your Possessions and the other Territories to any of them belonging or pertaining, and of your Empire of India, according to their respective Laws and Customs?
King:	I solemnly promise so to do.

Still, there is no hesitation.

Archbishop: Will you to your power cause Law and Justice, in Mercy, to be executed in all your Judgements?
King: I will.

Three responses have been given without painful pauses.

Archbishop: Will you to the utmost of your power maintain the Laws of God and the true profession of the Gospel? Will you to the utmost of your power maintain in the United Kingdom the Protestant Reformed Religion established by Law? And will you maintain and preserve inviolably the Settlement of the Church of England, and the Doctrine, Worship, Discipline, and government thereof, as by Law established in England? And will you preserve unto the Bishops and Clergy of England, and to the Churches there committed to their charge, all such Rights and Privileges, as by Law do or shall appertain to them, or any of them?
King: All this I promise to do.

Despite one bishop obscuring the words of the oath with his thumb as he is reading it, the King manages to say his words. No doubt relieved, he then signs the oath, twice dipping his pen in the ink, which gets all over his fingers.

Next, he walks over to the faldstool where he lays his right hand on an open bible and says: 'The things which I have here before promised, I will perform and keep. So help me God!'

The final hurdle has been jumped and the King's words, careful and deliberate but fluent, are heard clearly through the loudspeakers. He is intensely relieved that he has managed to say his lines with 'not a moment's hesitation or mistake' as he later writes to Lionel Logue, thanking him for his 'expert tuition and unfailing patience'.

The anointing

The Archbishop of Canterbury leads the communion service, after which the King and Queen kneel, as the choir sing 'Veni, Creator Spiritus' followed by Handel's 'Zadok the Priest'.

The King prepares for the most sacred part of the service: his crimson velvet robe, red satin under-robe, and cape are removed. Now dressed modestly in a white shirt and breeches, he sits in King Edward's Chair, facing the altar. The golden canopy borne by four Knights of the Garter, wearing deep blue velvet cloaks, is placed over him.

The Archbishop anoints George VI with holy oil, in the ancient sequence, starting with the palms of both hands, his chest, his finger and the top of his head. He has his back to most of the congregation at this point, but from the royal box Queen Mary watches her son and the scene brings back 'memories and emotions'[12] of her and George V's Coronation Day, twenty-six eventful years earlier. She wipes a tear from her eyes – a moment caught by cameras filming the ceremony, but one that will be edited out before the film is screened in cinemas.

Once consecrated, the Dean of Westminster helps the King into the Colobium Sindonis, but it appears inside out and the King's Groom of the Robes has to provide assistance. The next layer is the golden supertunica and girdle. The Lord Great Chamberlain's hands fumble and shake as he tries to dress the King, who lends assistance. The King then receives his royal regalia, including the golden spurs, the Sword of State, and the gold jewel-encrusted Orb. The Archbishop places the ring on the fourth finger of his right hand. Finally, he assumes the gold Imperial Mantle.

Holding a Sceptre in each hand, a shaft of sunlight catches the King's golden tunic as he waits for the Archbishop and the Dean to approach with the crown.

Worried that the Archbishop would not be able to tell the difference between the front and the back of St Edward's Crown, the King had tied a piece of red cotton to the front of it as a guide in rehearsals. Unfortunately, the red cotton has been removed and the Archbishop of Canterbury moves to place the crown on back to front – the King himself having to correct him, anxious that if the 7 lbs crown is not fitted correctly, it would be in danger of dislodging.

Peers don their coronets at the moment of crowning, while young Lilibet looks up to see the arches and beams at the top of the Abbey 'covered with a sort of haze of wonder'.[13]

Leaving the Coronation Chair, and walking to the throne in the centre of the Theatre, the King nearly trips when a bishop accidentally stands on the end of his robes and he has to 'tell him to get off pretty sharply'.[14]

But for those watching, the transformational power of the coronation ceremony in the ancient setting weaves its magic. The King looks more regal than ever before. The King and Queen appear deeply moved by the ceremony and are somehow able to convey their deep emotion so that the whole congregation feels it, too. To some, the King looks like a medieval knight, a rapt expression in his eyes, that gaze straight ahead.[15]

The homage

Next, the King walks to his elevated throne to receive the homage. He is lifted onto the throne by the Archbishop and senior officers of state, in the gesture that demonstrates the power of Church and State.

Sitting on his throne, with the sun streaming in, the King looks youthful and shy, yet also regal, as the Archbishop of Canterbury drops to his knees to lead the homage, then walks up the five steps and kisses the King's left cheek.

The royal dukes – the King's brothers Prince Henry and Prince George – also pay homage, followed by the usual pattern of a senior representative from each rank of the peerage who approach the King to pay homage, while others do so in their seats.

For some Edward VIII loyalists, the moment is charged with thoughts of what might have been; Channon is among those for whom regret still lingers as he thinks 'of that sad, more glamorous wistful Edward VIII alone with Wallis … no doubt listening in on the radio to the Coronation service of his brother, which ought to have been his own had he not reached the acme of folly and infatuation…'

But most understand that they are watching the right couple, 'two simple and good young people',[16] being crowned; unable to imagine the self-indulgent Edward VIII, let alone the twice-divorced American Wallis Simpson at the heart of such a solemn, religious British rite.

'You were right,' remarks a tearful Churchill to his wife Clementine. 'I see now that "the other one" wouldn't have done.'

The Queen's coronation

Queen Elizabeth has sat silently watching on, but now it is her turn and, as the sounds of the trumpets and the shouts for the King start to fade, she walks to her faldstool and kneels under a canopy held by four duchesses.

The Archbishop anoints her just once, on the crown of her head, and then blesses the Queen Consort's ruby ring, before placing it on the fourth finger of her right hand. The Queen Consort is crowned by the command of the King, rather than by the will of the people, so the ceremony is shorter and the Queen doesn't swear an oath.

The Archbishop then brings her crown from the altar and places it on to her head.

Once again, this is the cue for the ceremony's most dazzling moment, as the peeresses all put on their coronets at the moment of crowning. Lilibet watches 'arms and coronets hovering in the air and then the arms disappear as if by magic'. All have looked forward to this moment and it doesn't disappoint: 'a thousand white gloved arms, sparkling with jewels, lifting their tiny coronets and at the same moment, like fluttering swans … very white, graceful and lovely,' recalls Channon.

The Queen receives the Sceptre with the Cross and the Ivory Rod with Dove, and she turns and bows to the King before carrying her regalia over to her throne, beside the King.

For the woman born Elizabeth Bowes-Lyon, who married a shy second son and never expected to be Queen, the power of the ceremony, with its solemnity and splendour elevates her, in the eyes of her watching friends, beyond their circle. Among them is George Gage, her former beau who wanted to marry her, and a group of friends from more carefree, youthful days.

At the beginning of the communion service, His Majesty hands over St Edward's Crown, which is taken into St Edward's Chapel, and substituted for the Imperial State Crown, which the King assumes after the communion service. As the couple kneel to take communion, they achieve a private, spiritual moment; despite the crowds surrounding them, the Queen is 'not conscious of there being anyone else there'.[17]

Lilibet and Margaret have put on their own coronets, and now peer over the edge of the royal box surveying the scene.

For the assembled congregation, having been sitting for hours, the airless Abbey becomes stifling and the prayers seem never-ending. By this point, even the dutiful Lilibet is bored. She and Queen Mary thumb through their service booklets to see how much longer is left, and when Lilibet points to the word 'Finis' a few pages away, Dowager Queen and heir presumptive exchange a conspiratorial smile, before turning their attention back to the service.

But at last, it comes to an end, around two hours after it started, and the King and Queen adjourn to the chapel, as the procession out of the Abbey is arranged. The King is disrobed of his Royal Robe of State by the Lord Great Chamberlain and he is helped into his Robe of Estate. He now wears the Imperial State Crown.

The congregation watch spellbound as the procession uncoils and moves slowly down the Nave: the Queen following the King this time. They proceed out – carrying their regalia – as the National Anthem 'God Save the King' is sung.

With the Abbey doors now open, a cold draught has whipped around the royal box and the young princesses are glad to get up and file back down the aisle, as the orchestra strike up Elgar's 'Pomp and Circumstance'. They take a break in the dressing room by the West Door, where they have a welcome meal of sandwiches, stuffed rolls, orangeade and lemonade, before facing the crowds once again.

Those left in the Abbey face another wait, and surreptitiously produce their flasks and wrapped packages and consume their remaining supplies.

Above left: Queen Victoria on her Coronation Day. George Hayter's portrait shows the young Queen in her coronation robes, holding the sceptre and wearing the Imperial State Crown, with the Black Prince's ruby at the centre. (Wiki commons, public domain)

Above right: Queen Victoria's Coronation Medal. (Wiki commons, public domain)

Queen Victoria's Coronation by George Hayter. (Wiki commons)

Above: Queen Victoria in her coronation robes, painted by Charles Robert Leslie. (Wiki commons, public domain)

Left: Edward VII kneels and touches the bible, as he takes the coronation oath. (Wiki commons, public domain; Samuel Begg for the *Illustrated London News*)

Above: Edward VII's coronation procession, through central London. (Wiki commons, public domain)

Right: King Edward VII and Queen Alexandra in their coronation robes and crowns, 1902. (W&D Downey, Wiki commons, public domain)

The anointing of Queen Alexandra in 1902, by Archbishop of York William Maclagan. Four duchesses hold the canopy over her while her page boys kneel. (Laurits Tuxen, Wiki commons, public domain)

St Edward's Crown, photographed in 1952, with the sovereign's orb, sceptres and ring. (Wiki commons, public domain)

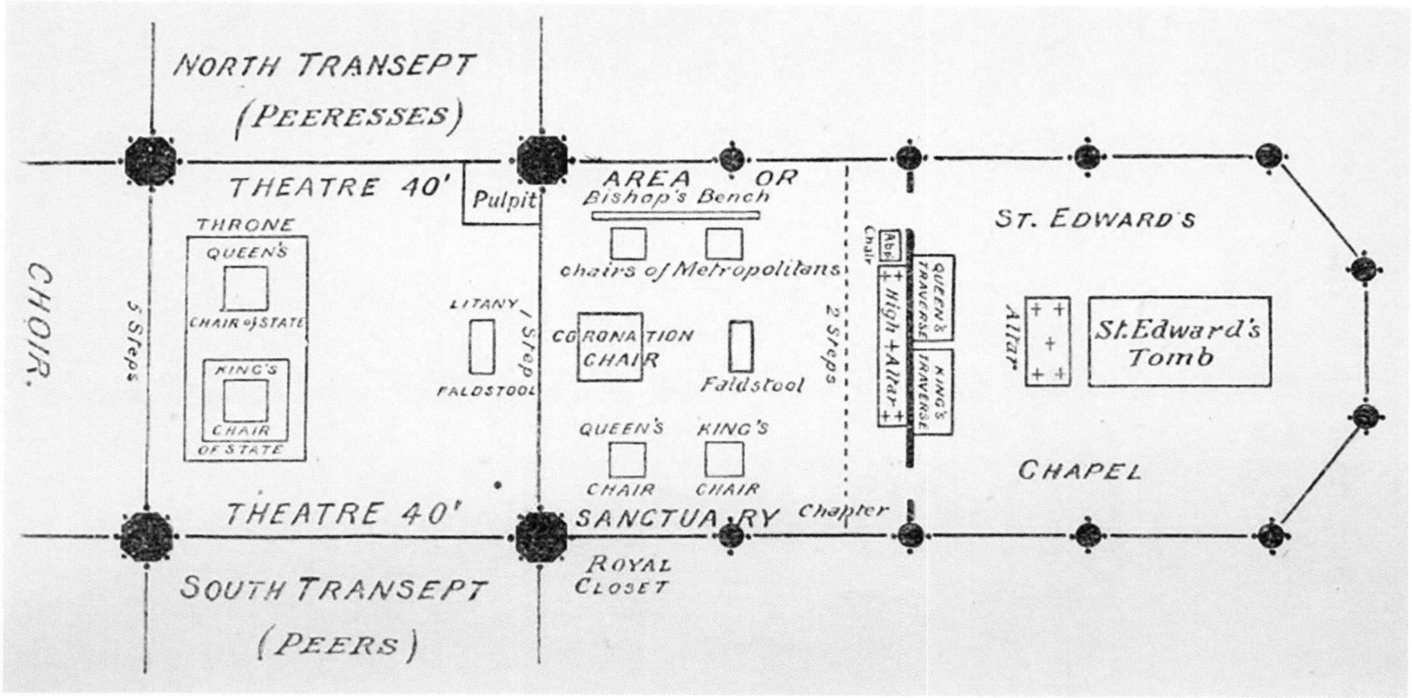

Diagram showing the layout of the Coronation Theatre inside Westminster Abbey. This sketch was done for the 1902 coronation of Edward VII, but all coronations have taken place in the Theatre. (Wiki commons, public domain)

Above left: King George V, in his coronation robes and crown, holding the orb and sceptre. (Wiki commons, public domain)

Above right: George V and his cousin Tsar Nicholas II of Russia, taken in Berlin in 1913. The two men enjoyed a close friendship and their remarkably similar looks meant they were at times mistaken for each other. (Wiki commons, public domain)

Left: George V and Queen Mary in their coronation dress, 1911. (Emery Walker, Wiki commons, public domain)

George V and Queen Mary at the Delhi Durbar, following their coronation in 1911. The newly crowned Emperor and Empress of India receive tributes from notable Indians in a ceremony no other monarch has taken part in. The King wears the newly made Imperial Crown of India, as the Imperial State Crown could not be legally moved from the United Kingdom. (Wiki commons, public domain)

The Royal Procession of the Regalia, 1911: the regalia is taken by Abbey clergy, via a side route, early in the morning on coronation day, to the High Altar. (Wiki commons, public domain)

Above left: Queen Elizabeth (later, the Queen Mother), in her coronation robes. Painting by Gerald Kelly. (Wiki commons, public domain)

Above right: The Prince of Wales, the future Edward VIII, with his sister Princess Mary, pictured just after their parents' coronation in 1911. (Wiki commons, public domain)

Below: The Queen, the royal family and the six maids of honour greeting crowds from the Buckingham Palace Balcony, 1953. (Library archives, Canada. Creative commons)

Above left: Queen Elizabeth II, on her coronation day, holding the orb and sceptre. Portrait by Cecil Beaton. (Wiki commons, public domain)

Above right: Queen Elizabeth II waves from the Buckingham Palace balcony following her coronation.

Below: Stamp of New Zealand, 2 and a half pence, featuring George VI and Elizabeth, to mark their coronation in 1937. (Wiki commons, public domain)

Prince George, the Duke of Kent, taken after the coronation of his brother George VI, with his wife, Princess Marina, the Duchess of Kent, wearing a tiara and small coronet. The couple wear coronation robes and Prince George also wears a large coronet. Prince George was killed in a plane crash five years after this picture was taken. (Wiki commons, public domain)

King George VI and Queen Elizabeth on their coronation day. (Wiki commons, public domain)

The Thrones for King George V and Queen Mary, in Westminster Abbey, 1911. The Queen Consort's throne is placed on a slightly lower level to the King's. (Wiki commons, public domain)

Coronation mug to commemorate the coronation of King George VI and Queen Elizabeth in 1937. (Wiki commons, public domain)

George VI on his coronation day, 12 May 1937. (Wiki commons, public domain)

Right: Edward VIII coronation mug. Retailers were left with thousands of items of 'coronation memorabilia' they couldn't sell after the abdication.

Below: Coronation crowds at Portman Street/ Oxford Street, 1953 by Ben Brooksbank. (Creative commons licence)

Left: The Imperial State Crown, worn by the monarch in the latter stages of the coronation ceremony, is altered for each sovereign. The crown features the Black Prince's Ruby at its centre and the magnificent Cullinan II diamond. (Wiki commons, public domain)

Below: The gold coach in the coronation procession, 2023. (Creative commons licence)

King Charles and Queen Camilla wave to the crowds from the Buckingham Palace balcony on their coronation day. (Open Government licence. Wikimedia commons)

The Prince and Princess of Wales, in their coronation robes, with their children seated opposite them in a semi-state landau, travelling directly behind the Gold State Coach, following the 2023 coronation in Westminster Abbey. (Wikimedia commons licence)

The King and Queen, with their family and attendants on the balcony of Buckingham Palace, May, 2023. (Pail Clark, Department for Culture, Media and Sport. Open Government licence)

Crowds surround the Victoria memorial outside Buckingham Palace and continue all the way down the Mall, on coronation day 2023. (Creative commons licence)

In the filing out of guests, the order of precedence is observed correctly – save for a moment of comedy when one of the officers, 'losing his humour and his head',[18] shouts, 'A baron has got out before the viscounts!' and while many greet the preposterous remark with laughter, some are genuinely angry at the breach of protocol. 'Members of the House of Commons don't wait for mere barons,' comes one indignant retort.

Although members of trades unions and other working-class organisations have been invited to the coronation, they are expected to know their place, and for the most part they play along nicely. 'The few Socialists and their little humdrum wives seemed subdued and impressed by the ancient service and the grandeur of the feudal capitalistic show,' notes the unfailingly snobbish Channon. But when one dares to question the feudal order, asking: 'Why should we sit behind these peer Johnnies?' he is given short shrift by Channon, who replies sharply: 'It's their show after all. You are lucky to be here at all.'

Eventually all emerge, blinking in the light, and are surprised to find it has rained.

The procession

To support the ambition for the occasion to show off the British Empire to the world, the route of the procession from the Abbey back to Buckingham Palace has been extended to over six miles in length, the longest coronation procession to date.

The crowds of people lining the routes, slightly damp from the rain, watch on as over 32,000 soldiers and sailors march past, followed by the carriages carrying foreign dignitaries, the royal family – and finally the King and Queen. Jolting along in the Gold State Coach, the King is wearing the Imperial State Crown and carrying the Orb and the Sceptre with the Cross; the Queen is wearing her crown and carrying her two sceptres. Their Majesties perform the delicate balancing act of bowing to the crowds, without dislodging their heavy crowns.

Around 660 yards of the Embankment, from the shadow of Big Ben to Charing Cross, is packed with 37,000 school children who, by the

King's express wish, have been invited to enjoy the day. It has been a huge logistical exercise to bring them all here, accompanied by 700 adult helpers who have supplied each child with a lunch of sandwiches, bottles of milk and packets of crisps, packed in bags that are waterproofed on one side so they can be sat upon once empty. The children have listened to the coronation via loudspeakers, and can now enjoy nearly four hours of procession in what one official described as 'the most exciting children's party ever held in London'.

There are 20,000 police officers lining the route along the Embankment and Northumberland Avenue, through Trafalgar Square, James's Street, Piccadilly, Regent Street, Oxford Street, Marble Arch and back to the palace via Hyde Park Corner.

Balcony appearance

The royal family appear on the balcony to be greeted by an estimated 50,000 people cheering and waving flags. In the spirit of scaling up, there are now four balcony appearances. Queen Mary, Lilibet and Margaret join the King and Queen on the balcony. Lilibet waves to the crowds, using the same hand-twirling motion she sees her grandmother doing. Queen Mary, whose steadfast presence throughout the day has signified not just her support for her family, but her loyalty to the crown itself, now turns to Bertie and says: 'It's not for me they are cheering, but for you my son.'[19]

Next, it's time for the official photographs, which involves posing patiently for some time 'under those awful lights', as Lilibet puts in. The resulting portraits by official photographer Dorothy Wilding are quite sober and a little flat in tone. The two young princesses are photographed with their parents, both wearing their cloaks and coronets, as the family of four gaze a little remotely into the camera.

The crown jewellers, including Mr Mann, are waiting in the wings, with the cases for the various bits of regalia and, once the photographs are taken, the regalia is placed in its cases and taken to the Privy Purse strong room at Buckingham Palace, where it is kept under lock and key until finally being collected on Friday, 14 May and returned to the Tower.

As the afternoon turns to evening, the King faces what for him must have been a terrifying prospect: his speech to the Empire at 8.00pm. An antique desk has been raised up in a small room at Buckingham Palace, so the King can stand to make the speech into a microphone, allowing more air to get to his lungs. Lionel Logue, who has worked so hard with him to prepare for this moment, is present to offer last-minute support and will wait in the next room along with Queen Elizabeth, whose presence always relaxes her husband, as the King delivers the ten-minute speech alone.

'It is with a very full heart that I speak to you tonight,' he begins, and the words sound clear, slow and deliberate – there is perceptible effort and emotion in his voice, but it continues steadily:

> Never before has a newly crowned King been able to talk to all his peoples in their own homes on the day of his Coronation. ... the Dominions are now free and equal partners with this ancient Kingdom, and I felt this morning that the whole Empire was in very truth gathered within the walls of Westminster Abbey.

Referring to the crown as a symbol of the unity of a global Empire, the speech attempts to align the medieval aspects of coronation, 'that infinitely beautiful ceremonial', with twentieth-century values. 'Its outward forms come down from distant times, but its inner meaning and message are always new: for the highest of distinctions is the service of others, and to the Ministry of Kingship I have, in your hearing, dedicated myself, with the Queen at my side.'

There is hesitation before only one word – 'distress' as the King remembers the less fortunate of his realm, but he continues confidently, and it is barely noticeable. 'A triumph' is Logue's verdict on the speech.

Relieved the speech is over, the King and Queen can relax a little – they change into evening dress – he with the blue ribbon of the Garter, and she in a diamond tiara, evening dress and white fur-trimmed cloak.

At 9.00pm they emerge onto the balcony once more, waving through the slight drizzle that has been present most of the day, and illuminated by the Buckingham Palace floodlights that have been installed since the 1911 coronation. The crowd cheer, sing the National Anthem and shout for them to return again and again. In the end, they come out onto the balcony, to wave and smile and smile and wave, three times, retiring finally at 11.30pm.

Lilibet will treasure her memories of the day. 'I thought it all very, very wonderful,' she records in her own account of the coronation, neatly handwritten on six lined pages ('From Lilibet by Herself'). But it's also been exhausting. Back in her bedroom at Buckingham Palace she finds her 'feet and legs ached terribly', and she falls into a long, deep sleep as soon as her head hits the pillow.

Chapter Fourteen

WAR AND PEACE

After the coronation, Bertie's relief that, even if everything had not been perfect, he himself had remained calm and played his part well was immense. He obviously felt deeply moved by the religious service. Writing to the Archbishop of Canterbury, Cosmo Lang, to thank him, he describes how he felt that 'Some One Else' had been with him throughout the day.[1] Queen Elizabeth also writes to express her gratitude to the Archbishop for 'such a spiritual and wonderful service', telling him that 'I was more moved, & more helped than I could have believed possible.'[2]

The Dean of Westminster tries to get to the bottom of why the Imperial Crown had been missing from the Jerusalem Chamber, causing him such stress. The Dean's concern now is to establish a clear procedure so that he can leave notes for his successor for future coronations. All the records he has checked show that in 1902 and 1911, the crown had been the Dean's responsibility.

On 14 May, he writes to the Garter, explaining his horror and consternation at the moment that he made the discovery. He sent for the warders, who explained that it had been removed on the 'Lord Chamberlain's orders'. He goes on to describe how, with the procession ready to go, he endured '10 minutes of miserable doubt & apprehension, as I really did not know what had become of it and as far as I knew, I was in charge'.

In a letter dated 19 May, he receives the reply:

> Dear Mr. Dean,
> Garter has told me of the fearful convulsions which we nearly caused you when you found that the Imperial Crown was missing from the Jerusalem Chamber.

> I am so sorry; it must have been an awful moment, because it would take quite a lot of saving up to buy another one, but apparently in this Office we never considered any other method of getting the Imperial Crown up from the Jerusalem Chamber. I suppose this is one of the details which gets overlooked.
>
> Anyway, a note will be made for any future coronation, so that you or your successor will not go through an agonising few moments.
>
> You have quite enough to do without the mental strain of that sort, and you were so kind to us in lending us your house to smoke that I feel very sorry to have given you so much trouble.
>
> Yours very sincerely
> Mr N. Gwartkin
> Lord Chamberlain's Office[3]

For the newly crowned King and Queen, there was of course lots more coronation-related activity to attend to. On 20 May, the review of the fleet at Spithead saw a huge display of naval power. Around 300 ships from Britain and other nations, including fifty British battleships, took part, stretching in two seven-mile-long lines between Portsmouth and the Isle of Wight. Foreign ships included Germany's *Admiral Graf Spee*, a pocket battleship, and the Soviet battleship *Marat* (formerly *Petropavlovsk*). 'The Review was wonderful,' noted Queen Mary, who added that 'almost the loudest cheer came from the Bolshevik ship!'[4] Another memorable moment came during the live evening broadcast, when the officer tasked with describing George VI's inspection of the fleet, Lieutenant-Commander Thomas Woodrooffe, started to speak. Reporting from his former ship HMS *Nelson*, after a drinking session with his old shipmates, Woodrooffe slurred incoherently for four minutes on air about how 'the whole thing's lit up like fairy lights' before his colleagues faded him out.[5]

The coronation was also commemorated by the issuing of coronation medals, coinage and stamps, and other memorabilia. Across Britain, towns and villages organised their own celebrations, while throughout the Empire military parades and parties marked the occasion.

Overall, the coronation was deemed a success and many in Whitehall must have breathed a sigh of relief. Through pageantry and public spectacle, military parades, carefully curated traditions and the power of the crown, Britain had shown off its imperial might, faced down the rising fascist dictatorships in Europe, and put the abdication crisis behind it.

But there were signs that the old order was under strain and the now equal 'dominions' were not going to stand too much more of the aristocracy bagging all the best roles. Mackenzie King, the prime minister of Canada, commented that he thought it was an anachronism in modern times for the ceremony to be confined to ecclesiastics and peers – noting that the only commoner to take part was Ramsay MacDonald and then only in his role as Lord President of the Council. He also suggested that the practice of only peers taking part in the homage should be revised before the next coronation took place. Dismissing the idea, the King's conservatively minded private secretary Alec Hardinge hints at the inherent conundrum trying to democratise the crowning of a hereditary monarch would entail:

> I am afraid that I do not agree with Mr Mackenzie King: one might just as well say that the whole ceremonial of the Coronation is an anachronism in these days, and there is obviously a limit, beyond which you cannot go, in making the ceremony democratic – nor do I think that anyone would wish it to be so.[6]

Certainly not the stickler for tradition Dowager Queen Mary, who wrote to David later in May, complaining that David had not answered her previous letters. She tells him that the 'Coronation and all the festivities connected with it went off very well and was beautifully organised. It was a great ordeal for Bertie & Elizabeth, but they did it extremely well and everybody was much impressed by the solemnity of it all.' Towards the end of the letter, she makes reference to her eldest son's chosen new life: 'I suppose you are very happy now & I send you my best wishes. Ever darling David, Your devoted Mama.'[7]

From his exile across the Channel, David had listened to the coronation ceremony of his brother and sister-in-law on the radio.

Later Wallis would write of the day: 'I fought to suppress every thought, but all the while, the mental image of what might have been and should have been kept forming, disintegrating and re-forming in my mind.'[8] Afterwards, from his exile, David kept up a barrage of phone calls to his brother. Speaking on the telephone, he would take advantage of Bertie's hesitancy and stutter to press his issues, including Wallis's royal status. After he became King and his brother had left the country, Bertie was still entangled in complicated and sometimes distressing legal and financial wrangles with David, now Duke of Windsor. Not least of these concerned the ownership of the Balmoral and Sandringham estates, which had been bequeathed to David, as privately owned properties. A settlement wasn't agreed until 1938, when Bertie ended up paying his brother £25,000 a year from his own funds and buying the two estates for nearly £300,000 (around £30 million in today's money).[9] As part of lengthy negotiations that took place, the money David received was made conditional on his agreeing that he would not travel to Britain without the King's express permission. The government pushed this clause on an unwilling David, who had imagined he would be able to move back and settle in England, after a few years abroad.

Alec Hardinge, who served as the King's private secretary, later recalled of George VI's early years: 'he had no training for the task now thrust upon him … his health, together with the impediment of speech, had placed him under a severe physical handicap.'[10] Fortunately for Bertie, he did have his wife Elizabeth at his side. Socially skilled, able to charm courtiers, royals and public alike, and with a reliable joie de vivre, Elizabeth's personality underpinned Bertie's emergence as a respected monarch and wartime leader.

During the Second World War, the King and Queen became key targets of Hitler's Luftwaffe, and Buckingham Palace was bombed nine times. On one occasion, a bomb blew the windows out of the King and Queen's sitting room and narrowly avoided killing them; their Majesties were photographed among the wreckage. The King and Queen gained respect and loyalty for remaining in London during the war. Questioned as to whether the family would relocate to the relative safety of Canada, the Queen famously replied, 'The children won't go without me; I won't leave the King – and the King will never leave.' Elizabeth and Margaret were moved to the relative safety of Windsor Castle.

While Winston Churchill, who was appointed prime minister in May 1940, emerged as the nation's undisputed leader through the war years, the King and Queen found their footing in showing solidarity with the people, carrying out public service, and presenting a united and positive front. During the war, the King awarded 30,000 medals to members of the armed forces.[11] They were frequently photographed among bomb sites, carrying out public engagements and later with their elder daughter Princess Elizabeth in her Auxiliary Territorial Service (ATS) uniform. Queen Elizabeth's natural charm and social astuteness smoothed the way with photographers, one of whom recalled:

> Queen Elizabeth made it seem a privilege for her to be photographed by us ... she even came to know what distance we focused for. It was normally five yards. And five yards away precisely, wherever she saw us, she would pause, smile, make the picture for us and wait until we had taken it.[12]

In another bitter blow for Queen Mary, in 1942 the King's younger brother, the Duke of Kent, who was serving in the RAF, was killed in a plane crash, at the age of 39, leaving his wife Princess Marina and three young children. The royal family's lingering connection to the Romanovs saw the Grand Duchess Xenia, sister of the late Tsar, installed by the King and Queen at Craigowan Lodge on the Balmoral estate for the duration of the war.

Despite Churchill's huge popularity as a wartime leader, in 1945 the public's appetite for change saw a new Labour Government win power. Changes at home, including the birth of the NHS and the welfare state, ran parallel to the continued loss of the Empire with prime minister Clement Attlee granting India its independence in 1947. The General Election of 1951 saw a narrow victory for the Conservatives, however, and Winston Churchill, now in his 77th year, became George VI's prime minister for the second time.

George VI's death at the age of just 56 came as a profound shock to his family. Although the King had been ill for some time, his wife and daughters had thought he was recovering and were optimistic about his future. Although in reality he had become increasingly frail over the last year, within the family they were still talking about 'the flu' and the need to take rest to get well. The bulletins that the palace issued on the King's health struck a cautiously upbeat tone. Although tests the previous year had revealed a malignant tumour on his lung, the doctors had withheld the cancer diagnosis from him and his family, as was common practice at the time. He underwent surgery in September 1951, to remove his left lung, a three-hour operation during which the doctors saw evidence of cancer in his right lung, too. Again, they kept that to themselves.

In mid-December, the King recorded his Christmas message to the nation. This had always been a very difficult task for George VI, due to his stutter and the anxiety it caused him around public speaking. Now, with his failing health, it was distressing and painful for everyone involved. Working with a BBC sound engineer, it took two hours to record the short messages, as he needed to rest after speaking a few words. 'Not only by the grace of God and through the faithful skill of my doctors, surgeons, and nurses have I come through my illness,' he said in a frail, failing voice that was uncomfortable to listen to.[13]

The King and Queen spent Christmas at Sandringham, with the largest gathering of the royal family there since the war. The King seemed to rally, and joined in the Boxing Day shoot, carrying a light gun. He also continued to smoke heavily. On 31 January, he was seen on the tarmac at London airport, waving off Lilibet and Philip, who were leaving for Kenya, their first stop on a tour that would also see them visit Australia, New Zealand, and Ceylon.

On Tuesday, 5 February, in bright, crisp sunshine, George VI went out on a day of shooting with a group of friends, estate workers and staff, and was described by someone present as being 'in great form'.[14] That evening, after a family dinner, Bertie planned the next day's shoot, and retired cheerfully at around 10.30pm. Next morning, his valet brought in his tea at 7.30am, and found him lying motionless in the bed. He had died of a coronary thrombosis. His wife rushed to his room as soon as she was notified, and found him looking as though he was in a deep sleep.

Later that day, she wrote to Queen Mary. 'What can I say to you,' she began, her shock palpable: 'It is impossible for me to grasp what has happened. Last night, he was in wonderful form & looking so well…'[15] She sympathised with her mother-in-law, who had lost another son, and shared her own sense of profound loss at the husband who was 'my whole life'.

The letters between Queen Mary and Queen Elizabeth that now sit in the Royal Archive at Windsor are touching in the way that the two offer comfort to each other in their shared grief. A family in shock following a sudden death now have to cope with organising a very public farewell – and the re-emergence of the Duke of Windsor, who arrives in London ahead of the funeral. For Queen Mary this is 'a most annoying moment in the middle of the misery and suffering we are going through just now', but she feels that David must be suitably accommodated and offers to put him up at her home, Marlborough House. She writes to her daughter-in-law to 'beg and beseech' her to meet David with her daughters and 'bury the hatchet after 15 whole years'.[16]

The majority of people still got their news from the radio and cinema newsreels, but in the immediate aftermath of George VI's death, there were signs of the media revolution to come that would eventually see royal events being broadcast live across the world. When George VI's coffin was pulled on a gun carriage from King's Cross Station to Westminster Hall, the procession was televised. Footage included dramatic images of the new young Queen Elizabeth, Princess Margaret and the Queen Mother all dressed in black veils, standing with Queen Mary in a long black dress, against the striking backdrop of Westminster Hall. Parts of the funeral procession in Windsor were also televised, though not the service itself, which took place in St George's Chapel. The nation mourned the King who had become a respected leader and figurehead during the darkest days of the Second World War. On behalf of the government, Winston Churchill laid a wreath at the chapel with a card attached on which were written the words inscribed on the Victoria Cross: 'For Valour'.

Chapter Fifteen

'MY WHOLE LIFE'

Princess Elizabeth's first important message to her people came from South Africa, where she was on tour with her family, on the occasion of her 21st birthday. Millions who listened to the simple but heartfelt speech related to its message of hope for a better future. Having come through the war, 'these years of danger and glory', the princess first committed herself to continue to live by the 'noble motto' of her ancestors – '*I serve*'. Then she made the promise to which she remained true for the next seventy-five years:

> I declare before you all that my whole life, whether it be long or short shall be devoted to your service and the service of our great imperial family to which we all belong. But I shall not have strength to carry out this resolution alone unless you join in it with me, as I now invite you to do: I know that your support will be unfailingly given. God help me to make good my vow, and God bless all of you who are willing to share in it.

Her grandmother, the dutiful but 'cold' Queen Mary, wept when she heard the speech. So did the old war leader, Winston Churchill. More importantly, she won over her people. Over the course of the next seven and a half decades, her straightforward promise at the age of 21 would be quoted and re-quoted countless times and she would be held to it in a very public way. She did not fall short.

It was a remarkable debut onto the world stage for a 21-year-old woman who had led a sheltered, if royal, existence up until that point. She was of course unaware that just a few short years later, she herself would inherit the throne to begin an extraordinarily long reign. The tone of her speeches over the years of her reign would often strike a similar note. She wasn't afraid to appeal to people's sense of fairness, of core values of service, care for others, shared effort and good manners. Come on, she seemed to insist, we can be nice to each other, work hard and achieve good things – that's who we are.

As much as there is no doubt George VI and his wife Elizabeth created a close and happy family unit of 'We Four', as the King referred to them, the young Princess Elizabeth's life was far from normal. Educated at home with her younger sister Margaret-Rose, her early childhood was spent happily enough with her parents, her nanny, her sister and her governess, Marion Crawford. When 'Crawfie' later wrote a memoir about those years, she painted a touchingly simple picture of a 1930s upper-class childhood, with its routines of walks, teatimes and family games in a pre-war, pre-digital era where the princesses looked after their toy horses and put on their own plays for entertainment.

Everything changed overnight for Princess Elizabeth when the man she knew as 'Uncle David' abdicated the throne in December 1936. Up until this point, the Yorks had lived a pleasantly royal life, without the pressures that came with being directly in line to the throne. Her Uncle David, once a frequent visitor at the Yorks' home on London's Piccadilly, went into exile and it would be nearly twenty years before Elizabeth saw him again. With her father now King, 10-year-old Lilibet became known as 'heir presumptive', allowing for the possibility that she might still gain a brother, who would take precedence over her in the line of succession. The Duchess of York was 36, and hadn't had a baby for six years, so while it was a possibility, as time went on the succession became clearer: Elizabeth was going to be Queen.

The family moved into Buckingham Palace, which in common with other new residents of one of London's most famous landmarks, they found inconvenient and not particularly comfortable. It was a five-minute walk to get outside to the garden; 'people need bikes to get around here,' was Lilibet's verdict.[1] When the bombs started to fall, the girls were moved to the relative safety of Windsor Castle, where their parents joined them at weekends.

From December 1941, single women and childless widows aged between 20 and 30 were called up to do war work, with the entry age soon dropping to 19. Those called up worked in vital industries, farming, public services and the women's military services, the largest of which was the ATS. Following Princess Elizabeth's 18th birthday in April 1944, her father reluctantly agreed to her long-held wish to join the ATS and take part in war work. The princess was issued with the uniform and spent several weeks training in Camberley. Her experience in the ATS was negotiated with the palace in great detail and as a result it was quite limited – she was driven back to Windsor at the end of each day, rather than sleep in barracks, and she didn't take part in physical training. Nevertheless, being seen to be willing to take part in the war effort, sharing some experiences of her generation, certainly helped the monarchy appear connected to its people. The princess was even photographed in army fatigues, to the horror of some of her aristocratic friends: 'Trousers!'

It was also during the war years in Windsor that Crawfie noticed that Lilibet seemed to have a new sparkle whenever a certain handsome sailor was around. Philip Mountbatten, a distant relative of the royal family, sometimes spent his leave from the navy at Windsor Castle. It was during one such visit over the Christmas period in 1947 that he watched 17-year-old Lilibet play Aladdin in the princesses' traditional Christmas pantomime. The pair kept in touch, swapping letters and photographs throughout the war.

When the end of the war came, Elizabeth and Margaret famously slipped out of Buckingham Palace with a small group of friends and minders to party in the streets with the celebrating crowds. But it wasn't until after VJ day that Philip returned to England from the Far East where he had been serving. Elizabeth and Philip started to meet more frequently, often eating dinner together with Margaret in the old nursery at Buckingham Palace. While Elizabeth was smitten, the romance wasn't all plain sailing. Philip's brusque, entitled manner didn't endear him to the household staff, and the royal family regarded him as rough and ill-mannered and were less than delighted about the developing relationship.

Philip did have some royal pedigree – his father was Prince Andreas of Greece, a younger son of the Greek monarch, and his mother Alice was a great-granddaughter of Queen Victoria. However, the Greek monarchy had a rocky history, and his father had been forced into exile. Philip had very limited means, and lacked a home and family of his own. By this time, the press were almost constantly running stories speculating over who would become the husband of 'the most eligible bride in the world'. Whenever Philip was mentioned, the newspaper stories would emphasise his foreignness. The palace issued denials concerning a forthcoming marriage, but behind closed doors, Elizabeth was planning their future together. In the end, the King and Queen reluctantly agreed to their daughter's wishes, but insisted the couple wait until she was 21 before they could go public and arrange a wedding.

Elizabeth's determination in pursuing her relationship with Philip in the face of such opposition has been described as the one rebellion in an otherwise extremely dutiful and obedient life. The couple married on 20 November 1947 at Westminster Abbey, the bride wearing a Norman Hartnell dress made of fabric purchased using clothing coupons. George VI, never a fluent speaker, could nevertheless eloquently convey his feelings as a letter writer. In one of his most moving letters, he wrote to his beloved eldest daughter: 'I was so proud of you and thrilled at having you so close to me on our long walk in Westminster Abbey, but when I handed your hand to the Archbishop I felt that I had lost something very precious.' The couple's first child and heir, Charles, was born in 1948, and Anne followed two years later. Philip continued his career in the navy, and they spent time in Malta where he was stationed.

Following George VI's death, Elizabeth succeeded to the throne at the age of just 25. Once again, she found herself obliged to move out of a comfortable family home – in this case Clarence House, which Philip had devoted himself to restoring for them – and into the much less comfortable Buckingham Palace. Once installed, the new Queen did her best to get to grips with her new role, insisting on ploughing through the daily red boxes alone, and as a result seeing less of her two young children. Family life wasn't improved by the establishment's continued suspicion of Philip. The Duke of Edinburgh had also made it clear that he resented not being able to pass on his own adopted surname of Mountbatten to his children, and was frequently at loggerheads with his still-influential mother-in-law. When he decided to start taking flying lessons, he also upset Churchill – who was reluctant for the Duke to embark on a risky hobby ahead of the coronation. The Queen, wanting her husband to find purpose, decided that he should become Chair of the Coronation Planning Committee.

The coronation date was set for June 1953 – an unusually long gap of eighteen months after the accession. The relatively long wait was mostly a matter of timing and logistics: coronations tend to take place in the warmer, lighter months – typically, May or June, and George VI having died in February, it would have been a difficult scramble to organise a large event in the space of a few months. As prime minister, Winston Churchill felt that more time was needed to get the country ready to maximise what could be, if pulled off well, a significant global coup for Britain, not to mention his own flagging premiership.

Two committees swung into action: the Coronation Committee, chaired by the Duke of Edinburgh, and the Coronation Executive Committee, chaired by the Earl Marshal. In a classic bit of royal understatement, in his foreword to *The Queen's Coronation: The Inside Story*, the Duke of Edinburgh recalls 'inevitable discussions, even arguments' during this planning period. His vice-chair, the Earl Marshal, Bernie Norfolk, was conservatively minded, a stickler for tradition, and had experience of organising such events. While bringing energy and some fresh ideas about how to incorporate the Commonwealth, Philip also had a knack for getting people's backs up.

While Britain's economy in the early 1950s was experiencing welcome growth, the country was still recovering from the war years. There were food shortages with some rationing still in place, and everyday life was drab and austere for most people. Homes lacked comfort and convenience – few had central heating, fridges or washing machines. In cities, slum housing was still common, with outside toilets and tin baths in the kitchen. People got their news and entertainment from radio, or cinema newsreels, with television still in its infancy. For the minority who did own a television set, the quality of both the programmes being shown and the images on small, grainy black and white sets were often poor. The BBC was the only television provider and saw their role as reflecting respectable conservative views, rather than breaking any new ground.

In the years running up to the coronation there had been some very limited television coverage of royal events. As well as the short film of part of the funeral procession of George VI, at Elizabeth's wedding to Philip in 1947, cameras had been present to film a few minutes of the couple processing up the Nave and out of the Abbey. The actual wedding service itself was deemed to be a private, religious matter, not appropriate for television. Around a million viewers did watch the television coverage, but far more listened on the radio.

The BBC wanted more access to the coronation than they had to George VI's state funeral, but their initial request to the Coronation Committee for permission to broadcast the ceremony was greeted with hostility. The committee's most senior figures all instinctively felt that televising the event would increase the pressure on the Queen and everyone else, and expose any mistakes that were made. Churchill pompously informed the House of Commons that it would be unfitting for the coronation to be shown as though it were 'a theatrical performance'.[2] The Archbishop of Canterbury, Geoffrey Fisher, was opposed on the grounds that it would threaten the religious solemnity of the occasion. There was also concern over how the bright lights needed by television crews would affect the look and feel of the ceremony. Considering that the cinema newsreel crews were to be allowed in the Abbey, the opposition to television wasn't wholly understandable and the BBC persisted, sending their persuasive and charming new Director of Television, George Barnes, to the palace to negotiate. Barnes received a boost when the newspapers came out in support of televising the coronation, with the *Daily Express* announcing that four out of five of its readers supported the idea. At the age of 78, Winston Churchill was still capable of reading the public mood and swiftly changed his stance. In October, he called a meeting with key figures including the Archbishop and the influential private secretary Sir Alan Lascelles, known as 'Tommy', at which he made clear that he now thought the coronation should be televised. On 28 October, Churchill was back in the House of Commons, explaining that the decision to televise the event would in no way detract from the 'utmost moral seriousness' of the event.

The Queen herself had not embraced the idea of the coronation being televised, but she accepted that the public mood was clear. It was agreed that four cameras would be permitted in the Abbey, but they would not be allowed to film the anointing or the Queen taking communion, considered the most sacred parts of the service. While the palace tried to restrict what the cameras did, the BBC's Outside Broadcast team were determined to show as much as they could. The decision to televise was a popular one and triggered a major shift in the nation's media consumption. Thousands of television sets were purchased in advance of the coronation, which became the first mass audience appointment television.

The Queen's Christmas message was not broadcast on television until 1957, following criticism from Lord Altringham that she was too remote a figure and needed to modernise. Back in 1952 though, her very first Christmas radio broadcast to the nation came from Sandringham. As she talked about her forthcoming coronation, her upper-class, rather prim, high voice showed no signs yet of modernisation, but her sincerity was obvious as she invited public participation in her forthcoming coronation, in the form of prayers:

> 'I want to ask you all, whatever your religion may be, to pray for me on that day – to pray that God may give me wisdom and strength to carry out the solemn promises that I shall be making.'

In the early 1950s, Britain was still militarised, still war-ravaged. Bomb sites littered cities, and military conscription, known as National Service, was in place for all men aged 18 to 26. The population was monocultural, smaller and more equal than it is today. Only 5 per cent of young people went on to university, most left school at 15. Although church attendance declined during the 1950s, it was much higher than it is today. Eighty per cent of the population regarded themselves as Christian and around a third believed the monarch was chosen by God. The royal household's influence extended to the arts world, with all plays intended for public performance having to be submitted to the Lord Chamberlain, for censorship.

The British Nationality Act of 1948 allowed all Commonwealth and colonial citizens to move to the UK, without any immigration controls. India was by now an independent republic, though still a member of the

British Commonwealth independent countries. Other Commonwealth countries where the Queen was head of state included Canada, Australia, New Zealand, South Africa, Pakistan and Ceylon.

Though still a great orator, at aged 78, Churchill was losing his once formidable intellectual powers. He was inclined to confuse names and faces – to such an extent that some baffling appointments were made in Downing Street because the prime minster had mixed up who he was giving jobs to.[3] His lifestyle had long involved overindulgence in food, heavy drinking and smoking and he had already suffered one stroke. When questions were asked about whether Britain could really afford a lavish – some would say indulgent – coronation for the new Queen, he batted them away. 'Everybody likes to wear a flower when he goes to see his girl' was his somewhat whimsical reply to one journalist's question about the extravagant cost of the coronation.

He was devoted to the young Queen, to whom he became something of a mentor. Always keen to attend his weekly meetings at the palace, which often lasted over an hour, the relationship between Churchill and Elizabeth had some echoes of that between Melbourne and Queen Victoria. On one occasion, asked by a journalist what they talked about, he replied, 'the racing, mostly'. Churchill was effusive in his praise and admiration for Elizabeth and devoted himself to coronation planning, which he very much hoped would put the successful 'Festival of Britain', organised by the Labour Government of 1951, in the shade.

Queen Mary, who had come through many sad losses, never really got over Bertie's death. Her robust constitution, curiosity and determination to carry on had sustained her through a long life, but now she started to age rapidly. Nevertheless, she lent her experience and support to the planning of her granddaughter's coronation. In May 1952, she went to Kensington Palace to study Queen Victoria's coronation robes, which she felt could form the model for the new Queen's.[4] The following February she drove through Hyde Park to look at the stands being erected in preparation for the coronation. Aware that her health was failing, and with her characteristic thoughtfulness and attention to detail, she let it be known that if she were no longer around to attend the coronation, her strong wish was that it would not be postponed, and that nobody attending should wear mourning. It was her preference to step away quietly. Queen Mary died on 24 March, aged 85, and was much mourned by all sections of British society. Formidable, yet revered, the great lady was almost sublimely regal, yet also relatable. The MP and diarist 'Chips' Channon famously said that a chat with Queen Mary 'was like talking to St Paul's Cathedral', yet she was also 'easy and pleasant to meet'.[5] Her death was followed by one month's formal court mourning.

The Court of Claims swung into action once again, fielding applications from all those who felt they had the right to play a part in the coronation. It was chaired by the Lord Chancellor, with the Duke of Norfolk and leading judges also examining the various requests. Some were nodded through on the evidence that the families concerned could trace their role back to the Middle Ages. Others were turned down – including, to his consternation, the Lord of the Manor of Worksop, a title belonging to successive Dukes of Newcastle, whose family had always had the privilege of presenting the monarch with a white glove, with which to hold the Sceptre. The ninth Duke had transferred the management of the Manor of Worksop, which included land ownership, to a limited company, and while he still felt that he could perform his duty, the claims court disagreed.[6] Instead, the task of carrying the glove was given to Lord Woolton, Chancellor of the Duchy of Lancaster.

The question of which foreign guests to invite, and where to accommodate them, once again took up considerable planning time and budget. Many had to be accommodated at hotels at a cost of around £15,000 (the equivalent of around £350,000 today). Most monarchies followed custom in sending their heirs. The Crown Princes of Norway and Denmark stayed at Buckingham Palace, as did the Duke of Edinburgh's mother Princess Alice of Battenburg, and his three surviving sisters and their German husbands. Philip's sisters had all married German aristocrats, and their involvement with the Nazi party during the war meant that they had not been invited to Elizabeth and Philip's wedding just five years earlier, but it was now considered that enough time had passed for their presence to be deemed acceptable.

The Duke and Duchess of Windsor's names never made it on to the guest list, despite David's hopes that they would be welcome. There was considerable concern that the lack of an invitation wouldn't deter him from making an appearance anyway, and in the end, the Archbishop of

Canterbury pressed Tommy Lascelles to write to the Duke's lawyers, stating unequivocally that it had been decided that the couple's presence would not be appropriate.

The government wanted to accommodate more guests from the Commonwealth this time, and also from trade unions and other groups representing different sections of society. They did cut back a little on invitations to peers – though peers and their wives, the peeresses, still made up the largest single group on the guest list.

In February, Churchill announced that an amnesty for wartime deserters would form part of the coronation celebrations, in order to restore men to their families and communities after many years on the run. Many of those who had gone AWOL from the services had obtained fake identity documents and ended up in Ireland. The offer was made to men who deserted between 3 September 1939 and 15 August 1945, thought to be 10,393 soldiers, 1,784 airmen and 863 sailors. Men currently in prison or awaiting trial for desertion were released.[7]

The Queen wanted Norman Hartnell, the couturier who had created her wedding dress, to design her coronation gown, and he was commissioned in October. Hartnell had initially been introduced to the royal fold by the Queen's aunt, the Duchess of Gloucester, who had asked him to design her wedding dress when she married Prince Henry. Queen Elizabeth the Queen Mother had also used Hartnell to design some of her increasingly distinctive dresses. Hartnell's flair for combining lavish, opulent yet elegant dresses, using exquisite beading detail, often over pale colours had a huge influence on royal fashion. There was a romanticism to Hartnell's designs which helped to elevate royal ladies. He was kept very busy in the run up to the coronation, as he was also designing the dresses for the maids of honour, the Queen Mother, Princess Margaret, the Duchess of Kent and Princess Alexandra. Work on the intricate embroidery of the Queen's dress took many months, with seamstresses working in a secluded, secure room shrouded in secrecy.[8] Following the example set by Queen Alexandra back in 1902, it was agreed early that the emblems of the countries of the United Kingdom would feature in the design. The English Tudor rose, the Irish shamrock and the Scottish thistle feature in early sketches, along with the daffodil for Wales. But Hartnell was firmly corrected by the Garter King of Arms, who insisted the daffodil be replaced by the leek. Hartnell went home and dug up a leek from his vegetable garden, but found it a creative challenge to incorporate the humble root vegetable into his beautiful design.[9]

The Queen personally appointed her six maids of honour, who would accompany her on her walk up the Nave, and carry the train of her robe. The criteria for this prominent position in 1953 were that you must be the unmarried daughter of an earl, duke or marquess; and the right height and size (read, tall and slim). Titles were essential, double or triple-barrelled surnames a nice-to-have. Those who made the cut were: Lady Rosemary Spencer-Churchill, Lady Mary Baillie-Hamilton, Lady Anne Coke, Lady Jane Vane-Tempest-Stewart, Lady Jane Heathcote-Drummond-Willoughby and Lady Moyra Hamilton.

The Earl Marshal, current Duke of Norfolk, took up his customary responsibility of organising the coronation. He had experience as he'd managed the 1937 coronation. Unlike some of his predecessors, Bernie Norfolk was a meticulously organised planner who left nothing to chance. He was also highly experienced, having also organised the state funerals of George V and George VI. He will go on to organise the state funeral of Winston Churchill in 1965, and the investiture of the Prince of Wales in 1969. Anne Glenconner (formerly Coke) remembers the twelve rehearsals that she attended as being formal affairs, where Bernie Norfolk would consult his ninety-four diagrams, depicting different parts of the ceremony, every minute and movement accounted for. His attention to detail included arranging for his bald head to be powdered several times during the ceremony, due to the presence of overhead cameras.

The maids of honour wore black suits, with hats and gloves, for the many rehearsals, including one with the Queen herself where they walked up and down the White Drawing Room in Buckingham Palace, a curtain being substituted for the long train. 'I was being instructed on how to walk, how to stand, how to hold the train and how to move,' recalls Lady Anne.

Getting the Abbey itself ready for the big day took almost a year, and it was shut to the public for months. Tubular scaffolding was used to build tiers of extra seating that reached almost to the high ceiling. To create better acoustics, the floors were laid with felt. Stands were erected outside the Abbey for 96,000 paying guests.

For the final rehearsal, everyone was ordered to wear their real costumes. For the pages, including the 13-year-old Andrew Parker Bowles, future husband of Camilla, that meant carrying ceremonial swords. At one point, the Gold Sticks had to be diverted to dealing with the jousting boys, who hadn't been able to resist drawing the swords.[10] The maids of honour wore six identical ivory silk long dresses with gold embroidery and matching gold and pearl headdresses. The Duke of Norfolk had instructed everyone to wear the dresses, but keep them covered up as the design was meant to be a secret. As Lady Anne Coke left the Abbey, a breeze blew up her shawl and waiting photographers snapped the dress. Of course, the photo made the front pages the next day, leaving a horrified Lady Anne dreading an angry call from the Duke of Norfolk which, to her relief, didn't materialise.[11]

The coronation planners tried to think of everything. To help them cater for the planned street parties, every household was to be permitted an extra pound of sugar, with caterers able to claim additional fat and sugar for crisps and cakes.

Back at Buckingham Palace, the Queen's own significant preparations for the day included spending time going through her papers in her study, while wearing the crown on her head, to help her get used to its weight.

After the austerity of the post-war years, the nation was ready to party. People wanted something to celebrate; some colour, glamour, sparkle and, yes, pageantry. The coronation of 1953 was a moment that millions looked forward to, talked about, read about and planned for. It had to deliver more than ceremony, it had to restore the gaiety of the nation. Could a 25-year-old woman at the centre of an ancient ritual really do all that?

Of course, the Queen's characteristic calm and dry humour always saw her through. Passionate about horse-racing, she had a thoroughbred running in the upcoming Derby. 'You must be feeling nervous, ma'am,' suggested a sympathetic lady-in-waiting on the eve of the coronation. 'Of course I am,' the Queen replied, not missing a beat, 'but I really do think Aureole will win.'[12]

Chapter Sixteen

CORONATION DAY 1953

The Coronation of Her Majesty Queen Elizabeth II, of the United Kingdom of Great Britain and Northern Ireland and of her other Realms and Territories, Defender of the Faith.

Date:	Tuesday, 2 June 1953
Guests:	8,251
Cost:	£912,000
Weather:	Rainy, grey and wet; one of the coldest June days of the century

Early morning

As a cold, grey dawn breaks over London, the capital is already a hive of activity. Keen to get a good view of the day's events, people line the pavements – some have slept out for days, despite the rain, to be a part of the thirty-eighth coronation to be celebrated at Westminster since 1066. The atrocious weather puts few people off on the day. Crowds continue to surge into London, determined to enjoy themselves. Half a million people gather along the route of the processions, their mood expectant. By 5.00am, each side of Whitehall is packed solid and loud speakers in the trees are playing party tunes and many in the crowd join in singing. Spontaneous singalongs also pop up; 'It's a Long Way to Coronation' (to the tune of 'It's a Long Way to Tipperary') being a favourite. Many people are in military uniform and most others are plainly dressed in everyday wear – clothes rationing is still in place in post-war Britain, so new outfits have not been an option.

The mood is one of genuine excitement and celebration. While it may be an exaggeration to say Britain in 1953 was a nation of ardent royalists, on 2 June, it is probably true. Everyone joins in.

Those with roles to play have an early start, too. The presence of television lights and cameras galvanises hairdressers and dressers to go full-on. Lady Anne remembers having 'ridiculous amounts of make-up' put on her and her mother who would also be in the procession. 'In daylight, we both looked extraordinary with blusher as red as our lipstick and great dark eyebrows.'

Outside the Abbey, many of those with a coveted ticket have arrived too early and stand about in small groups. The dress code for women is 'full-length dresses with hats', for men 'mourning dress or lounge suits'; there are lots of robes and uniforms. Someone spreads the news that the British Expedition, led by Sir Edmund Hillary, has been the first to reach the summit of Mount Everest. The news travels up and down the line of waiting guests and through the crowds beyond. All remark on the timing: 'What a Coronation gift for our Queen!'

Richard Dimbleby, who will broadcast commentary live to the nation for the BBC, is another early arrival. He has slept on his boat docked at Westminster Pier, and is picked up by a police launch at 5.15am, getting him to the Abbey by 5.30am, ready to take up his seat in the sound-proofed commentary box up in the gallery behind the High Altar.

Photographer Cecil Beaton also has a seat up in the rafters, where he sits sketching and taking photographs. Suffering from nerves and a hangover, he sucks on barley sugar and peers over the edge of the balcony, where he can see straight down the Nave.

As guests are let in and make their way to their seats, they mingle with television crews who are testing their equipment. But the Abbey, this early in the morning, draped in gold and blue, still has an air of tranquility. The early arrivals can watch as the regalia is borne in from the Jerusalem Chamber, in the procession of the Abbey clergy.

The peers and peeresses are once again out in force – they have around 1,000 seats allocated in the Abbey, with the peers in the South Transept and the peeresses in the North Transept – a vision of white-gloved swan-like arms and dazzling jewellery. The aristocracy have been urged this time to abandon their custom of arriving at the Abbey in the family's dusted-off and creaky horse-drawn carriage; the Earl Marshal has made it clear that they should arrive in cars or via the London underground. But old aristocratic traditions die hard and one or two, including the Marquess of Bath, have fought back against the diktat, even roping in Churchill to support their cause. The Duke of Devonshire has moved the old family coach to London from Chatsworth, along with two horses, and sets off with his family from Mayfair at 6.00am. But the coachman gets lost and the Duke, in full robes, has to lean out the window and shout up directions, which gives the watching crowds a good laugh. The Earl of Shrewsbury has an even more stressful time when the horses pulling his carriage are frightened by the large crowds and refuse to move at all.[1]

Once they reach the Abbey, space is tight and bags are not allowed. Many of the peers and peeresses have put sandwiches and malted milk tablets in their coronets to keep them going. It's also cold, and no one has been allowed to bring a coat.

In living rooms up and down the country, neighbours, families and friends start to gather to watch on television. The estimated 20 million viewers planning to watch the ceremony at home have been advised that the BBC will start broadcasting the test card an hour and a quarter before the programme itself, so that they can switch on to warm up their sets and adjust the aerials. A commentator for French television is at the Abbey, and across the Channel large numbers of people tune in. Among them are the Duke and Duchess of Windsor, watching with a small group of friends at the Parisian home of American heiress Margaret Biddle. The Duke keeps up a running commentary throughout the ceremony.

Cars start arriving carrying members of the royal family, as well as foreign dignitaries. The prime ministers of the Commonwealth countries include Robert Menzies from Australia and Dr Malan, leader of the Purified National Party in South Africa, who had a pro-Hitler, anti-black stance.

Queen Salote of Tonga makes a statement, wearing a deep pink robe made from the bark of a hibiscus tree and a foot-tall headdress of red feathers from the sacred kula bird. Larger than life at around six foot three inches and weighing 20 stone, she ignores the rain and seems as excited to see the crowds as they are to see her. Riding in the carriage with the diminutive Sultan of Kelantan, they make an odd couple.

Up in his seat, Cecil Beaton watches 'that great old relic' Winston Churchill arrive, dressed in the uniform of Lord Warden of the Cinque Ports, a ceremonial post he was appointed to by King George VI. He is cloaked with the robes of the Order of the Garter. Now aged 79, he has recently deigned to accept entry into the most noble order, despite having previously refused it,[2] as 'it was the Queen's wish'. In a scene reminiscent of the Duke of Wellington's reception at Queen Victoria's coronation in 1838, the old war leader is greeted with the resounding cheers, applause and excitement that are his due.

As thousands of colourfully dressed people file through the Abbey's doors, the scene inside is 'like a medieval tapestry'.[3] The Duke of Edinburgh's family is led by his mother, Princess Alice of Battenburg. She is wearing a grey nun's habit of floor-length cloak and flowing veil, having founded a nursing order of Greek Orthodox nuns in 1949.[4]

The processions of the Princes and Princesses of the Blood Royal, with the royal arms emblazoned on their tabards, include Princess Alice, who is attending her fourth coronation – one of only a handful of people who manage this feat.

Queen Victoria's 80-year-old granddaughter Princess Marie-Louise is here. She seems flustered at the difficulty of climbing the stairs to the royal gallery and bundles her long train over her arm in order to do so.[5]

The Queen Mother and Princess Margaret arrive in the Irish State Coach, fairy-tale like. Twenty-two-year-old Margaret is stunning in her embroidered white-gold Hartnell dress. The Queen Mother wears a white satin dress with gold embellishments, and a full skirt, with Queen Mary's robe from 1937. Her own robe from 1937 had such a long train it would not have been appropriate for today, and would have been difficult to shorten.[6] They have their own small procession through the Abbey. Once part of the central family of four, they are now a sideshow; as Lilibet has assumed a huge role and responsibilities, so theirs have diminished. At times a forlorn expression passes over Margaret's features; years later she will recall her sadness on this day: 'I had just lost my beloved father, and, really, I had just lost my sister, because she was going to be so busy and had already moved to Buckingham Palace.' She has kept her relationship with Group Captain Peter Townsend, her late father's equerry, pretty well under wraps, and doesn't yet know how exposing today will be. The Queen Mother, now 52 and a widow, turns for a moment as she passes the empty throne, before following the Lord Chamberlain up to the royal gallery, overlooking the Theatre.

Amidst the richness of the colours, the blue and gold, the crimson, the white miniver, the scarlet robes and diamonds and pearls and rubies, the chatter and movement and excitement, the Theatre in front of the High Altar retains its stillness and simplicity. St Edward's Chair, unadorned and alone, is waiting.

In contrast, the choir stalls are ablaze with the colourful dresses, uniforms and national costumes of the foreign guests.

Just before 10.00am the choir sing the litany and the buzz of anticipation intensifies. The Dean of Westminster leads clergy in bringing the regalia from the altar to a table by the Great West Door, leaving it under the care of the Lord Great Chamberlain.

Sensing the royals are about to arrive, the entire congregation stand up. When green-uniformed ladies appear carrying carpet sweepers and start a final clean of the carpet, they realise they've stood too early. The organist starts playing 'Greensleeves' and everyone laughs.[7]

At 10.26am the Queen and Duke of Edinburgh leave Buckingham Palace in the Gold State Coach, pulled by eight grey gelding horses: Cunningham, Tovey, Noah, Tedder, Eisenhower,[8] Snow White, Tipperary and McCreery. The horses' names could be a metaphor for the day itself: nods to the biblical, the fairy-tale, twentieth-century innovation, wartime alliances, popular songs and one or two nobody really understands. The geldings pull together well and look splendid as they carry their monarch on the nineteen-minute journey to the Abbey. They are surrounded by a thousand guardsmen; Viscount Johnnie Althorp (father of Princess Diana), an equerry to the Queen, rides with the mounted Household Cavalry troops.[9] Lord Louis Mountbatten has ridden behind the coach on horseback, and found it hard to keep his lively horse to a dignified walk – on arrival at the Abbey, he hands the reigns to a Life Guard trooper and tells him 'somewhat tetchily – and unrealistically'[10] to take the horse away and exercise it. Queen Mary had thought Philip should be riding alongside the coach on horseback, too – rather than sitting in it next to the Queen.

The six maids of honour have been given small vials of smelling salts, which they store in their white gloves, as they wait together for the arrival of the Queen, just outside the entrance to the annexe. When the Archbishop of Canterbury greets them, Rosie Spencer-Churchill shakes his hand vigorously, and the vial in her gloves breaks and releases a pungent smell. 'What on earth have you done?' exclaims an unamused Archbishop as the girls dissolve into giggles.[11]

The Gold State Coach pulls up and out jumps the Duke of Edinburgh. Keen to ensure the day is perfect, he starts to rush around the waiting maids of honour, checking everything is in order. For Lady Anne, his behaviour only adds to the tension. Everyone in the stands around Parliament Square are on their feet cheering.

They move to gather up the Queen's train using its silk handles, as the Duke of Norfolk stands on the steps of the Abbey in his ducal robes, white knee breeches and stockings, ready to greet her, exactly as he did in 1937 for George VI.

The Duke of Edinburgh, who is wearing the full dress uniform of an admiral of the fleet, goes inside to put on his robes of a royal duke, and the Queen and her procession get ready for their walk up the Nave. The Queen turns to her maids of honour and says: 'Ready, girls?'

As they enter through the West Door a tremor of excitement runs through the congregation and the trumpets sound. All eyes are on the young Queen – the guests in the Abbey, plus an estimated 18 million people watching on television. The congregation stand up in unison.

The orchestra strike up and the choir sing 'I Was Glad'.

Flanked by her supporting bishops, The Bishop of Bath and Wells and the Bishop of Durham, the Queen is calm and poised as she walks slowly and deliberately. The maids of honour, realising that she is walking slightly more slowly than her rehearsal-stand-in did, find they have to adjust their pace, yet still stay in time with each other, to avoid tripping on her 21-foot train of crimson velvet. The Queen's Norman Hartnell gown is made of shimmering white satin embroidered with gold and silver thread and pastel-coloured silks. Pearl and crystal details create a glittering effect as she moves. The tiered skirt of the dress is just visible under the robe of state and does indeed feature the humble leek – beautifully elevated by a sparkling dew of diamonds – rose, thistle and shamrock, representing the United Kingdom and also the emblems of Commonwealth nations that the Queen has specifically asked for: the maple leaf of Canada, the wattle flower of Australia, the fern of New Zealand, the lotus flower of India, wheat, cotton and jute for Pakistan, the protea of South Africa, and another lotus flower for Ceylon.

The six maids of honour are all wearing diamond brooches, in the shape of the letters 'ER', designed in the Queen's own handwriting – a gift the Queen has sent them just the day before. They are followed by the Mistress of the Robes – the Dowager Duchess of Devonshire – and several ladies in waiting.

'Vivat Regina Elizabetha!' shout the Westminster schoolboys, who have been up since the crack of dawn and long since eaten all the sandwiches and barley sweets they were given for the day.

The Queen kneels in prayer in front of her Chair of Estate, as the Spurs, the Orb, the Sceptre, the Rod, and the Staff are laid upon the altar cloth.

The recognition

The Queen rises and her rich crimson cloak is spread out by her maids of honour on the gold carpet. The Archbishop turns to the north, south, east and west, asking each in turn:

> 'Sirs, I here present unto you Queen Elizabeth, your undoubted Queen. Wherefore all you are come this day to do your homage and service, are you willing to do the same?'

The Queen curtseys to each of the four sides, a rare occurrence for her, and a gesture she has decided on herself, despite opposition from the Garter King of Arms who felt it would be seen as a sign of weakness for a sovereign to do so, preferring a small nod of the head.[12]

From each side in turn comes the resounding answer: 'God Save Queen Elizabeth!' accompanied by the sound of trumpets.

The oath

The Queen's voice remains clear and steady as she confirms that she will 'govern the Peoples' of all her realms and territories 'according to their respective laws and customs' and delivers her responses to the Archbishop.

For the first time in the history of the coronation service, the Dean of Westminster hands the Bible to the Moderator of the General Assembly of the Church of Scotland, the only non-Anglican participant in the ceremony, who walks with the Archbishop of Canterbury to the Queen. Together they hand the bible into her charge: 'the most valuable thing that this world affords.'

The Moderator says: 'Here is Wisdom; this is the royal Law; these are the lively Oracles of God.'[13]

The Queen moves to the High Altar, kneels and lays her hand on the bible. She confirms her promise: 'The things which I have here before promised I will perform and keep. So help me God.' She kisses the bible before signing a copy of the oath.

There is movement in the royal gallery, as 4-year-old Prince Charles is brought in to sit with the Queen Mother and Princess Margaret. Dressed in a white silk shirt with lace cuffs, his hair has been smoothed into place with a cream he later describes as 'the most appalling gunge'.[14] A footstool is brought in to help him see over the barrier and he watches the scene below him intently, with his chin resting on his hands. From time to time he turns to his granny and asks a question; she is seen patiently explaining what is happening.

The anointing

The Archbishop, with his hand on the ampulla, prays for the Queen, who is kneeling. The Lord Great Chamberlain and Mistress of the Robes remove her train, sparkling collar and precious stones. Now stripped of majestic trappings, she walks solemnly to St Edward's Chair where four heralds and four Knights of the Garter step forward to bear the cloth of gold canopy which will shield this most religious part of the ceremony from the gaze of the congregation, and the television cameras are diverted for this most solemn moment. One of the knights, the Duke of Wellington, is also attending his fourth coronation; having been a page in 1902, a member of the Royal Household in 1911, and a Gold Staff Officer in 1937.[15]

Long-term friend and lady-in-waiting to the Queen, Lady Pamela Mountbatten, watching, knows how important the consecration is to the Queen personally.

The Queen is anointed on her hands, chest and head with a new batch of holy oil, which has been made up for today. Although there was plenty left over from 1937, it was lost when a bomb hit the Deanery of Westminster during the war.[16] The Archbishop's blessing can be heard clearly. The canopy sags in the middle and shakes rather, as one of the knights has advanced Parkinson's.[17]

The crowning

The choir sing 'Zadok the Priest' and all rise for the crowning moment; one onlooker describes the Queen as sitting, looking 'terribly alone'.[18]

Maid of honour Lady Anne Coke, standing watching nearby, having been on her feet for hours with little to eat, starts to feel dizzy, and feels herself start to sway.

It is the Lord Great Chamberlain's job – the Marquess of Cholmondeley, assisted by the Mistress of the Robes – to help with the Queen's costume changes. It's one of those appointments where the hereditary selection process hasn't exactly produced the right man for the job. Probably never having had to dress himself, let alone anyone else, he has already stretched Bernie Norfolk's patience in rehearsals by his inability to do up hooks and eyes – in the end, the Duke has ordered them to be replaced by poppers, which he pushes with violent force.[19] The plain white robe is removed and the Queen is helped into the Colobium Sindonis and the Supertunica and girdle of cloth of gold. She stands for a moment, shimmering in the gold garments, before returning to St Edward's Chair.

Lady Anne's vision blurs and, anxious not to ruin the ceremony, she breaks her vial of smelling salts, but they have little effect. 'I must not faint,' she tells herself firmly, thinking of all the millions watching this moment. Fortunately, 'Black Rod', aka Lieutenant General Sir Brian Horrocks, standing nearby notices her plight and, with the help of a nearby pillar, the distinguished war hero manages to support the swooning maid until she recovers.

The Queen is invested with the Stole Royal and the Robe Royal. She receives the emblems of Majesty including the Orb, the Sceptre, its Star of Africa diamond shining against the dark oak of the Coronation Chair; and the Queen's Ring, placed on the fourth finger of her right hand. Surrounded by the emblems of monarchy, it is her personal demeanour that those watching remember the most. 'Here was no anxious entry into an uneasy heritage,' said one. 'Rather, by her absorbed attention, serenity and assuredness, she conveyed that she knew what she was taking on, and she embraced it willingly, confidently, but with humility.'[20]

At Archbishop Fisher's suggestion, the ancient ceremony of the bracelets, last seen at the coronation of Elizabeth I in 1559, has been reintroduced. Symbolising the bond that unites the monarch and her peoples, the new bracelets have been presented as gifts from the Governments of Commonwealth countries. Glints of gold are seen as the Archbishop clasps them on the Queen's wrists.[21]

The Queen assuredly carries the jewelled 'Sword of State' to the altar, where she places it – surrendering her worldly power to God. It is Lord Salisbury who performs the symbolic act – redeeming the sword in exchange for one hundred freshly minted shillings.

The Queen sits holding the golden Sceptre in her right hand and the Rod in her left.

The Archbishop's voice falters with emotion as he prays over the crown, which alone remains on the altar. 'Bless, we beseech Thee, this Crown, and so sanctify thy servant Elizabeth, upon whose head Thou this day dost place it…'

The Dean carries the crown on a velvet cushion as a hush descends in the Abbey. A small gold star has been placed on the front of the crown to assist the Archbishop in getting it the right way round. He raises the crown above the Queen's head and holds it there momentarily, as he has been advised to do by Richard Dimbleby in rehearsals, before bringing it down into place.

The peers and peeresses don their coronets – in a sweeping movement, the white-gloved peeresses appearing to move like a flock of swans.

The congregation cry, 'God Save the Queen!' Trumpets sound. Outside the cannons roar. Then a hush descends, both inside and outside the Abbey. Outside, the rain starts to pour down hard.

The weight of St Edward's Crown is now on her head, but the Queen carries it gracefully, with apparent ease.

The homage

The Archbishop leads the Queen to the throne on the dais, and together with the bishops, knights and officers of state, lifts her onto the throne, symbolising the combined power of Church and State. The Archbishop kneels, in the first act of homage. The bishops kneel, too and they all do their homage to her.

Next, it's Prince Philip's turn. Handing his coronet to his page, he kneels before his wife and utters his vow: 'I, Philip, do become your liege man of life and limb, and of earthly worship; and faith and truth I will bear unto you, to live and die, against all manner of folks. So help me God.' He rises and kisses her left cheek, before retreating backwards and returning to his chair.

Some senior dignitaries and courtiers detect irreverence in his expression. There is a suspicion that the Duke is not taking this ceremony as seriously as they are.

The royal dukes – the Duke of Gloucester and the young Duke of Kent, age 17, whose father was killed in the war when he was just 6 – also do their homage. The Earl Marshal, Duke of Norfolk, leads the dukes, followed by a representative of each tier of the peerage: the Marquis of Huntley, the Earl of Shrewsbury, Viscount Arbuthnot… each repeat the vow, on behalf of himself and his fellow noblemen of the same rank, who say the words where they sit, kneeling and removing their coronets. Bottom of the aristocratic pecking order are the barons; led by the premier baron of England, Lord Mowbray, whose fellow peers are amused to watch mothballs falling from his robes as he kneels before Her Majesty.[22]

'God Save the Queen, long live Queen Elizabeth! May the Queen live for ever!'

In a first for a coronation, at the beginning of the communion service, the congregation are invited to join in the singing of the hymn 'All People That on Earth Do Dwell'. As the music fades, the Queen moves to the altar and hands St Edward's Crown, the Sceptre and the Rod to the Lord Chamberlain. She makes her offering, an altar cloth and an ingot of pure gold, and she and Prince Philip kneel on their faldstools. The cameras divert as they take communion; for three minutes, viewers at home are left looking at an altar cloth on their screens.

The Archbishop leads a prayer for the Duke, 'who with all humble devotion offers himself for Thy service in the dignity to which Thou hast called him…'

By long royal tradition, there is no crowning ceremony for Philip, who will remain 'Prince Consort', as the husband of a reigning monarch.

The communion service over, the congregation listen to the exquisite sound of William Walton's 'Te Deum', as the Queen retires to St Edward's Chapel, where she takes off the heavy St Edward's Crown and changes from the Robe Royal into the newly made Purple Robe of State, edged with ermine and embroidered around the border in gold, with the Imperial State Crown. Her maids and a few attendants are with her. The Archbishop of Canterbury offers round a flask of brandy, though the Queen declines.

Outside, the procession forms up, the whole Theatre becoming 'a swirling kaleidoscope of brilliant colour'.[23] The Theatre is a mass of scarlet uniforms, and robes, rich blue mantles and white silk, ushers in green satin, Knights of the Garter wearing red velvet surcoats and blue Garter mantles. Interspersed among them are the pages, attending the peers and peeresses – boys aged 12–15, wearing the livery colours of those they attend, with white breeches and stockings, lace cravats and ruffles, and wearing swords.

After the Orders of Knighthood came the bearers of the Standards of Ceylon, South Africa, Australia, Pakistan, New Zealand, Canada, the Union Standard, the standard of the Principality of Wales, and the Royal Standard, borne by Field Marshal the Viscount Montgomery.

The prime ministers of the members of the Commonwealth move from the choir stalls to join the procession, most prominent among them being Sir Winston Churchill, who turns to take a last look at the throne, the Coronation Chair and the High Altar.

Then the Queen reappears, looking exquisitely young, beautiful and regal, carrying the Sceptre with the jewelled Cross shining brightly, and the Orb. She turns to look upwards to the royal gallery where her mother and sister sit. Perhaps she is remembering when she sat with her granny, sixteen years earlier, and watched her parents being crowned.

The orchestra play fanfares, followed by the National Anthem, followed by Elgar's 'Pomp and Circumstance', 'Land of Hope and Glory', as the Queen processes through the Abbey to the West Door. As she steps outside, the waiting crowds erupt as they see the Queen make her way to the annexe, where Coronation Chicken is served during a brief break.[24]

Inside the Abbey, guests – stiff from hours of sitting – start to move towards the exits.

During a quiet, unguarded moment, Princess Margaret chats to Captain Peter Townsend, the former fighter pilot she has fallen in love with. When the princess casually leans forward and flicks a piece of fluff off Townsend's jacket, the moment is caught by the watching cameras. It's a seemingly insignificant gesture, yet its intimacy is enough to signal to the world's press that something is going on between the princess and the handsome, but divorced, group captain, and trigger one of the biggest scandals in royal history.

The crowds outside wait patiently in the rain for the Queen to reappear, and climb into the Gold State Coach. As she does so, the sun makes a rare appearance. The Duke of Edinburgh at her side, they set off for the much larger, seven-mile procession through London. Ten thousand servicemen and servicewomen take part; two thousand from the dominions and a further five hundred from the colonies, including Cyprus, the Soloman Islands, Trinidad and the Bahamas. Twenty-seven bands play as they march. Contingents from the Commonwealth countries, including South Africa, New Zealand, Australia, Pakistan – and the mounted Royal Canadian Police and the Gurkhas get especially loud cheers.

A large contingent from the British armed forces includes the women's regiments from each of the three armed services. With wartime memories still fresh in people's minds, and Britain's defence spending and armed forces still taking a huge chunk of the national budget, many of those watching are also in uniform. The crowd recognise and cheer war heroes, including Field Marshal Montgomery ('Monty'), commander of the Allied Land Forces on D-Day.

Princess Alice shares a carriage with Princess Marie-Louise, who has drunk a glass of neat gin after mistaking it for water. She nearly falls out of the coach, and her tiara slips down as she leans out of the window, waving to the crowds.[25]

Through the rain-soaked streets they go. People lucky enough to be in the covered stands have handed their umbrellas to those exposed on the pavement below – and when the weather clears the umbrellas are passed carefully back through the rows to their owners. The service has been broadcast to the crowds, via loudspeakers. When people glimpse the Gold State Coach itself, the Queen waving a white-gloved hand and bowing her head to the crowds, they surge forward waving little flags.

The exuberantly cheerful Queen Salote is loved by the crowds, as she keeps the roof of her carriage down, pretending not to understand the tiny Sultan's requests to have it closed as the rain pours down. By the time they arrive at Buckingham Palace, they are soaking wet.

The Queen arrives at Buckingham Palace and mingles with her guests. Charles and his younger sister Anne, who at two and a half had not been taken to the Abbey, hide under their mother's dress; Charles has his eye on the crown, but is prevented from swiping it off a table. He must wait another seventy years to get his hands on it.

As the Queen's party make their way down the long palace corridors to be photographed, the mood is one of excitement at the occasion and relief that everything has gone off well. Exhilarated, the Queen starts to run, and her maids run after her.

In the Throne Room, Cecil Beaton has set up two backdrops, so one group can be arranged while he shoots the other.

The Queen Mother has got her way with the choice of her favourite photographer. Prince Philip had wanted his friend Baron to take the photographs. Now he tries to take over Beaton's shoot, telling people where to stand and when to smile and generally 'being frightfully bossy'.[26] Beaton becomes increasingly irritated, but the Duke persists with his interference. Eventually, the photographer puts his camera down, saying, 'Sir, if you would like to take the photographs, please do so.' He starts to walk away, to the horror of the Queen and the Queen Mother. Philip backs off and the session resumes.

Several hours after the end of the coronation ceremony, a solitary peer, in full robes and carrying his coronet, is seen walking to St James's Park Station and taking the underground to Sloane Square, to the amusement of fellow passengers.[27]

The balcony appearance

When the Queen walks out alone onto the balcony of Buckingham Palace to greet her people, she is hit by the deafening sound of a crowd that covers every available inch of space down the Mall to Admiralty Arch and in the surrounding parks. She is joined by her family.

The Queen is visibly moved by the support she receives. She smiles and waves tirelessly, the small figures of Charles and Anne waving, too.

Then comes the roar of approaching jet fighters, and they watch as the planes fly overhead, dipping their wings to the new monarch. The crowd cheer their appreciation of the display – but also now they are cheering for the fighter pilots who have played such an important part in the war, and to whom they owe their freedom.

The maids of honour are also on the balcony. Lady Anne feels the noise from the crowd physically hit her. 'The flypast was a magnificent tribute, simultaneously a look to the future and a reminder that we had escaped, that we were free and at peace… I could see and feel the Queen's pride as we all shared a distinct feeling of unity and hope.' Senior Maid of Honour Lady Rosemary Spencer-Churchill leaves promptly afterwards for Blenheim Palace, her ancestral home, where her mother is expecting her to help with the ox roast for the family meal – a relaxation of the meat ration to permit ox roasts being one welcome coronation initiative.[28]

The broadcast

Introduced by Churchill, the Queen addresses her people in the evening: six years after her broadcast in South Africa, on the occasion of her 21st birthday, she renews her promise to the nation:

> The ceremonies you have seen today are ancient, and some of their origins are veiled in the mists of the past. But their spirit and their meaning shine through the ages never perhaps, more brightly than now.
>
> I have in sincerity pledged myself to your service, as so many of you are pledged to mine. Throughout all my life and with all my heart I shall strive to be worthy of your trust.

Towards the end of the speech there's a valiant attempt to link the day's dressing up, oath-uttering, oil-anointing and crowning activities with the disparate British Empire and the emerging Commonwealth.

> There is also this. I have behind me not only the splendid traits and the annals of more than a thousand years, but the living strength and majesty of the Commonwealth and Empire, of societies old and new, of lands and races different in history and origins but all, by God's will, united in spirit and in aim.
>
> Therefore I am sure that this, my Coronation, is not the symbol of a power and a splendour that are gone, but a declaration of our hopes for the future, and for the years I may, by God's grace and mercy, be given to reign and serve you as your Queen.

At the end of the speech, the National Anthem plays and, this being 1953, everyone – whether at home or at a public gathering – stands up.

The Queen reappears on the balcony at 9.45pm to switch on the illuminations. As she presses a switch, a garland of lights shines all around the palace and up the Mall and beyond.

On the South Bank, there's a fireworks display, setting the night sky ablaze in colour. London's West End is abuzz with parties, with people from different backgrounds mixing in a way they wouldn't normally do in class-conscious Britain.

But this is the 1950s. Lady Pamela Mountbatten, daughter of Lord Louis Mountbatten, the last Viceroy of India, watches the fireworks with her father and mother Edwina. They sit with Jawaharlal Nehru, the Cambridge-educated Indian nationalist who is now the first prime minister of the Indian republic. Lady Pamela overhears a woman behind her saying: 'Look – there is Lady Mountbatten. And that's the Indian Nehru next to her. How *can* she let him sit so near?' When Nehru touches her mother's arm to point something out, the horrified woman behind says: 'Look, he is touching her. How *can* she let him? It's disgusting.'[29]

But even if the reality didn't always quite match the aspiration, the prevailing mood was undeniably one of national celebration, togetherness and optimism. As the royal party finally retired, exhausted but satisfied with how things had gone, for many the day ended late, in the spirit it was begun – with singing, laughter and hopes for a brighter future.

Chapter Seventeen

CONTINUITY

In the aftermath of the coronation, there was much talk of the wonder of it all, the magnificence of the ceremony and what it meant for the country. The Queen wrote to the Archbishop of Canterbury, thanking him for making 'the strain of that long day so much easier to face'.[1]

Four days after the coronation, the Queen awarded Edmund Hillary a knighthood.

Coronation-related events continued through the month, with a grand display of naval power taking place at Spithead on 15 June. Over 300 ships from the UK and twenty-two other countries took part. The Queen reviewed the fleet from aboard the royal yacht, HMS *Surprise*.

Less than a fortnight after the coronation, Princess Margaret's romance with Peter Townsend was splashed all over the newspapers. The royal family had known for months, but had hoped to keep a lid on it – the last thing they wanted was for the scandal to eclipse positive coronation-related stories. Many news reports depicted the relationship as frankly unthinkable, some suggested it must be a false rumour, unable to comprehend that a princess could fall for an older, divorced man.

The Queen herself was not unsympathetic to Margaret, and would have liked to have helped make her sister happy. But in these early, quite difficult years of her reign, she was a naturally conservative character, much younger than those experienced men who were advising her – chief among them the long-term courtier Alan Lascelles and the prime minister Winston Churchill. Her husband, the Duke of Edinburgh, was distrusted by both the Queen Mother and Queen Mary, and tensions abounded over what his role really was.

The Queen asked Margaret to wait for a couple of years. The Royal Marriages Act stated that she needed the monarch's permission to marry until she reached the age of 25. But even after that, as a member of the royal family, she did need the approval of parliament. By 1955, new prime minster Anthony Eden proposed that if Margaret were to marry Townsend she would need to give up her royal title and live, preferably abroad, as plain 'Mrs Townsend'. Still grieving for her father, uprooted from her home, distanced from her sister and kept apart from the man she had fallen in love with, it was an unenviable choice. Princess Margaret, the King Emperor's daughter, came to realise that being Her Royal Highness was too much for her to give up and she ended the relationship. Who is to say whether, had she lived in more accepting times, a union between Margaret and Townsend would have given her more lasting happiness than she later achieved by marrying photographer Anthony Armstrong-Jones.

The Royal Commonwealth Tour of 1953–54 was a chance for the new Queen to cement the monarchy's relationship with the dominions. The Queen took her coronation dress with her and wore it to open parliaments in New Zealand, Australia and Ceylon. The dress was not particularly suited to hot climates, as when the sun warmed the diamanté and metalwork embroidery, it became so hot that it burned her skin, even through underlayers of petticoats.[2]

The second Elizabethan era was one of great change. Through the dying days of the Empire and the emergence of a more modern society, technological, social and political changes, Queen Elizabeth II remained a constant, reassuring figurehead. She emerged as a monarch with considerable diplomatic skill on the world stage, who both provided leadership and sought to share in national challenges and emergencies at home. When the Covid pandemic arrived in March 2020, the Queen addressed the nation from Windsor Castle where she was isolating with the Duke of Edinburgh. In a short speech that referenced the nation's history in pulling together and the need to find new ways of keeping in touch, she said, 'I am certain we are up to that challenge,' conveying a gravitas that comes from wisdom and experience in a way that elected politicians of the day cannot necessarily match.

Her death in September 2022 at the age of 96 marked the end of an era. Many expressed their gratitude for a monarch who had been a constant, exemplary public servant. During her many decades on the throne, she was adept at changing with the times, yet what many people valued was that she always seemed to stay the same. Physically she aged, her hair greyed then whitened, but in appearance and what she wore she was deliberately consistent. People understood that she was authentic because she stayed true to herself, her personality, her values and her life's purpose – 'I serve'.

Unusually for a monarch, due to Scottish law, a death certificate was issued, which was signed by Princess Anne and made public. The cause of death was stated as 'Old Age'. It was known that the Queen had been suffering from a number of conditions in her final years. Princess Anne, in an interview with Canadian television, said that her mother had expressed concern that it would make things more difficult for others if she died at Balmoral, adding, 'I think we did try to persuade her that shouldn't be part of the decision making process.'[3] But she obviously gave much thought to her final months, even continuing with essential constitutional duties when required. She was photographed at Balmoral, with new prime minister Liz Truss, in her sitting room, the decor of which hadn't changed in decades.

There was a satisfying sense of tying up loose ends at the end of a long life well lived. She had settled the matter of Camilla's future title – always left rather ambiguous due to sensitivities over Princess Diana – by issuing a statement saying that it was her 'sincere wish' that Camilla would become 'Queen Consort' when the time came.

The timing of her death was impeccable. Earlier in August, when parliament is in recess and everyone has left London for their summer holidays, would have been an inconvenience. But in early September, the weather is still good, the processions looked stunning, crowds didn't freeze and, perhaps with an eye on making things easy for her successor, it gave a clear six months to organise a coronation in May. Perfect. No one wants a winter coronation.

The Queen's coffin was driven from Balmoral to Buckingham Palace, and later removed to Westminster Hall to lie in state for four days, during which 250,000 people queued for up to twenty-four hours to file past and pay their last respects. Once inside the great hall, phones and cameras were banned, and the scene was majestic and dignified as people walked slowly, silently by the coffin, which had the Imperial State Crown and the Orb bolted onto the top.

King Charles and his siblings stood vigil by the coffin, in a sign of changing times his sister Princess Anne was among them, which felt entirely appropriate. Next day, Prince William led the grandchildren in their own vigil. Prince Andrew and Prince Harry were granted permission to wear their military uniforms for the vigils, despite having relinquished all connections with the forces on retiring from royal life.

The grand state funeral of Queen Elizabeth II in 2022 was another chance for Britain to produce a flawless display of pageantry, and the event saw the largest gathering of world leaders ever to take place in Britain, with major airports struggling to cope with the number of private jets arriving. According to BBC figures, the funeral and processions were watched by a worldwide television audience of around 66 million, including 43 per cent of the British population, and 11 per cent of the French population.[4] Afterwards, at a Committal service in St George's Chapel Windsor, her family watched on as the Imperial State Crown, along with the Orb and Sceptre, was finally removed from the top of the coffin. 'I rather weirdly felt a sense of relief,' recalled the Princess Royal of that symbolic moment of closure, when she knew 'that responsibility has been moved on'.[5]

Chapter Eighteen

A Smooth Transition

From the moment the news of Queen Elizabeth II's death was announced, the nation watched as a meticulously planned set of events unrolled at pace. Times of change, moments of succession – these are what monarchies survive or perish on and a sense of urgency prevails. Remember the Archbishop of Canterbury and the Lord Chamberlain banging on the doors of Kensington Palace at the crack of dawn on that morning in 1837? If the monarchy is to fulfil its role as a force for continuity and stability, then these moments are when it needs to be seen to be doing that.

The new King Charles III addressed the nation on the evening of the Queen's death, paying tribute to his mother, and renewing her 'promise of lifelong service'. It was a fitting tribute in which he eloquently quoted Shakespeare: 'may flights of angels sing thee to thy rest'. But he also promptly got down to business, announcing that William and Kate would become Prince and Princess of Wales. The speech, which was well received, signalled the start of a slick operation, to ensure a smooth and assured succession.

The new King returned to London from Balmoral for the Accession Council on 10 September, where the formal proclamation and Charles's inaugural speech were televised for the first time. Long gone, of course, is any talk of Empire, as the new King speaks of his intention to strive to uphold constitutional government and to 'seek the peace, harmony and prosperity of the peoples of these Islands and of the Commonwealth Realms and territories throughout the world'. In the speech, he deliberately, delicately articulates his position as an unelected head of state in a twenty-first-century democracy: he will, he says, be 'upheld' by the affection and loyalty of the peoples, while being 'guided by the counsel of their elected parliaments'.[1]

Membership of the Privy Council had by this time far outgrown the space in St James's Palace, so Privy Counsellors were forced to take part in a ballot to secure a space at the Accession Council. Automatic invitations had only been granted to the most senior members – including former prime ministers and archbishops. All went well, until Charles sat down to sign the oath to preserve the Church of Scotland, and found the small desktop on which he was expected to write was cluttered with objects. His irritation was apparent as he gestured to an aide to clear it – all, of course, caught by those ever-present television cameras.

Medieval traditions were adhered to, with the Garter King of Arms, the most senior Herald, reciting a proclamation from the balcony of St James's Palace, which was then repeated at the City of London, the devolved capitals and then in towns all over the United Kingdom. These proclamations drew small crowds, who enjoyed the traditional bulletin and small slice of pageantry, even if it was not exactly 'breaking news'.

King Charles also met representatives from both houses of parliament, in Westminster Hall, and there followed visits to Scotland, Wales and Northern Ireland. It was a demanding schedule, and one that took its toll on a 73-year-old man who had just lost his mother. Signing the visitors' book at Hillsborough Castle, his pen started leaking, once again triggering an outburst of temper that hit the headlines: 'Every stinking time…' he seethed.

Charles's accession coincided with a tumultuous time in British politics. Prime minster Liz Truss had been in office for just four days – and she would last only another forty-five. The new King had time for just two weekly audiences with his first prime minister at Buckingham Palace, before she announced her intention to resign. Following a disastrous 'mini-budget' that had resulted in the pound crashing to an all-time low against the dollar, she had been under increasing pressure from within her own party to go. In contrast to the musical chairs going on in Downing Street, Charles, the elder statesman with decades of public service and centuries of tradition behind him, appeared to offer experience and stability.

All in all though, it was a fairly seamless accession, and one that helped the public to see Charles in a new light. Polls suggested the public approved of his actions and three-quarters of people thought he was demonstrating 'good leadership'.[2] The new King was a very familiar figure, in the public eye since his birth due to his place in the royal family, he was also known for his charity work and as a passionate advocate for the environment. People knew what they were getting.

Having waited even longer than Edward VII to inherit the throne from a long-lived monarch meant Charles had a lifetime of ups and downs already behind him, all played out in the media; documented in the tabloids, in books, on the internet, via documentaries and television interviews. When Charles was a young child, his parents made long tours of the Commonwealth, often being away for months and he appears to have had a slightly distant relationship with his mother, who was busy getting to grips with her role as Queen. He was sent to a remote Scottish boarding school where the very physical regime and isolated location didn't suit his temperament and he was unhappy. At age 20, he attended his own investiture as Prince of Wales at Caernarfon – in a similar ceremony to the one his Great Uncle David, the last Prince of Wales, had gone through back in 1911. A new coronet was made for him for the occasion, as the Duke of Windsor had taken his father George VI's coronet with him into exile and refused to return it.

After a history degree at Cambridge, Charles served in the Royal Air Force and Royal Navy in the 1970s. During his youth, the prince was considered highly eligible and romantically linked with a string of girlfriends. In 1980, at the age of 29, he began dating Lady Diana Spencer and the 19-year-old was hounded by the press, with speculation growing that the two would marry. While Charles didn't face the pressure that his great-great-grandfather Edward VII endured to marry a foreign princess, there's no doubt from his comments at the time and since that he felt a pressure from his family and a responsibility to marry a 'suitable' girl. Despite the age gap and their different interests, and the fact that they hadn't had very much time alone together, Charles proposed the following February and the couple were married in a huge royal wedding at St Paul's Cathedral in July 1981. During the 1980s and until her death in 1997, Diana dominated the headlines, with the media seemingly having an insatiable appetite for the princess who at times courted their attention. The marriage broke down after the birth of the couple's two sons, William and Harry, with both Charles and Diana later confessing to infidelity. Charles returned to his former love, Camilla Parker Bowles, who began a slow and difficult journey to gain public acceptance as partner to the heir to the throne.

Despite Charles's rocky private life, which sometimes dented his popularity with the British people, who often sided with Diana, he did gain respect for his charity work and public service. As well as championing causes such as the environment, he created the Prince's Trust, which helped over a million young people find a firmer footing in life. Charles gained the Queen's blessing to marry Camilla at St George's Chapel, Windsor, in 2005. The bride wore a pale blue silk dress-coat; the Queen wore white, the same colour that Camilla had chosen to wear at Charles and Diana's wedding back in 1981. Camilla was never known as 'The Princess of Wales', instead being known as the 'Duchess of Cornwall', with the suggestion that she would be styled 'Princess Consort' when Charles became King. As the Queen grew older, Charles increasingly took on duties to represent her, particularly abroad, and people became accustomed to the sight of Camilla accompanying him. As Duchess of Cornwall, she also took on her own share of charity and public service work, including speaking out against domestic violence. Still, there was a question mark over her title. The King's wife has the right to be called the Queen, but would Camilla use that title? Would the public accept it?

While Queen Elizabeth II's death was marked with respectful television and radio coverage, tributes and a huge floral display in the parks surrounding Buckingham Palace, there was no prolonged public mourning. Following the death of George VI, the official period of public mourning had lasted for over two months; after Queen Elizabeth II died it was set at just ten days. Within twenty-four hours of the death of Queen Elizabeth II, parliament had been recalled.

The sense that it was best to get on with things was reinforced when a date for the coronation was fixed just four weeks after the Queen's death. There was no long pause as there had been in 1953, no dithering around about timings. It was announced on 11 October that the coronation would take place on Saturday, 6 May – which left seven months to get everything organised.

This initial announcement seemed to suggest that there would be no huge surprises or changes to 'the way we have always done things'. As expected, the coronation would take place at Westminster Abbey, be conducted by the Archbishop of Canterbury, and the ceremony would include the coronations of the King and Queen Consort. It was His Majesty's sincere wish that the coronation looked towards the future, while also being rooted in long-standing traditions. Over the course of the following months, it would become clearer how exactly the organisers were going to strike the balance between the future and the past.

Sir Clive Alderton, the King's private secretary, was appointed to chair a Coronation Organising Committee at Buckingham Palace, while the prime minister appointed Oliver Dowden MP to oversee the government's involvement in the coronation, and the Archbishop of Canterbury, Justin Welby, was in charge of the liturgical aspects, in consultation with the Dean of Westminster. The Earl Marshall was also involved, and became a strong champion of the coronation concert that took place on the day after the coronation itself.

Charles had no doubt given plenty of thought to the role of the monarchy within a modern society. While he trod a careful line, with considerable grace, between looking to his own future role, without in any way anticipating his mother's passing, he did occasionally give voice to his thoughts on modernising the monarchy. In 1994, when asked about the monarch's role as 'Defender of the Faith', he said: 'I personally would rather see it as Defender of Faith, not *the* faith, because it means just one particular interpretation of the faith, which I think is sometimes something that causes a problem.'[3] The remark caused much discussion around the monarch's role as head of the Anglican Church, in a much more diverse society.

There was also much speculation about what was termed a 'slimmed down' monarchy under Charles, presumably comprised of Charles and Camilla, William, Harry and their families. But since then Harry and Meghan have departed for California in a blaze of negative headlines. The King's brother, Andrew, has been stripped of all his titles, and been forced to retire from public life, living as 'Andrew Mountbatten

Windsor', following his friendship with Jeffrey Epstein, a convicted paedophile. Queen Elizabeth and Prince Philip have died. The monarchy has slimmed down of its own accord, and the public have become familiar with the core group of Charles and Camilla, William and Kate and, on a few key occasions throughout the year, their three young children, Prince George, Princess Charlotte and Prince Louis. This smaller group is supported by Princess Anne, and Edward and Sophie, the Duke and Duchess of Edinburgh, and the lesser-known but still active working royals, the Duke and Duchess of Gloucester.

Dubbed 'Operation Golden Orb', planning for the coronation took into account the success of the 1953 event, while understanding that much would need to be changed and scaled back. While there aren't huge numbers of people around who were adults in 1953, who remembered the coronation happening or even attended it, thanks to film, photography, books and articles many do have an idea of what the occasion was like. Compared with Queen Victoria's coronation, when years later, Abbey staff had difficulty saying with certainty which crown she wore, there were many more records available to those who wanted to remind themselves what happened. For Charles himself, not only had he been present, watching intently as a small boy, he also has memories of the time.[4]

But how do you match the splendour and extravagance of 1953? Like Queen Elizabeth II herself, it is a tough act to follow. Britain in the early 1950s was a very different place. In the decades since, the population of the UK has risen by around 30 per cent, from 51 million in 1952, to 67 million in 2021. The 2011 census recorded that ethnic minorities formed up to 15 per cent of the population in England and Wales.[5] In the early 1950s, Britain's global Empire and associated large armed forces meant there were 863,000 British troops posted abroad in 1952, in countries including Germany, Egypt, the West Indies, Malaya and Hong Kong. In 2022, the British armed forces had shrunk to one-fifth of their previous size, with a total of 150,800 regular forces. By 2023, the Empire had gone, in its place the Commonwealth had grown to fifty-six members. Fourteen of these are 'Realms', with King Charles as head of state – giving a unique global dimension to the British monarchy, that no other modern monarchy has.

Another key difference with the 1953 coronation that organisers have to grapple with is the huge cost of security now required to put on a large-scale public event. The rise of international terrorism has meant that policing central London during such occasions requires far more resource than it did in 1953, when the large numbers of police who lined the route were present primarily to ensure the public's safety, rather than react to potential threats.[6]

The monarchy has a constitutional association with religion, yet Britain is increasingly a secular country. In a 1956 survey, 34 per cent of those asked thought that the Queen was 'especially chosen by God'.[7] Fast forward to 2023 and there are now far fewer churchgoers and the Church of England enjoys less support than it once did. Very quickly following his succession, Charles tried to set out how he saw himself in relation to the multiple faiths of his subjects, having obviously given the issue much thought. At the Privy Council gathering on 10 September, he spoke of himself as a committed Anglican Christian, stating: 'at my Coronation I will take an Oath relating to the settlement of the Church of England'. He then talked about his vision of Britain as a 'community of communities' and of his duty as sovereign to protect the right of others to practise other faiths, or live secular lives.

On a more prosaic level, the coronation planning committee faced the usual questions and challenges: who to invite and where to put everyone.

Bernard Norfolk, the Earl Marshal who had organised the coronations in 1937 and 1953, had died in 1975, leaving four daughters who, due to the laws of primogeniture, were unable to inherit the title. Astonishingly perhaps, dukedoms in the United Kingdom still cannot be inherited by women, which means that the great office of state of Earl Marshal cannot be held by a woman, since it is attached to the dukedom. The Dukedom of Norfolk, along with the office of Earl Marshal, therefore passed to a second cousin once removed, Miles Fitzalan-Howard, who died in 2002. The title was then inherited by his son, Edward Fitzalan-Howard, who became the 18th Duke of Norfolk, who had been involved in organising the funeral of Queen Elizabeth II in 2022. In April 2022, Fitzalan-Howard was disqualified from driving for six months, due to a motoring offence. His barrister argued in mitigation that he needed to be able to drive to organise the coronation.[8]

In reality, organising the coronation was a team effort; key players included Sir Charles Alderton, the King's private secretary, and Oliver Dowden, on behalf of the prime minister. There was a large weekly meeting of the Coronation Organising Committee, with lots of sub-committee offshoots.

The public side of the coronation was managed by the Department for Culture, Media and Sport. The Earl Marshal was responsible for some of the ceremonial aspects of the service, while the Archbishop of Canterbury, alongside the Dean of Westminster, managed the order of service, and came up with ideas around how to involve other faiths in an Anglican ceremony, while retaining all legally binding oaths and rituals. It was agreed early on that the whole thing should last around one hour and forty-five minutes – about the length of a football match, including half time.

The King remained very involved in decision making. His deep interest in matters relating to faith, and long experience in dealing with British institutions and the Commonwealth, meant he was the key decision-maker for the coronation planning, in a way that his mother in 1953 hadn't been. Reflecting his personal passion for music, he particularly wanted to involve a range of musical styles, including female composers and gospel singers.

Since 1953, the position of the aristocracy had also radically changed. In 1999, under Tony Blair's Labour government, the right of hereditary peers to sit in the House of Lords was abolished, although concessions made by the government to get the bill passed meant that ninety peers, elected by those eligible, were allowed to remain, as well as the Earl Marshal and the Lord Great Chamberlain. The 800 members of the House of Lords are now made up of representatives from all parties, as well as independent members. These changes were reflected in the decision to exclude almost all hereditary peers, except for a few with specific roles from the coronation. The number of seats for parliamentarians was also reduced from 1,500 in 1953 to just 100, to be selected by ballot and with no room for spouses. This was a significant departure from all previous coronations. The Earl Marshal, keen to avoid the sight of a few hereditary peers crowning themselves, set strict rules for peers who did attend, stressing they shouldn't bring their aristocratic toys, such as the family coronet.

The convention that other heads of state past and present do not attend coronations may have come in handy when the Duke of Windsor threatened to show up in 1953, but Charles III and his team saw no problem with heads of state attending if they wished to. Compared with 1953, there were now three times as many nation states, so that's an awful lot of invitations.

The Coronations Claims Office, a modernised version of the Coronation Claims Court, was set up, staffed by civil servants, it being felt that country's most senior judges were not required to adjudicate on who carried which bits of regalia. There were, somewhat surprisingly, 429 claims, though most were not considered relevant – for example, those that simply claimed a right to attend the service. Those claims that were judged to be valid were submitted to the Royal Household and the Earl Marshal for consideration as to whether they would be required at the ceremony. Thirteen claims were approved, including senior civil servant Antonia Romeo, holder of ancient title of 'Clerk of the Crown in Chancery', who had claimed an ancient right 'to record the proceedings and have five yards of cloth'. She was given a front-row seat in the North Transept, and the right to record the event with pen and paper. The cloth never materialised.[9]

The judgements of the claims process revealed that hereditary peers would still have a role in a twenty-first-century coronation. The Earl of Erroll, Merlin Hay, one of the ninety hereditary peers to retain a seat in the House of Lords, was granted the right to have a silver baton or staff as Lord High Constable of Scotland and to have a place in the King's Procession into Westminster Abbey. The Earl of Loudon, Simon Abney-Hastings, became the only Australian to take part in the ceremony, being granted the right to bear a Golden Spur in the King's Procession. From his hometown of Wangaratta, Victoria, Abney-Hastings announced that he was 'delighted and sincerely honoured to accept the invitation'. His neighbours in the small Australian town were surprised to find out they had an earl in their midst, despite a 2004 Channel 4 documentary *Britain's Real Monarch*, arguing that Abney-Hastings did in fact have a rightful claim on the British throne itself. As direct descendants of George Plantagenet, the brother of Edward IV and Richard III, some historians have claimed that Edward IV was illegitimate, and therefore as the oldest legitimate brother George and his direct heirs should have inherited the crown. The low-key earl seemed keen to avoid any possible awkwardness over the matter, however, indicating that he would not seek the crown itself; adding that he and the royals were on amicable terms and exchanged Christmas cards each year.[10]

For most unsuccessful claimants it was a lacklustre rejection email from a nameless civil servant – not even a signed letter from the Earl Marshal to keep in their scrapbook. But in an attempt to let them down gently, they were advised that they were at liberty to try again at future coronations.

This ruthless standing down of the aristocracy upset some. Journalist Petronella Wyatt, daughter of a Tory peer, writing in the *Telegraph* accused the palace of 'pandering to the woke' in organising a coronation that would lack the pomp and pageantry that made it special. 'It is particularly disturbing that the Earl of Derby has not been asked to provide falcons, as his family have done since the 16th Century. These little things deprive people of their purpose in life.'[11]

It was decided that Queen Camilla would reuse one of the previous Queen Consort's crowns. The Queen Mother's beautiful circlet was considered diplomatically unsuitable, due to the fact that its centrepiece is the magnificent 105-carot Koh-i-Noor diamond. Several nations, including India, have claimed that the diamond was effectively stolen and should be returned. Camilla therefore opted for Queen Mary's crown, which was altered to reduce the eight arches to four, increase the width, and re-set with pieces from the Cullinan diamond, the largest gem-quality diamond ever mined. Pieces of the Cullinan diamond also feature in the Sceptre with Cross and the Imperial State Crown.

The monarch himself would of course be crowned with St Edward's Crown, and later don the Imperial State Crown, both of which were in need of some refurbishment by royal jeweller Mappin and Webb. Having carefully measured the King's head, Mark Appleby became the first crown jeweller in history to be faced with the task of cutting up St Edward's Crown in order to insert four seven-millimetre gold strips to expand the width slightly.[12]

In the BBC documentary *Charles III – The Coronation Year*, the television crew accompany Charles and Camilla to inspect the work in progress. They are fascinated by the painstaking and precise craftsmanship of the jewellers. They also meet royal milliner Philip Treacy, who has been commissioned to produce the soft inner lining of each crown – the so-called 'cap of maintenance'. Without the cap, explains Treacy, the crown may cut the wearer's forehead – and would certainly leave an unsightly mark. The cap also prevents the crown 'becoming a necklace'.[13]

Throughout the coronation planning process, media speculation over whether or not Harry and Meghan, the Duke and Duchess of Sussex, would show up on the day continued. For many weeks, no response to their invitation was forthcoming. Now residing in an upmarket suburb of Los Angeles with his American wife and their two young children, the King's second son had published a tell-all memoir just months earlier, which followed on from a television interview with Oprah Winfrey. By the time they received their coronation invitation, Harry and Meghan's relationship with the royal family had reached a new low; suggestions that his brother William had physically attacked him, his sister-in-law Kate had not been supportive of Meghan, and even made her cry over bridesmaids' outfits, that Camilla's need for positive PR had sometimes been secured at the expense of Harry, and even allegations of racism within the royal family, were among the 'revelations' in the book and television interview. The Queen issued a compactly worded statement; 'recollections,' she said, 'may vary'. Charles said nothing, throughout, which was probably the wisest course of action – opinion polls showed his popularity was unaffected.

Another row threatened to blow up around the 'Stone of Scone', also known as the 'Stone of Destiny'. This rectangular block of sandstone is an ancient symbol of Scottish monarchy, and is traditionally positioned underneath St Edward's Chair during coronations. Having been used for the inauguration of Scottish kings hundreds of years ago, it was stolen by Edward I of England in 1296, who had St Edward's Chair crafted especially to hold the stone. Since 1308, the stone has been used for coronations in England, but in 1996, following demands from the Scottish government, it was returned to Scotland to be put on display at Edinburgh Castle, with the proviso that it would be loaned to the Abbey for coronations. In the run up to the 2023 coronation, voices in Scotland who had long campaigned for independence, including former First Minister Alex Salmond, called on current first minister Humza Yousaf to refuse to allow the stone to be loaned to England, in protest over Westminster blocking a second referendum on Scottish independence, following the 2014 referendum when a majority of Scots voted to stay in the United Kingdom. However, Mr Yousaf, a republican who voted 'Yes' to Scottish independence, attended a farewell ceremony in Edinburgh and allowed the stone to be transported to England.

Sometimes the modernising spirit of innovation and inclusion simply misfired. A media storm blew up around proposals released by the Archbishop of Canterbury's office suggesting that the traditional homage by the now-redundant peers would be replaced by 'the homage of the people'. The idea was that for the first time, ordinary members of the public would play an active role in the coronation. Following the Prince of Wales's homage, the Archbishop would invite the people to swear true allegiance to their undoubted King by saying: 'I call upon all persons of goodwill to make their homage, in heart and voice, to their undoubted King, defender of all.'

Millions up and down the country and throughout the world would then respond in unison, presumably to their television sets: 'I swear that I will pay true allegiance to Your Majesty and to your heirs and successors according to law. So help me God.'

The hope, according to Lambeth Palace, was that people would say the homage out loud, wherever they were, and there would be a 'sense of a great cry around the nation and around the world of support for the King'.

The Great British Public were having none of it. It turned out that they did not welcome the opportunity to 'cry out and swear allegiance' and the proposal was interpreted through the media as an order to pay homage, which got people's backs up. This was not 1953 and deference was thin on the ground. The anti-monarchist campaign group Republic said the proposals were 'offensive' and 'tone deaf' and the gesture held people in contempt. While a few game MPs went on television to say they were delighted with the invitation and would be doing their homage, in an online poll for ITV's *Good Morning Britain*, 86 per cent of respondents said they would not be joining in.[14]

Charles's biographer and friend Jonathan Dimbleby, in an interview with the BBC,[15] said that the very idea of the public paying homage to him would be abhorrent to the King, saying 'he has never wanted to be revered'. The idea, he implied, must have come from the Archbishop and was well-intentioned but ill-advised, since it had just given everyone a chance to say 'well, I'm not going to pay homage'. There was swift backtracking at the palace, as they sought to make it clear that this was simply an optional invitation, to anyone who happened to want to join in, rather than 'an expectation or request'. 'Brits will not have to pay homage to King Charles!'[16] declared the headlines as they reported on the 'major last-minute change' the widespread criticism had forced. The Archbishop's response? 'What would this country be if we didn't find something to argue about. That's part of who we are.'

Another recurrent theme in the media in the run up to the coronation was how much this was all going to cost the British taxpayer. As with the funeral of Queen Elizabeth II, the largest part of the budget was going to be spent on security costs. For that state funeral, the first since Winston Churchill's in 1965, security and policing had cost £73.7 million, with the total cost of the funeral and ten-day mourning period including the lying in state at Westminster Hall coming to £162 million.

Can you really do coronations, in the twenty-first century? Is coronation fever still a thing? While it may be a wild exaggeration to compare the sense of excitement to that of 1953, interest in the royals is still high, with all leading newspapers having dedicated royal editors and devoting whole sections to royal news. In mid-April, the Royal Collection Trust, a department of the royal household, launched their range of commemorative china, made in Stoke-on-Trent, and featuring a mug, cup and saucer, with prices ranging from £30 to £75 per piece. It quickly sold out, with some pieces later appearing on eBay with price tags of up to £1500.[17] Also popping up on the auction site were coronation coins, of which 1,000 had been made, each carrying the message: 'The Coronation of their Majesties King Charles III and Queen Camilla'.

Amid all noise and speculation, rehearsals for the coronation continue at the Abbey, at Buckingham Palace and at Lambeth Palace. Some were even filmed, for the BBC documentary, and key players like Justin Welby spoke to the media about how things were going. In this way, things had come full circle from 1838, when Lord Melbourne had advised the young Queen Victoria that a quick look around the Abbey the evening before would suffice. In 2023, the rehearsals became part of the event itself – a source of funny family stories, of interesting historical snippets – a way of getting people interested in the event. Later in the year, when the BBC documentary was screened, some scenes from the rehearsals even went viral on social media. When Prince William is taken through his role in the homage, at one point, the Archbishop turns to him and says: 'If you ever get lost in this, sir, just look confident and bow and that will carry you through everything.' Since 1953, the emergence of reality television alongside a more open, relaxed society means that allowing people to see behind the scenes is communications stardust. Watching the warmth and light-hearted jokes between family members, while rehearsing a huge solemn occasion, is perhaps the best royal PR around. At one point, debating which side of the King's face it is appropriate to kiss, William tickles his father under the chin and jokes: 'Your left cheek is better!' During another moment, while rehearsing the Queen's crowning, the Archbishop struggles to get the King's attention. 'Darling, we need a nod!' shouts Camilla helpfully and the ensuing chuckles help ease the tension among people who have, after all, never done this before and know that they will be performing their duties in front of a watching world.[18]

On the evening before the coronation, there was little time for nerves, as the King entertained the foreign delegations at a reception at Buckingham Palace. There were simply too many of them for a state banquet, but he had made time to meet all the Commonwealth heads of state individually in the preceding days.

Chapter Nineteen

CORONATION DAY 2023

The Coronation of His Majesty King Charles III of the United Kingdom of Great Britain and Northern Ireland and of His other Realms and Territories, King, Defender of the Faith, and of Her Majesty Queen Camilla, His Consort.

Date: Saturday, 6 May 2023
Guests: 2,000
Cost: £72 million[1]
Weather: Heavy rain

Early morning

Once again, London is on the move from very early morning. Compared with 1953, there is much more robust crowd control in place along the Mall, and the entire processional route, with steel fences and gates which are closed by police when areas reach capacity. Hundreds of people have camped out along the route in order to secure a good view – with small encampments of royalists flying union flags and sharing cups of tea along the Mall. Large screens have been erected in the neighbouring parks to accommodate those who can't get a place along the route.

The interior of the Abbey bursts with colour; the rich blue and gold fabrics and carpets of previous coronations are in evidence, along with, for the first time, flower arrangements. Featuring seasonal spring flowers from gardens, farmlands and allotments across the United Kingdom, the floral arrangements pay tribute to the King and Queen's love of the natural world and passion for gardening. Royal florist Shane Connolly has even installed a small meadow of wild grasses, cowslips, primroses and violets by the West Door, which is soon buzzing with bees.[2]

Guests have been advised to wear full ceremonial day dress with medals and decorations, or morning coat or lounge suits for men; day dress for women with an optional hat or fascinator. The early birds are rewarded with the best seats as, aside from members of the royal family, senior representatives of the realms and world leaders, there are no reserved seats. The Gold Sticks guide arrivals to a section of seating, determined by the colour of their ticket. Guests have also received precise instructions around 'facilities'; being advised that the very limited toilet facilities in Westminster Abbey will be available between 7.30am and 10.00am, before closing for the duration of the service and reopening at 1.30pm. Most guests prudently monitor their fluid intake.[3] Conversations are struck up between guests, most of whom have been issued a single ticket so have not been able to bring a spouse.

The Earl Marshal has been at pains to head off any potential upstaging by the few peers and peeresses who have been invited this time around, stipulating no tiaras, coronets or coronation robes are to be worn. Although peers are permitted to wear their standard parliamentary robes, worn for the State Opening of Parliament. However, a few disgruntled peers, who do not sit in the House of Lords, have appealed directly to the King, and he has overruled the Earl Marshal, saying that those who want to wear their family robes should be allowed to do so. But it remains a firm 'no' to bringing along other aristocratic emblems, such as coronet, pages and horse-drawn carriages. This is no longer the aristocracy's show.

The majority of the congregation are not members of the aristocracy at all. Many have been invited because they are associated with the King and Queen's various charities, or are frontline workers in the emergency services. The largest group of invitees are holders of the British Empire Medal (BEM). Awarded for outstanding contributions to community service of some kind, holders have typically made a significant impact at a local level, for example through charity work or volunteering. The Cabinet Office identified 400 BEM holders, ensuring geographical and gender parity, and sent them invitations.

Some royal-adjacent stalwarts have been cut loose; Lady Pamela Hicks, daughter of Charles's mentor Louis Mountbatten and long-time friend of the late Queen, has been gently let down. Others, like Camilla's ex-husband Andrew Parker Bowles, one of the pages at the 1953 coronation, have received an invite.

Limos crawl through the streets surrounding the Abbey and queue to allow their passengers to alight. At the late Queen's funeral, the Foreign Office had organised a coach to bus in foreign leaders and ease traffic pressures. It was an initiative that had infuriated many of them, including President Macron of France, so has not been repeated.

Meanwhile, the King and Queen have been driven to Buckingham Palace from Clarence House, where they will be joined by their immediate supporters and household staff, and they will put on their robes.

Ninety-nine heads of state from around the world accepted an invitation. All foreign representatives have been allowed two seats per guest – some are accompanied by a spouse, others by an aide. Jill Biden, first lady of the United States, arrives with her granddaughter Finnegan Biden, who wears a summery caped yellow dress by designer Markarian, with a floral headpiece, while her grandmother wears a chic cornflower-blue suit with gloves. Walking side by side, they make a statement in the colours of the Ukrainian flag, and they take their seats in the Abbey. As countries have been seated in alphabetical order, Dr Biden is next to Olena Zelenska, wife of the Ukrainian president.

Invitations have not been sent to leaders of Russia, Belarus, Iran, Myanmar, Syria, Afghanistan and Venezuela, with whom Britain currently does not maintain diplomatic ties.[4]

Guests arriving are able to escape from the heavy rain via a covered walkway leading to the Great West Door, which is flanked by a pair of tall yew topiaries, surrounded by wild flowers. Inside, the Tomb of the Unknown Warrior is adorned with floral tributes symbolic of remembrance, including bluebells and forget-me-nots for constancy of love, daffodils for chivalry and cowslips and lilac for memories of youth. King Charles's favourite hellebores feature in beautiful displays in the Choir.

At 10.00am, a procession of faith leaders and representatives enter the Abbey and proceed to their seats. They include the Chief Rabbi, who has spent the night at St James's Palace on the invitation of the King, so he could adhere to Jewish custom that motorised transport is avoided on Saturdays – the Jewish Sabbath.

At 10.15, the governors-general, prime ministers and representatives of countries of the realm process up the Nave, led by the bearers of the national flags. The flags are placed in special stands on the north side of the Sacrarium. They enter in alphabetical order, so Antigua and Barbuda is first, followed by Australia, the Bahamas, Belize, Canada, Grenada, Jamaica, New Zealand, Papua New Guinea, St Christopher and Nevis, Saint Lucia, St Vincent and the Grenadines, Solomon Islands, and Tuvalu. First ministers of the devolved nations of the United Kingdom attend, together with representatives of all political parties, including those with a republican agenda, such as Northern Ireland's Sinn Féin. Humza Yousaf attends in a kilt, with prime minster Rishi Sunak and his wife Akshata Murty bringing up the rear.

At 10.25 comes the procession of foreign royals. Members of surviving European monarchies include: King Willem-Alexander and Queen Maxima of the Netherlands, as well as King Felipe VI and Queen Letizia of Spain, and Prince Albert II and Princess Charlene of Monaco. Queen Margarethe of Denmark is absent, after undergoing back surgery – later in the year, she will announce her abdication at the age of 83, after a fifty-two-year reign.

The non-working members of the royal family arrive together. Prince Andrew, yet to lose his royal titles, is among them, wearing his Garter robes, for which he must have gained the King's permission. Zara and Mike Tindall are there, with Princess Beatrice, in a pink dress with puffed sleeves from British brand Beulah, London. She is accompanied by her husband Edoardo Mapelli Mozzi, a British property developer descended from Italian nobility. Her sister, Princess Eugenie, heavily pregnant with her second child, is with her husband Jack Brooksbank. Sandwiched in between his cousins is Prince Harry, who wears a mourning suit with a row of medals. He walks up the Nave alone; his wife Meghan has stayed in California with their children.

As a non-working royal, Harry has no formal role in the coronation and he sits with his cousin Princess Eugenie in the third row. This is the first time he has come face to face with members of his family since the publication of his bombshell memoir *Spare*, in January.

Also in the third row is Prince Andrew, King Charles's younger brother, who is also now a non-working royal. There are fewer rows of royals than is usual for such an occasion, with curbs on distant cousins and extended family members bringing their spouses and children. At Prince William's insistence, Kate's family have been included – Michael and Carol Middleton arrive with their children Pippa and James.[5]

Princess Anne arrives, with her husband Timothy Lawrence. The King's sister's look is full-on pageantry: she wears her uniform as Colonel of the Blues and Royals, with dark green velvet thistle robe and collar, Garter Sash, Garter Star, Thistle Star, GCVO Star, full-sized medals, KCVO Star and Companion of the Order of the Bath neck decoration. As she takes her seat in row two, her tall black hat with a large red feather sticking out the top obscures Prince Harry seated directly behind her, leading to speculation that the seating arrangement has been deliberate.

Princess Anne is playing the role of Gold Stick, one of the close protection officers who will ride alongside their Majesties' carriage in the return procession, hence her military uniform – she has also joked that the role 'solves her dress problem'.[6]

The Duke and Duchess of Edinburgh arrive with their children. Sophie, Duchess of Edinburgh, wears a white high-necked dress with lace detailing under a robe of purple and crimson.

At 10.30am the King and Queen board the Diamond State Coach at Buckingham Palace, which is pulled by six Windsor greys. Their Majesties are literally carried by history: the coach has been made from materials that include timber from Lord Nelson's flagship HMS *Victory*, an original counterweight from Big Ben, a Battle of Britain Spitfire and Hawker Hurricane, a Dambusters Lancaster and part of a musket ball from the Battle of Waterloo. They are surrounded by around 200 men and horses from the Household Cavalry, plus a mounted band. The pace is brisk and, upsetting the usual rank-conscious order of such events, they inadvertently arrive at the Abbey ahead of the Prince and Princess of Wales, who are running nearly two minutes late.

This causes an awkward situation and as the King and Queen wait in their carriage outside the Abbey, the King is seen muttering irritably, according to a lip reader saying, 'We can never be on time… There's always something… This is boring.'[7] William and Kate's car seems to have got stuck behind the King's carriage and there is no choice now but for them to follow behind the King and Queen, rather than go ahead. Later, there is a suggestion that William and Kate's decision to make a social media video of the coronation held them up.

Queen Camilla processes up the Nave first, wearing a beautiful white coat-dress designed by Bruce Oldfield, plus the crimson Robe of Estate made for Queen Elizabeth II in 1953. Embroidered on her dress in gold are the floral emblems of the home nations: a rose, thistle, daffodil and shamrock, as well as other flowers and even a tribute to her beloved Jack Russells, Beth and Bluebell. She is flanked by the Bishop of Hereford and the Bishop of Norwich, and followed by four pages of honour, who include three of her grandsons and her great-nephew. Thirteen-year-old twins Gus and Louis Lopes are at the back – Gus being given the right side, so that he can hold the robe with his left hand – his right arm is in a cast, after he broke it in a recent bike accident. Behind the twins are the Queen's companions, known in rehearsals as 'the bridesmaids',[8] wearing long white gowns, similar in style to Camilla's coronation dress: her sister Annabelle Elliot and long-term friend Fiona, Marchioness of Lansdowne, who later recalls of the moment, 'I was quite busy concentrating on walking very slowly and not tripping up.'

The beauty of one of King Charles's favourite pieces of music 'I Was Glad' reverberates around the Abbey as the processions in all their colourful and regalia-laden splendour move through the Nave into the Choir, as it has since Hubert Parry composed it for Edward VII's coronation 121 years ago.

'Vivat Regina Camilla,' and 'Vivat Rex Carolus,' shout the Westminster schoolboys from on high, the only Latin that now appears in the coronation ceremony.

The King's crimson Robe of Estate is the same one worn by his grandfather George VI, and great-grandfather George V. His procession includes senior clergy: the Dean of Westminster, the Bishop of London, and the Archbishop of York. The heralds and more junior officers of arms the Pursuivants follow him, including the current 'Unicorn Pursuivant of Arms', a Scottish title created after 1381.

The King's four pages include his grandson, William and Kate's oldest child 9-year-old Prince George, looking very smart in his knee-length scarlet coat with gold trimmings. The King looks composed and serene as he acknowledges friends in the congregation, including former Lord Chamberlain David Airlie, the only person present who was also at both the 1953 and 1937 coronations, when he served as a page.[9]

Proudly bearing the regalia in the procession from the Great West Door to the High Altar are aristocrats who have fought for their claim on their ancestral privileges. Bearing the Queen's crown is the current Duke of Wellington, who is wearing the coronation robes worn by his famous ancestor the first Duke of Wellington at Queen Victoria's Coronation in 1838, when the war hero was so loudly cheered. But this time, other regalia have been shared out more imaginatively. The Orb is carried by nursing pioneer Dame Elizabeth Anionwu and the beautiful Sceptre with Dove is borne by Baroness Benjamin, both members of the Order of Merit. The Sword of State is borne by the Lord President of the Council, MP Penny Mordaunt.

The Prince and Princess of Wales, left with no choice due to their late arrival, bring up the rear, dressed colourfully in their coronation robes. Kate wears a white embroidered dress by Alexander McQueen, one of her favourite design houses. There has been some speculation over which tiara the future Queen will wear, and now she reveals a new piece; a sparkling silver headpiece in a leaf pattern, hand embroidered with silver thread and adorned with crystals. The stunning design is the work of Notting Hill milliner Jess Collett, who started her business thirty years ago with a loan from the Prince's Trust. Kate wears statement pearl and diamond earrings that belonged to her late mother-in-law Princess Diana. In a mother–daughter moment, Princess Charlotte looks beautiful in a matching single-strand headpiece and caped white dress, also by Alexander McQueen.

Eight-year-old Princess Charlotte holds the hand of her younger brother Prince Louis, who looks unusually subdued as they process up the Nave behind their parents. At 5 years old, he is present for the beginning of the two-hour service, but takes a planned break with his nanny midway through.

The King and Queen walk to their Chairs of Estate, and the Prince and Princess of Wales move to their seats in the South East Lantern, with Charlotte and Louis sitting between them.

In another first for a coronation ceremony, Samuel Strachan, Child of His Majesty's Chapel Royal, now greets His Majesty: 'Your Majesty, as children of the Kingdom of God, we welcome you in the name of the King of Kings.'

King Charles's reply articulates the new theme for the coronation ceremony: 'In His name and after His example, I come not to be served, but to serve.'

In stating that he is there to serve the people, the message sets this coronation apart from past ceremonies, where the implication was that the monarch is chosen by God – and the people serve the monarch. The King and Queen stand in front of their Chairs of Estate with their heads bowed for a few moments of private prayer and reflection.

After an introduction from Justin Welby, Archbishop of Canterbury, Sir Bryn Terfel sings the 'Kyrie Eleison', composed for the ceremony, in both English and Welsh.

The recognition

The King faces the High Altar as the Archbishop presents him, uttering the traditional words of the recognition, followed by the congregation's cries of, 'God Save King Charles!'

The King then moves to face the south, west and north, where the same words are repeated, and there is a trumpet fanfare after each one. In another innovation, the Archbishop is joined at the remaining sides in turn by the first black member of the Order of the Garter, former politician Baroness Amos; then Lady Elish Angiolini, the first female Lord Advocate of Scotland; and then Christopher Finney GC, chairman of the Victoria Cross and George Cross Association.

The oath

It's now time for King Charles to take the oath, which the law requires him to do, but first the Archbishop says a few words that underline the King's interpretation of his role in defending all faiths.

> Your Majesty, the Church established by law, whose settlement you will swear to maintain, is committed to the true profession of the Gospel, and, in so doing, will seek to foster an environment in which people of all faiths and beliefs may live freely. The Coronation Oath has stood for centuries and is enshrined in law. Are you willing to take the oath?

The King replies simply: 'I am willing.'

He then places his hand on the bible and takes the coronation oath, as the Archbishop asks: 'Will you solemnly promise and swear to govern the Peoples of the United Kingdom of Great Britain and Northern Ireland, your other Realms and Territories to any of them belonging or pertaining, according to their respective laws and customs?'

Unlike in 1953, the 'other Realms' have not been named. The King responds: 'I solemnly promise so to do.'

While King Charles kneels on his faldstool, with both of his hands on the bible, the Archbishop says: 'Will you to the utmost of your power maintain the Laws of God and the true profession of the Gospel? Will you to the utmost of your power maintain in the United Kingdom the Protestant Reformed Religion established by law?'

Next comes the 'Accession Declaration', where Charles is required to swear on the bible that he will ensure that only Protestants can succeed to the throne:

> I Charles do solemnly and sincerely in the presence of God profess, testify, and declare that I am a faithful Protestant, and that I will, according to the true intent of the enactments which secure the Protestant succession to the Throne, uphold and maintain the said enactments to the best of my powers according to law.

A pen is proffered for the King to sign the oath and the Accession Declaration. Many onlookers hold their breath as it momentarily appears that the pen might not work… but after a split second, the ink flows and the King signs his name – and a third pen debacle is avoided. The choir sing 'Prevent Us, O Lord' by William Byrd.

In another new addition, Charles now offers a prayer where he again makes reference to other faiths.

'Grant that I may be a blessing to all thy children, of every faith and belief, that together we may discover the ways of gentleness and be led into the paths of peace; through Jesus Christ our Lord, Amen.'

'Gloria in Excelsis' sing the choir, as the King returns to his Chair of Estate and the service continues with prayers and readings.

The Prime Minister Rishi Sunak reads the Epistle, from Paul's letter to the Colossians 1:9–17, from the pulpit.

All stand as the Ascension Choir, the first gospel singers to perform at a coronation, sing the 'Alleluia' based on Psalm 47 1–2, another specially composed piece.

The Archbishop's sermon, which he keeps short, reiterates the day's theme – that with the privilege of power comes a duty to serve: 'service is love in action'.

The anointing

The King and Queen kneel on their faldstools; the choir sing the 'Veni Creator' in English, Welsh, Gaelic and Irish, and the Dean brings the ampulla from the altar.

The King and Queen are divested of their robes of state, to the accompanying 'Zadok', but the watching viewers see only a moment of the King in his shirt before members of the Household Division place a screen around the Coronation Chair, so that the King will have some privacy for this most sacred part of the service. The screen has been made especially for today and it features an elaborately embroidered 'Tree of Life' design, with leaves bearing the names of the fifty-six countries of the Commonwealth, with the King's Cypher positioned at the base of the tree to represent the King as a servant of his people. It is a sturdy construction compared to the rather flimsy canopies used in previous coronations. It helps that, rather than four elderly knights, its limed oak poles are held upright by officers from the Household Division.

The Dean of Westminster pours some of the consecrated oil from the ampulla into the spoon. Based on the oils biblical kings Solomon and David were anointed with, oil has been mixed and consecrated in Jerusalem for the occasion. The Archbishop, who has suggested the oil smells of lavender, carefully anoints the King, now dressed only in a simple white shirt, on his hands, breast and head '…as Solomon was anointed king by Zadok the priest and Nathan the prophet…'

The moment somehow feels private. 'There was a sense of the presence of God that was utterly indescribable,' recalls Welby. Clive Alderton has resisted BBC demands that this section of the service be televised, believing that the King needs this spiritual moment in private.

The screen is removed and Charles kneels again at his faldstool, while the Archbishop prays. He is then helped into the Colobium Sindonis, the Supertunica and the girdle, and he takes his seat in the Coronation Chair.

All the while, Conservative MP and Lord President of the Council, Penny Mordaunt, who is tasked with carrying the heavy Sword of State for fifty minutes – a task she has trained for with press-ups – is concentrating hard on maintaining an expressionless face, so as to blend in to the background. It doesn't work – unbeknownst to her, everyone has noticed her and social media is abuzz with comments on her outfit and impressive sword-carrying skills. 'Got to say it, Penny Mordaunt looks damn fine!' tweets Labour MP Emily Thornberry. 'The sword-bearer steals the show!' The first woman to perform the role, Mordaunt has commissioned a £2,000 dress from design label Safiyaa, and matching hat, both in eye-catching blue and gold.[10]

The presentation of the regalia

The spurs, made in 1661 and presented to King Charles II as a symbol of courage in battle, are now presented to King Charles III by the Lord Great Chamberlain, as the Archbishop says: 'Receive these spurs, symbols of military honour and chivalry: May you be a brave advocate for those in need.'

Now comes some choreographed symbolic sword action, which Penny Mordaunt seems to understand, even if viewers are left baffled. First, she exchanges the Sword of State for the lighter Jewelled Sword of Offering, and presents it to the Archbishop, who holds it before the altar, praying that King Charles will use the sword 'to resist evil and defend the good'.

He hands the sword back to Mordaunt, who places it in the King's right hand. The King then rises and the sword is clipped to his girdle – he sits again, as the Archbishop says another prayer.

Finally, the King stands, the sword is unclipped from the girdle and the King surrenders it to the Dean of Westminster, who places it on the altar. All of this is, admits the Reverend Mark Birch, Canon of Westminster Abbey, is 'cloaked in the mists of Medieval chivalry' and might not make a lot of sense to us.[11]

Mordaunt then places the redemption money – a bag of newly minted coins bearing His Majesty's effigy – in the Alms dish. The Keeper of the Jewel House unsheathes the sword, hands it to the Lord President of the Council, and it's Mordaunt's job to carry it…

This is an Anglican service, as the law and constitution require. But Charles's determination to make it inclusive means that representatives of all the main faiths are present in some capacity.

Lord Kamall, a Muslim academic, carries the bracelets, known as 'armills'.

The Robe Royal is presented to the King by Jewish peer Baroness Meron, with the Groom of the Robes bringing the Stole, which Prince William helps his father into. The King's Stole Royal, a silk band worn around the monarch's neck following the anointing, is new. The one used in 1953 included the names of Ceylon, South Africa and Pakistan as realms, which are now of course republics, Ceylon now being Sri Lanka.

The Archbishop of Armagh leads the presentation of the Orb, followed by Scottish scientist and Hindu Lord Patel's presentation of the coronation ring.

Bearing the glove is Lord Singh of Wimbledon, a cross-bench peer and prominent member of Britain's Sikh community. The King puts the glove on his right hand, 'that you may hold authority with gentleness and grace…' intones the Archbishop.

Scottish and Welsh representatives bring forward the Sceptre with Cross and the Sceptre with Dove, and these are placed in the King's hands.

The crowning

All stand for the crowning moment. Justin Welby has spent weeks repeating to himself 'square front, oval back' to help him with the perennial 'which way round?' question. (St Edward's crown has a square emerald at the front, an oval one at the back.) Now, the Archbishop raises St Edward's Crown high in the air, before bringing it down onto King Charles's head, securing it firmly ('You have to jam it on',[12] the King has advised in rehearsals), then, slightly bizarrely, he appears to take it off and put it back on again, before bending down slightly to check it's on properly, before standing back and saying loudly: 'God save the King!'

To which the congregation respond heartily: 'God save the King!'

And the trumpet fanfare sounds, the Abbey bells ring and gun salutes can be heard from Horse Guards Parade. Gun salutes are also fired at the Tower of London, and all Saluting Stations throughout the United Kingdom, Gibraltar, Bermuda and on ships at sea.

The King, wearing the crown and holding the sceptres, is escorted to the throne which, as tradition dictates, he is lifted into by the Archbishops. Once enthroned, he is relieved of the sceptres.

The homage

As is traditional, the Archbishop of Canterbury is the first to pay homage, kneeling before the King.

Next comes Prince William, who kneels in front of his father and, placing his hands between the King's, says the time-honoured words: 'I, William, Prince of Wales, pledge my loyalty to you and faith and truth I will bear unto you, as your liege man of life and limb. So help me God.'

He stands, touches the crown, in the gesture that means he will help the King bear it, and kisses his father. The King responds quietly: 'Thank you, William.'

There are no further homages at the Abbey this time – replaced by 'the people's homage'. The congregation stand, and the Archbishop asks them and the viewers at home, in wording that now includes a caveat (You don't have to do this, folks!):

> 'I now invite those who wish to offer their support to do so, with a moment of private reflection, by joining in saying "God save King Charles" at the end or for those with the words before them to recite them in full.'

The Archbishop leads the people – in the Abbey, in front of their televisions at home, or anywhere else in the world – in the first-ever people's homage: 'I swear that I will pay true allegiance to Your Majesty, and to your heirs and successors according to law. So help me God.'

A fanfare sounds, there are more shouts of, 'God save the King!' and the sceptres are returned to Charles.

The choir sing the anthem 'Confortare', composed by Sir Walford Davies for the coronation of King George VI.

The Queen's coronation

Now it's Camilla's turn, and she moves to kneel on the faldstool in front of her Chair of Estate, while the Dean brings the ampulla and spoon from the High Altar. The Archbishop then anoints the Queen, as she will be known from today, dropping the 'Consort', on her forehead, using the oil sparingly, as he has promised to do.

The Queen's ring is then presented to her and she puts her hand alongside the ring, but it is not placed on her finger this time.

Next, the Dean marches off to fetch the Queen's crown, and hands it to the Archbishop, who appears to forget to look to the King for a nod of approval, and instead cracks on with swinging the crown above Camilla's head, before bringing it down more slowly onto her head. At one point, the Queen appears to flinch away from the crown, but she is not having last-minute second thoughts – merely trying to move the train of her dress to prevent the Archbishop tripping over it. She looks a little nervous as the large crown is placed firmly on her head, and puts up a tentative hand to adjust her hair, but once it's in place, the effect is instantly regal.

The Queen Consort's Rod with Dove and Sceptre with Cross are then presented to her.

For Camilla, who was once 'the other woman', and so hated by the public and hunted by the press she was effectively under house arrest, this is a remarkable full-circle moment of acceptance. Her destiny has not been to sit up high in a gallery of royal mistresses watching proceedings, like her great-great-grandmother Alice Keppel did in 1902, but to sit in the Theatre itself, with the Archbishop crowning her Queen.

At the end of the Queen's coronation, the choir sing Andrew Lloyd-Webber's newly written piece 'Make a Joyful Noise', based on the words of Psalm 98, 'Make a joyful noise unto the Lord for he hath done marvellous things.' The Queen is escorted to her throne in the Theatre and, after curtseying to the King, she is enthroned by the Archbishops.

All stand for the hymn 'Christ is Made the Sure Foundation', and the King and Queen and their attendants retire briefly to St Edward's Chapel, where they are divested of their crowns and the mood is light-hearted as the key players are relieved and elated and it becomes 'a bit of a party'.[13] On their return, the King touches the bread and wine that is prepared for the Holy Communion.

The Archbishop ends the prayers at the start of the communion by inviting everyone to say the Lord's Prayer in their own language.

Afterwards the procession starts to form up in the Theatre, to the sound of the choir singing the 'Te Deum', composed for the 1953 coronation by William Walton. The King and Queen head for St Edward's Chapel where the King is helped into his purple Robe of Estate, made for George VI, and the Imperial State Crown. The Queen now dons the only new robe made for this coronation: her newly designed Robe of Estate, beautifully embroidered with bees and butterflies and twenty-four plants with personal associations. Sewn in exquisite detail, her birth flower, lily-of-the-valley, is there as well as delphiniums, the King's favourite flower, and the flowers of the home nations, this time including daffodils for Wales, rather than the leek.

Their Majesties emerge to a trumpet fanfare, then all sing the National Anthem as the procession starts to move. The royal family drop low curtsies and bows as the King passes. On they go, led by the Earl Marshal and the ever-present Penny Mordaunt, now carrying the slightly lighter

Jewelled Sword of Offering, back through the Abbey to the West Door, accompanied by the sound of the orchestra playing Elgar's 'Pomp and Circumstance', and Parry's 'March from the Birds'. Camilla looks more relaxed now and Charles smiles at familiar faces.

At the West Door, the King is greeted by faith leaders and representatives from the Jewish, Hindu, Sikh, Muslim and Buddhist faiths, who say: 'Your Majesty, as neighbours in faith, we acknowledge the value of public service. We unite with people of all faiths and beliefs in thanksgiving, and in service with you for the common good.'

Although the script, as dictated by the Liber Regalis, has been stuck to, other faiths have been included, and women have featured much more prominently than in any previous coronations. Different faith leaders have been happy to accept their invitations, and the tweaks and additions feel right.

The King and Queen proceed out of the Abbey and into the Gold State Coach, pulled by six Windsor greys, for the return procession to Buckingham Palace. This is a much larger procession, the like of which has not been seen on London's streets since 1953. More than 4,000 troops march, with 3,000 supporting.

In another first, all the bass drummers in the nineteen marching bands can hear each other via earpieces, so they can all keep time. All sections of the armed forces are represented in the procession, along with 400 troops from the Commonwealth and the King's other realms, except India and South Africa, who have chosen not to take part. This is thought to be for political reasons over the UK's staunch support of Ukraine. Both India and South Africa have recently abstained from a UN vote calling on Russia to leave Ukraine.

Princess Anne is riding directly behind the Gold Coach, in the role she has been asked to play today – as 'Gold Stick', the monarch's closest protection officer. Other members of the royal family follow in carriages, led by the Prince and Princess of Wales with their children, the oldest, George, having joined them after completing his duties as page.

Back at the Abbey, Prince Harry gets into a car alone, managing to get a flight back home to California that sees him arrive by 19.30 local time, so he is able to wish his 4-year-old son Archie a happy birthday in person.[14] The King's second son will not take part in the carriage procession, the balcony appearances or be in the official photographs, taken by Hugo Burnand.

In another coronation first, the troops marching in the procession head straight for the Buckingham Palace gardens, where they form up to greet the King and Queen as they go out onto the terrace for an impressive three cheers.

The rain has eased off a bit by this time, but the weather remains poor and, disappointingly, the planned flypast has had to be cancelled. But the King and Queen, in their coronation robes and crowns, emerge on the Buckingham Palace balcony for that once-in-a-reign moment when the noise from the crowds hits them like a wave. Led by King Charles, the days when the late Queen had all manner of relatives fan out in a long line – and journalists would have to look up who they all were and provide numbered guides – are gone; the balcony appearances are limited to 'working royals' to use the term du jour. That means the Prince and Princess of Wales, Princess Anne, and Edward and Sophie, Duke and Duchess of Edinburgh, and the Duke and Duchess of Gloucester. But Anne's husband Timothy Lawrence is also there, as well as William and Kate's children, George, Charlotte and Louis, and the Edinburghs' children. Today the King has also invited the page boys and Camilla's two companions to join in the moment – one that Annabel Elliot later describes as 'mind-blowing'.[15]

There is an extended family gathering, with a buffet meal and drinks flowing as everyone celebrates a successful and historic day. But celebrations wrap up relatively early, compared to 1953.

Chapter Twenty

MOVING FORWARD

On Sunday evening, the royals turn out again for the special coronation concert at Windsor Castle in front of 20,000 ticket holders and a television audience of millions. The concert features a wide range of musical styles and a stunning light show. Big-name performers like Katy Perry, Take That and Lionel Richie delight the crowd and at the end, Prince William takes to the stage and pays tribute to his father's work for the environment and understanding of the importance of embracing people of all faiths. He invokes his grandmother, the late Queen, who he says is up there 'keeping an eye on us', and ends by saying, 'Pa, we are all so proud of you.' It goes down well, though some commentators are quick to point out that he didn't mention Camilla. In the wake of Prince Harry's memoir *Spare* being released, the question of the real nature of the relationship between the King's sons and his wife has been much raked over in the media. One of Harry's assertions in the book, which he has since reiterated in television interviews, is that William and Harry asked Charles not to marry Camilla. There were also suggestions that Camilla's need for positive PR was sometimes secured at the expense of Harry and Meghan.

Many more events and celebrations followed the coronation, some of which were attended by members of the royal family. An extra bank holiday was granted on Monday, 8 May, and a suggested celebratory three-day itinerary had been issued by the palace, although with the furore around the 'people's homage', they were careful not to appear to impose it on anyone. Fortunately, the rain of Coronation Day itself eased off on the Sunday, which was designated for street parties and community lunches. The bank holiday Monday was dubbed 'The Big Help Out' – a nationwide recognition and celebration of voluntary work.

More than 400,000 people, including police, ambulance workers, choristers and military personnel received a medal in recognition of their contribution to the coronation. Made of silver nickel, the medals have the royal cypher on one side and images of the King and Queen on the other. The coronation medal was also given to frontline workers in the police, emergency services, prison services and armed forces members with five years' service, as well as living recipients of the George Cross or Victoria Cross.

In July 2023, King Charles attended a service at St Giles's Cathedral in Edinburgh, to receive the Honours of Scotland. Wearing the robes of the Order of the Thistle, he inspected the Scottish Sceptre, in a gesture that respected Scottish traditions, but stopped short of holding the Sceptre, which might have looked too much like a second coronation. The union between England and Scotland is cherished by the royals.

According to opinion polls, King Charles and the monarchy enjoyed a boost in popularity following the coronation, with 63 per cent of people in one Ipsos poll saying they were satisfied with the job the monarchy were doing. The same poll, however, also showed a rise in the number of people in favour of a republic, at 28 per cent.[1]

Nowadays, with almost thirty years having passed since the tragic and untimely death of Princess Diana, a whole generation has grown up without ever having known the King's empathetic, scene-stealing, glamorous, dangerous ex-wife. Settled into his role as King, and seemingly happy in his marriage to Camilla, Charles seems relatively relaxed, cautiously optimistic and enjoys an easy rapport with the members of the public he meets every day.

When the King was diagnosed with cancer less than a year after his coronation, he was relatively open about it, and his ongoing treatment. By levelling with the public in this way, he headed off much of the speculation, rumours and questions that might have dominated the headlines. While people may be asking how long he has left, they also see him carrying on with a 'business as usual' approach that instils calm and often admiration.

For the remainder of King Charles's reign, large-scale public pageants are unlikely to feature heavily again. After the late Queen's Diamond Jubilee celebrations, her state funeral and then a coronation taking place in under two years, there will be now be an interlude – until of course, George, Charlotte and Louis grow up and the prospect of royal weddings loom on the ceremonial horizon. Pageantry, ceremonial and the unique aesthetic the monarchy offer has, however, continued to play a role, both domestically and in projecting Britain's image on the world stage. When prime minister Keir Starmer arrived in Washington for talks with the newly re-elected President Donald Trump in February 2025, a key weapon in his arsenal for winning over a tempestuous US president was a shiny invitation to Balmoral to meet King Charles – followed by a lavish no-holds-barred state visit that took place against the backdrop of Windsor Castle in September. Royalty and the trappings that go with it are still a draw, and a diplomatic asset.

There may be issues ahead. Harry has openly spoken of his wish for reconciliation with his family, and even though it was a message delivered via a media interview, as a parent, it will be difficult for Charles not to respond in some way. While no doubt he would love a better relationship with his estranged son, it seems that repairing trust damaged by media interviews is a difficult hurdle to overcome.

Following further allegations around their relationship with Jeffrey Epstein, Andrew Mountbatten Windsor and his ex-wife Sarah Ferguson were given notice to leave the Royal Lodge, the palatial mansion in Windsor for which Andrew paid a peppercorn rent. As well as generating unwelcome negative scrutiny of the royals, the episode sparked wider questions around the royal family's living arrangements, and in December 2025 a parliamentary inquiry was launched into the Crown Estate, which leases properties to members of the royal family. Charles has not yet made clear his plans for his own multiple properties. Alongside Highgrove, Birkhall – on the Balmoral Estate – and Clarence House in central London, Charles has inherited Sandringham, Balmoral, Windsor Castle and Buckingham Palace, which he uses as an office rather than a home. While the coronation was generally well received for its spectacular pageantry, its attempts at inclusivity and its spirit of national celebration, the biggest criticisms of the day came over how much was spent on it. Charles himself is known for his high-end tastes, a love of luxurious living that has been called extravagant. In the years following the coronation, how will the new reign of Charles III strike the balance between a monarchy that can visibly serve the people, and deliver the grand moments, while not appearing overly indulgent in times when people are struggling with the huge rise in the cost of living in a post-Covid world?

Chapter Twenty-One

WILLIAM AND CATHERINE

King Charles III is now in his late 70s, and while he has always been very fit and healthy, he was diagnosed with an unspecified cancer early in 2024, for which he has undergone treatment. For those who are involved in the huge amount of planning and organising that is required to put on large public events, thoughts will be turning to what a coronation might look like when William succeeds to the throne.

Prince William, like his father before him, does not intend to speculate about his own accession and coronation in public. He has said in the past that he doesn't like to think too much about it, given that succeeding to the throne himself means losing beloved members of his family. One of the aspects of coronations that tends to get less focus is that, for the sovereign whose ceremony it is, the day is often tinged with grief over the recent loss of a parent.

Despite enjoying extraordinary wealth and privilege, the royal family face similar challenges to other families when it comes to dealing with personal issues. Now in his early 40s, William has already lived through some tough times that will have both shaped his own character and given him greater insight and empathy into the lives of others. His childhood often looked picture-perfect, with its exclusive prep schools, ponies and holidays spent at the royal family's country estates, yet was also difficult for a shy child growing up with the paparazzi, who he would come to hate, always present. His parents' failing marriage ended in a very public separation when William was just 10 years old, and they later divorced. While many children go through the breakdown of their parents' marriage, few have to endure their mother and father giving television interviews admitting adultery, or constant tabloid headlines and accusations. While there was never any question that Charles and Diana loved their sons, the very public nature of their marriage breakdown cannot have been easy for William and Harry. After some years spending school holidays sharing long car journeys between their parents' homes, the brothers were staying with their father in Balmoral in August 1997 when the news came through from Paris that Diana had been involved in a car accident. William was 15 when he lost his mother, and had to cope with his own grief as well as that of an unusually emotional public when he walked with his brother, father, uncle and grandfather behind her coffin through the streets of central London.

For a while, it seemed that the shared early experiences that William and Harry went through had resulted in a supportive and good-humoured bond between them, but that too fell apart when Harry met and fell in love with American actress Meghan Markle. In his book *Spare*, Harry describes how William raised concerns about Harry's relationship moving too quickly, and even talks about an alleged physical scuffle that took place between the brothers.[1]

It was William who, after the death of his grandmother, organised the surprise joint appearance of the short-lived 'Fab Four' – William and Kate, Harry and Meghan, at Cambridge Gate near Windsor Castle. William drove both couples in a black Land Rover, and they spent around forty minutes meeting crowds and taking in the floral tributes. The crowds were delighted and a message of unity in grief had been sent, even if the body language, particularly between Kate and Meghan, was at times awkward, and both couples later indicated that they had found the experience difficult.[2] Since then there appears to have been little contact. It is thought that William and Harry have not spoken now for some years – on the occasions when they have been in the same room, they have avoided each other.

In January 2024, it was announced that the Princess of Wales was to undergo major abdominal surgery for an unspecified medical condition. In March, after much speculation about her health, she revealed in a short video address that she had cancer, later undergoing gruelling rounds of chemotherapy. With three very young children, and also worried about his father's battle with cancer, William later described the experience as 'brutal', adding that 2024 had been 'the hardest year in my life'.[3]

Having come through all of this, what is William actually like? Remarkably sane and down to earth, seems to be the consensus among those who have had dealings with him. William is certainly a very different character to his father, moulded by different experiences. Less academic perhaps, less spiritual, with tastes that include supporting Aston Villa and watching box sets while enjoying takeaways. Grounded in a family life that is more Middleton than Mountbatten, he appears to have dealt with the trauma of his adolescence. Although they also have grand residences in Kensington Palace and on the Sandringham Estate in Norfolk, William and Kate have recently made Forest Lodge in Windsor Great Park their main family home.

While William respects his father's faith and work, he has resisted doing things which might not feel authentic for him. For example, he hasn't undergone a formal investiture as Prince of Wales, or sought to learn Welsh, though he and Kate have regularly visited Wales in an effort to build strong links with the country. He hasn't been seen wearing a kilt when appearing in public in Scotland, despite the royals' tradition of donning Scottish dress when north of the border. While he was said to be a great admirer of his father's coronation, palace officials have indicated he might want to scale back some of the rituals when his time comes – the ancient presentation of the glove being picked out as one that might not have made a lot of sense to him.[4]

William himself has often paid tribute to his grandmother, and expressed his desire to follow her example. But, as he has acknowledged, Elizabeth and Philip were of their generation and he knows that he himself faces different challenges. When it comes to his coronation, organisers will certainly be looking more to what happened in 2023, than 1953. So many significant changes were made for Charles III's coronation, while keeping the essential ceremony and traditions at its heart, that in a sense the foundations for a twenty-first-century coronation have been built. William and Catherine could simply refresh a few aspects of the design. While for the most part, the changes were well received, those that didn't work so well can be ironed out. After the media storm around 'the people's homage', we can be pretty sure that idea will be laid to rest, but whether or not the whole notion of paying homage will be looked at again remains to be seen.

Although throughout the second half of the twentieth century, and the first quarter of the twenty-first century, hereditary privileges have been marginalised in public life, the existence of a hereditary monarchy has not been significantly challenged. Queen Elizabeth II and King Charles have both enjoyed broad support from the people. But monarchies can never be complacent, and the least convinced are the younger 18–34 year olds, who may or may not change their views as they age.[5]

The UK is the only European monarchy that still has a religious coronation, rather than a constitutional investiture, where a monarch swears an oath to observe the constitution. King Charles is known to have a strong faith, as did Queen Elizabeth II, whose Christmas broadcasts, especially in her later years, often had a strong Christian message. William is not known to be a regular worshipper, although the family attend church on key dates throughout the year. For the monarchies of Belgium, Netherlands and Spain, there are no religious requirements, but in Britain there is a requirement for the monarch to be 'in communion with' the Church of England. Most religious writing assumes the coronation will continue to be an Anglican service, centred around the Eucharist, but finding a place for other denominations and religions – however, it has been mooted that a secular service could celebrate the nation's diversity in way that an Anglican service cannot.[6] Another suggestion that has been mooted is that there would be an additional multi-faith service outside of London, perhaps in York or Edinburgh, as well as the Anglican service at Westminster Abbey.

William met his wife Catherine while both were studying at St Andrews University, and when they went on to marry, the fact that Kate was a 'commoner' from a middle-class family was not seen as a barrier. William's children will certainly enjoy similar freedom to choose who they marry. The Succession to the Crown Act in 2013 introduced gender equality into the line of succession, meaning the eldest child of the monarch will be the heir, whether a boy or girl, and also removed the prohibition on heirs marrying Roman Catholics, although they themselves must not be Roman Catholics.[7] Prince George will no doubt be relieved that he will not be obliged to seek out a non-Catholic foreign princess as a life partner, or worse have a marriage arranged for him.

How many of the fourteen realms where King Charles is currently head of state will have become republics by the time of William's accession remains to be seen. There were suggestions that out of respect for the late Queen, who was regarded with affection, countries such as Australia would hold off becoming republics until after her death. While the subject of republicanism regularly rears its head in the countries where King Charles is head of state, several years into his reign, only Barbados has taken that step. William, like his father, has made clear that the decision as to whether to become a republic and break ties with the British monarchy is entirely a matter for the people of those countries themselves, and he will respect their decision.

Whether William and Kate would be willing to undertake long, gruelling Commonwealth tours as Elizabeth and Philip did, while their children are school age, is another matter. The dominions are now fully self-governing territories, who would be free to determine their own foreign policy in the event of a war, and the couple have at times received a mixed reception while on shorter tours. Reducing the number of realms in which the monarch is head of state might also help William and Catherine avoid being the target of campaigns for historical justice and reparations. During their week-long tour of the Caribbean in March 2022, to celebrate the Queen's Platinum Jubilee, the couple were put in situations which drew negative press coverage for being insensitive and invoking colonialism.[8]

The British monarchy has enjoyed remarkable longevity and stability, and King Charles III is still sovereign over a larger area than any other head of state in the world. In the absence of events that threaten monarchies, such as losing significant wars, prolonged economic crisis, or political instability, it has been relatively plain sailing for the House of Windsor. There hasn't been a deeply unpopular monarch, whose behaviour has crossed a line. It might not have been so, had swift action not been taken at key turning points: the young Victoria determinedly created distance between herself and the unpopular Georges; the government took firm action in forcing the abdication of Edward VIII, who history has revealed as a deeply flawed character who would have made an unsuitable King. More recently, Charles has taken decisive action in removing his brother Andrew from working membership of the royal family, and later removing all his titles, and insisting he move out of Royal Lodge, his lavish mansion on the Windsor estate, following his ill-judged friendship with the paedophile Jeffrey Epstein. While the long, and much admired reign of Queen Elizabeth II no doubt helped the survival of the monarchy, Charles and William may face more public scrutiny.

Unlike Edward VII, or his own father, both of whom followed very long reigning monarchs, William has the advantage of having been closely involved in his father's coronation. Attending rehearsals, playing his role on the day itself alongside his family, being able to see close up how the whole thing worked will have given him great insight that he can use to shape his own views. Importantly, he also insisted that his wife's family were closely involved. He knows that their presence when the time comes will provide vital support for his family, and it will help that they have been through it before.

So, will the nation celebrate the coronation of William and Catherine at Westminster Abbey? Certainly, opinion polls show that both the Prince and Princess of Wales enjoy consistently positive approval ratings. If, when the time comes for them to step up, they can build on the firm foundation of public service work and down-to-earth family values they have espoused to date, then there is no reason why not. But history shows that people like their monarchs to deliver on regal, large-scale, unifying events as well as the day-to-day charity work. The pomp, the pageantry, the colour, the glamour and the religious solemnity of a coronation can deliver a transformational experience that refreshes national pride and interest in having a monarchy – the future William V may do well to remember that.

NOTES

Chapter One: What Are Coronations For?

1. Buckingham Palace Press Office
2. Charlot, p. 81
3. Tanner, p. 18
4. Hardman, p. 240
5. www.spectator.co.uk/writer/richard-chartres

Chapter Two: The New Young Queen

1. www.britannica.com/biography/Victoria-queen-of-United-Kingdom/Accession-to-the-throne
2. Queen Victoria's journals, 20 June 1837
3. Queen Victoria's journals, 2 February 1839
4. Queen Victoria's journals
5. Martineau, p. 410
6. Queen Victoria's journals, Thursday, 15 June 1837
7. Queen Victoria's journals
8. www.telegraph.co.uk/royal-family/2025/03/15/meghan-royal-influencer-princess-of-wales-ancestor-first
9. Martineau, p. 411
10. Martineau, p. 412
11. Victoria's Journals, Monday, 26 June 1838
12. Martineau, p. 411
13. Marshall, p. 16

14. Ridley, p. 4–5
15. Strong, p. 288
16. Charlot, p. 117
17. Plunkett, 2003, p. 22.
18. Queen Victoria's journals, Saturday, 24 June 1838
19. Men and women over 21 were allowed to vote from 1928
20. *God Save the Queen: A Sermon preached in Godalming Church on occasion of the Coronation of our most Gracious Queen*, Rev. W. R Fremantle, J. Nisbet & Co, London.
21. 'The people were very happy, and they ate and drank there at the Lord's altar.

    ...The people celebrated and poured olive oil on Solomon's head to show that he would be their next king. They also poured oil on Zadok's head to show that he was their priest.' Chronicles 29:21–23.
22. www.rct.uk/collection/75002/queen-victorias-imperial-state-crown-frame
23. Charlot, p. 119
24. RA/VIC/ADD/U/134
25. Charlot, p. 117
26. RA/VIC/ADD/U/336/38
27. Queen Victoria's journals, 27 June 1838
28. Queen Victoria's journals, 27 June 1838

Chapter Three: Coronation Day 1838

1. Queen Victoria's journals
2. RA/VIC/ADD/U/134
3. Queen Victoria's journals
4. Martineau, p. 79–80.
5. Wilson, p. 86
6. Strong, p. 308
7. Charlot, p. 119
8. Queen Victoria's journals

9. Probably Henry Purcell's version based on Psalm 122, 'I was glad when they said unto me', originally composed for the coronation of James II. More recent coronations have used music by Hubert Parry, composed in 1902.
10. Charlot, p. 121
11. https://web.archive.org/web/20140201202053/http://www.queenvictoriaonline.com/Queen-Victorias-coronation.html
12. RA/VIC/ADD/U/336/38
13. Greville, in Charlot, p. 122
14. https://web.archive.org/web/20140201202053/http://www.queenvictoriaonline.com/Queen-Victorias-coronation.html
15. Charlot, p. 123
16. William Howley was a former bishop of London. As the Archbishop of Canterbury he had opposed the Great Reform Act of 1832, which led to his carriage being attacked on the streets of Canterbury
17. Deuteronomy 16:16
18. Tanner, p. 32
19. Historic Royal Palaces Factsheet Crown Jewels
20. https://web.archive.org/web/20140201202053/http://www.queenvictoriaonline.com/Queen-Victorias-coronation.html
21. RA/VIC/ADD/U/134
22. RA/VIC/ADD/U/134
23. John Rolle (1750–1842), Baron Rolle of Stevenstone, was a Tory MP from 1779 onward. Lord Rolle 'rolling' down the stairs became the butt of many jokes. Harriet Martineau recalls 'A foreigner in London gravely reported to his own countrymen, what he entirely believed on the word of a wag, that the Lords Rolle held their title on the condition of performing the feat at every coronation.' Martineau, p. 41
24. Charlot, p. 121
25. Queen Victoria's journals
26. Tanner, p. 140
27. RA/VIC/ADD/U/336/38
28. RA/VIC/ADD/U/336/38
29. Queen Victoria's journal, 28 June 1838
30. RA/VIC/ADD/U/336/38

Chapter Four: The Victorian Age

1. https://en.wikisource.org/wiki/1911_Encyclop%C3%A6dia_Britannica/Greville,_Charles_Cavendish_Fulke
2. Queen Victoria's journal
3. https://web.archive.org/web/20140201202053/http://www.queenvictoriaonline.com/Queen-Victorias-coronation.html
4. Longford, p. 8
5. Longford, p. 8/9
6. Wilson, p. 90
7. Wilson, p. 79
8. Wilson, p. 92
9. Ridley, p. 65
10. The Representation of the People Act 1918 enfranchised all men over 21 and all women over 30 who met minimum property qualifications. The Representation of the People (Equal Franchise) Act (1928) gave the vote to all men and women aged over 21

Chapter Five: Edward VII and the Reinvention of Monarchy

1. Ridley, p. 15
2. Ridley, p. xii
3. Canadine, p. 7
4. Ridley, p. 66
5. Dagmar became Empress of Russia, and mother to Tsar Nicholas, who was murdered alongside his family in the Russian revolution of 1917
6. Priestly, p. 17
7. Queen Victoria to Vicky in Fulford, *Dearest Mama*
8. Williamson, p. 152
9. Ridley, p. 73
10. Ridley, p. 351
11. Pope-Hennessy, p. 371

12. RA, Princess of Wales to Grand Duchess of Mecklenburg-Strelitz, 24 Jan 19020
13. Ridley, p. 357
14. www.thecourtjeweller.com/2025/04/queen-alexandras-rarely-seen-coronation-dress-now-on-display-at-buckingham-palace.html
15. RA/VIC/MAIN W.36/1a: Privy Council Minutes
16. Tanner, p. 140
17. Pope-Hennessy, p. 371
18. RA/VIC/ADD/U/28
19. Priestly, p. 26
20. www.tandfonline.com/doi/full/10.1080/09615768.2021.1885328#d1e100

Chapter Six: Coronation Day 1902

1. Strong, p. 348
2. Strong, p. 353
3. Strong, p. 327
4. Lord Roseberry
5. Ridley, p. 367
6. Ridley, p. 369
7. Tanner, p. 141
8. www.rct.uk/collection/404466/the-anointing-of-queen-alexandra-at-the-coronation-of-king-edward-vii. Danish artist Laurits Tuxen, 'Queen Alexandra's Special Artist to the Coronation'
9. Tanner, p. 141
10. Edwardians: Age of Elegance exhibition (2025), curator's notes
11. Tanner, p. 141
12. RA/PP/EDVII/A13420/1902
13. Ridley, p. 368

Chapter Seven: A Popular King

1. RA/QM/PRIV/GEOV/AA/34
2. RA/PPTO/PP/EVII/MAIN/A/13420

3. RA/PPTO/PP/EVII/MAIN/A/13420
4. www.english-heritage.org.uk/visit/places/osborne/history-and-stories/history.
5. Strong, p. 336
6. Priestly, p. 41
7. Priestly, p. 31

Chapter Eight: Stepping Up

1. Ridley, *Never a Dull Moment*, p. 10
2. Ridley
3. RA/GV/PRIV/AA29/32
4. RA/GV/PRIV/GVD/1892, 14 January
5. Pope-Hennessey, in Ridley, p. 70
6. Pope-Hennessey, p. 202–206
7. Duke of Windsor, p. 27
8. Ridley, p. 89
9. Duke of Windsor, p. 75
10. Strong, p. 328
11. RA/QM/PRIV/AA/1911, 2 April
12. RA/QM/PRIV/CC25/100, 7 May 1911
13. Pope-Hennessy, p. 430
14. Royal Collection Trust, www.rct.uk/collection/75030/queen-marys-coronation-dress
15. Pope-Hennessy, p. 435
16. RA/QM/PRIV/GEOV/AA/34
17. Ridley, p. 168

Chapter Nine: Coronation Day 1911

1. Strong, p. 327
2. www.tatler.com/article/princess-louise-duchess-of-argyll-queen-victoria-daughter-biography
3. Pope-Hennessy, p. 441
4. Ridley, p. 169

5. Tanner, p. 28
6. Gosling, p. 19
7. Duke of Windsor, p. 77
8. Duke of Windsor, p. 77
9. RA/GV/PRIV/GVD/1911, 22 June
10. www.rct.uk/collection/31704/queen-camillas-crown
11. Tanner, p. 143
12. Tanner, p. 143
13. Alexander Murray, Master of Elibank. Quoted in Strong, p. 330
14. RA/GV/PRIV/GVD/1911, 22 June
15. Pope-Hennessy, p. 442
16. Duke of Windsor, p. 78
17. RA/GV/PRIV/GVD/1911, 22 June

Chapter Ten: George and Mary

1. RA/GV/PRIV/GVD/1911, 22 June
2. RA/GV/PRIV/GVD/1911, 22 June
3. RA/GV/PRIV/GVD/1911, 23 June
4. RA/QM/PRIV/CC25/107, 25 July 1911
5. Ridley, George V, *Never a Dull Moment*, p. 53
6. Duke of Windsor, p. 186
7. George V diaries, quoted in *A King's Story*, p. 187
8. Duke of Windsor, p. 187
9. Duke of Windsor, p. 187–188
10. Duke of Windsor, p. 74

Chapter Eleven: The Uncrowned King

1. Duke of Portland, p. 63
2. RA/GV/PRIV/AA34/6
3. RA/GV/PRIV/AA34/6
4. RA/GV/PRIV/AA34/6
5. www.spherelife.com/insider-london/historys-first-royal-photoshop

6. From *Henry 'Chips' Channon: The Diaries* by Chips Channon published by Hutchinson. Copyright © Georgia Fanshawe, Henry Channon and Robin Howard as the Trustees of the diaries and personal papers of Sir Henry Channon, 2021. Introduction and notes copyright © Simon Heffer 2021. Reprinted by permission of The Random House Group Limited.
7. Lady 'Baba' Alexandra, quoted in Larman, p. 28
8. Larman, p. 31
9. Lascelles, p. 367
10. Lascelles, p. 361

Chapter Twelve: The Crown Lands on the Second Son's Head

1. Strong, p. 322
2. Shawcross, p. 224
3. RA/LC/LCO/MAIN/583/1937
4. May 12 Observation Project, p. 7
5. Tanner, p. 145
6. Strong, p. 343
7. Sydney Morning Herald, https://trove.nla.gov.au/newspaper/article/17305392
8. RA/PS/PSO/GVI/PS/COR/1000
9. Larman, p. 22
10. Bedell Smith, p. 308
11. Channon, p. 676
12. RA/QM/PRIV/CC/12
13. RA/PS/PSO/GVI/COR
14. Tanner, p. 146
15. Tanner, p. 146

Chapter Thirteen: Coronation Day 1937

1. RA/GVI/PRIV/PERS
2. RA/GVI/PRIV/PERS

3. Bedell Smith, p. 310
4. May 12 Observation Project, p. 6
5. Channon, p. 679.
6. LetterfromDeanofWestminster,14May(Archive,WestminsterAbbey)
7. Tanner, p. 147
8. https://trove.nla.gov.au/newspaper/article/36883307
9. RA/GVI/PRIV/PERS
10. Strong, p. 340
11. Strong, p. 368
12. RA EDW/PRIV/MAIN/A/3183,3244
13. 'From Lilibet By Herself', Royal Collection Trust
14. RA/GVI/PRIV/PERS
15. Tanner, p. 149
16. MP Leo Amery, quoted in Bedell Smith, p. 318
17. Shawcross, p. 239
18. Channon, p. 681
19. Picked up by a lip reader: quoted in Bedell Smith, p. 317

Chapter Fourteen: War and Peace

1. RA/MRH/GVI/FUNC/18
2. Shawcross, p. 239
3. Westminster Abbey Muniment, 58642C. By kind permission of the Dean and Chapter of Westminster
4. RA/QM/PRIV/CC/12
5. www.bbc.com/historyofthebbc/anniversaries/may/thomas-woodrooffe-at-the-coronation-fleet
6. RA/PS/PSO/GVI/PS/COR/1000/3/47
7. RA/EDW/PRIV/MAIN/A/3183,3244
8. Windsor, Wallis, p. 298
9. Bedell Smith, p. 305
10. Hardinge, p. 187
11. Acott Williams, p. 67
12. Acott Williams, p. 68
13. Bedell Smith, pp. 555–556

14. Maurice Fermoy, quoted in Bedell Smith, p. 558
15. RA QM/PRIV/CC/12
16. RA QM/PRIV/CC/12

Chapter Fifteen: 'My Whole Life'

1. Crawford, p. 80
2. Turner, p. 125
3. Turner, p. 56
4. Pope-Hennessy, p. 620
5. Channon, *The Diaries 1943–57*, p. 862
6. Hardman, p. 230
7. www.theguardian.com/theguardian/2012/feb/24/archive-1953-pardon-deserters-wwii
8. Vickers, p. 67
9. Vickers, p. 66
10. Brown, p. 144
11. Glenconner, p. 63
12. The Queen's horse Aureole came second in the 1953 Derby

Chapter Sixteen: Coronation Day 1953

1. Hardman, p. 194
2. Churchill was initially offered the Order of the Garter in 1945, shortly after losing the election. He reportedly said: 'I can hardly accept the Order of the Garter from the King, when the British people have given me the "Order of the Boot".'
3. Glenconner, p. 66
4. Hicks, p. 204
5. Hardman, p. 195
6. Shawcross, p. 468
7. Vickers, p. 90
8. A famous general during World War II, Dwight D. Eisenhower became the 34th president of the United States in 1953
9. Glenconner, p. 67

10. Hicks, p. 202
11. Glenconner, p. 68
12. Vickers, p. 78
13. Hutchinson, p. 35
14. Dunlop, p. 201
15. Tanner, p. 140
16. Hardman, p. 208
17. Hardman, p. 197
18. Tanner, p. 141
19. Glenconner, p. 61
20. Tanner, p. 141
21. Tanner, p. 150
22. Hardman, p. 198
23. Hutchinson, p. 40
24. Glenconner, p. 74
25. Vickers, p. 105
26. Glenconner, p. 77
27. Tanner, p. 151
28. Hardman, p. 311
29. Hicks, p. 205

Chapter Seventeen: Continuity

1. Vickers, p. 108
2. Vickers, p. 109
3. BBC documentary: *Charles III: The Coronation Year*
4. Morris, p. 7
5. BBC documentary: *Charles III: The Coronation Year*

Chapter Eighteen: A Smooth Transition

1. www.bbc.co.uk/news/uk-62862233
2. https://yougov.co.uk/politics/articles/43747-britons-first-impressions-king-charles-iii

3. Dimbleby, p. 642
4. Dimbleby, p. 642
5. Morris, p. 8
6. Morris, p. 10
7. Morris, p. 9
8. www.telegraph.co.uk/royal-family/2022/09/26/duke-norfolk-bids-avoid-driving-ban-role-organising-king-charless
9. Hardman, p. 231
10. www.theguardian.com/uk-news/2023/apr/25/simon-abney-hastings-15th-earl-of-loudon-australian-man-wangaratta-king-charles-coronation-great-golden-spurs
11. www.telegraph.co.uk/columnists/2023/02/21/pandering-woke-coronation-charles-begins-suicide-note
12. Hardman, p. 203
13. Hardman, p. 207
14. https://theweek.com/news/royals/960690/homage-of-the-people-should-public-pledge-allegiance-to-new-king
15. www.bbc.co.uk/news/uk-65493188
16. www.mirror.co.uk/news/royals/brits-wont-pay-homage-charles-29906842
17. www.telegraph.co.uk/money/consumer-affairs/king-charles-coronation-souvenirs-sell-seven-times-worth
18. BBC documentary: *Charles III: The Coronation Year*

Chapter Nineteen: Coronation Day 2023

1. www.bbc.co.uk/news
2. The Coronation Roll
3. www.independent.co.uk/life-style/royal-family/king-charles-coronation-westminster-abbey-b2333746.html
4. www.reuters.com/world/russia-belarus-iran-myanmar-not-invited-king-charles-coronation-uk-source-2023-05-02
5. Hardman, p. 284
6. Princess Anne interview with CNN

7. www.theguardian.com/uk-news/2023/may/07/king-charles-we-can-never-be-on-time-coronation-lip-reader
8. Lady Lansdowne, BBC documentary, *Charles III: The Coronation Year*
9. Hardman, p. 295
10. www.tatler.com/article/dress-worn-by-penny-mordaunt-in-starring-coronation-role-goes-on-display-in-the-house-of-commons
11. BBC documentary, *Charles III: The Coronation Year*
12. Hardman, p. 257
13. Annabel Elliot quoted in Hardman, p. 303
14. www.bbc.co.uk/news/uk
15. Hardman, p. 310

Chapter Twenty: Moving Forward

1. www.ipsos.com/en-uk/boost-personal-ratings-king-charles-and-prince-william-after-coronation-support-republic-also

Chapter Twenty-One: William and Catherine

1. Prince Harry, *Spare*
2. Hardman, p. 92
3. www.dailymail.co.uk/femail/article-14059041/Prince-William-hardest-year-Prince-Wales-cancer.html
4. Hardman, p. 379
5. https://theconversation.com/king-charles-inherits-crown-with-support-for-monarchy-at-record-low-but-future-not-set-in-stone-190448
6. Morris, p. 11
7. Morris, p. 12
8. www.theguardian.com/uk-news/2022/mar/25/william-and-kate-caribbean-tour-slavery-reparations-royals

BIBLIOGRAPHY

Beakon, Robert, *Cosmo Lang: Archbishop in War and Crisis*, I.B. Tauris, 2012

Bodley, J. E. C., *The Coronation of Edward VII,* Methuen & Co, 1911

Borman, Tracy, *Crown & Sceptre: 1000 Years of Kings and Queens*, Hodder & Stoughton, 2022

Brown, Craig, *A Voyage Around the Queen*, 4th Estate, 2024

Cannadine, David, *George V: The Unexpected King*, Penguin, 2014

Channon, Henry 'Chips', *The Diaries 1918–38*, ed. Simon Heffer, Penguin Random House, 2021

Channon, Henry 'Chips', *The Diaries 1943–57,* ed. Simon Heffer, Penguin Random House, 2022

Charlot, Monica, *Victoria, the Young Queen*, Blackwell, 1991

Crawford, Marianne, *The Little Princesses*, Odhams Press, 1952

Dimbleby, David, *Keep Talking: A Broadcasting Life*, Hodder & Stoughton, 2023

Dimbleby, Jonathan, *The Prince of Wales: A Biography*, Little Brown, 1994

Dunlop, Tessa, *Elizabeth and Philip*, Headline Publishing Group, 2022

Fremantle, Rev W. R., *God Save the Queen: A Sermon Preached in Godalming Church on occasion of the Coronation of our most Gracious Queen*, J. Nisbet & Co, 1838

Glenconner, Anne, *Lady in Waiting*, Hodder & Stoughton, 2019

Gosling, Lucinda, *Royal Coronations*, Shire Publications, 2013

Hardinge, Helen, *Loyal to Three Kings*, William Kimber, 1967

Hardman, Robert, *Charles III*, Macmillan, 2024

Hart-Davis, Duff (ed.), *King's Counsellor, Abdication and War: The Diaries of Sir Alan Lascelles*, Weidenfeld & Nicolson, 2006

Hibbert, Christopher, *Queen Victoria, A Personal History*, HarperCollins, 2000

Hicks, Pamela, *Daughter of Empire: Life as a Mountbatten*, Windsor Paragon, 2013

Jennings, Humphrey and Madge, Charles (eds.), *Mass-Observation Day Survey: May 12 1937*, Faber and Faber, 1987

Jobson, Robert, *The Windsor Legacy*, Blink Publishing, 2025

Larman, Alexander, *Power and Glory: Elizabeth II and the Rebirth of Royalty*, Weidenfeld & Nicolson, 2024

Larman, Alexander, *The Windsors at War*, Hachette, 2023

Longford, Elizabeth, *Queen Victoria*, Sutton Publishing, 2005 edition (first published 1999)

Lynn, Dame Vera, *Some Sunny Day*, HarperCollins, 2009

Marshall, Dorothy, *Lord Melbourne*, Weidenfeld & Nicolson, 1975

Marshall, Howard, *Coronation Day*, Hutchinson & Co Ltd, 1953

Martineau, Harriet, *Autobiography*, ed. Linda H. Peterson, Broadview Press, 2007

Morris, Dr Bob, *The Coronation of Charles III*, The Constitution Unit, University College London, 2022

Nicolson, Harold, *King George the Fifth: His Life and Reign*, Constable, 1952

Phillips, Adrian, *The King Who Had to Go*, Biteback Publishing Ltd, 2016

Pope-Hennessy, James, *Queen Mary: The Official Biography*, Hodder & Stoughton Ltd, 2019

Portland, Duke of, *Men, Women and Things: Memories of the Duke of Portland*, Faber & Faber, 1937

Priestley, J. B., *The Edwardians*, Sphere Books Ltd, 1972

Prince Harry, *Spare*, Penguin Random House, 2023

Queen Victoria's Coronation: The Form and Order of the service performed and ceremonies observed in The Coronation of Her Majesty Queen Victoria, Eyre and Spottiswoode, 1838

Ridley, Jane, *Bertie: A Life of Edward VII*, Vintage, 2013

Ridley, Jane, *George V: Never a Dull Moment*, Penguin Random House, 2021

Strachey, Lytton, *Queen Victoria*, Penguin, 1971

Strong, Roy, *Coronation: A History of the British Monarchy*, William Collins, an imprint of HarperCollins, 2022

Tanner, Lawrence E., *The History of the Coronation*, William Clowes & Sons Ltd, 1953

Tanner, Lawrence E., *Recollections of a Westminster Antiquary*, John Baker, 1969

Tinniswood, Adrian, *The Long Weekend: Life in the English Country House Between the Wars*, Jonathan Cape, 2016

Turner, Barry, *Thorns in the Crown*, The History Press, 2022

The Complete Ceremonies and Procedures observed at the Coronations of the Kings and Queens of England, Boot & Son, 1902

Shawcross, William (ed.), *Counting One's Blessings: The Selected Letters of Queen Elizabeth, The Queen Mother*, Macmillan, 2012

Vickers, Hugo, *Coronation: The Crowning of Elizabeth II*, The Dovecote Press, 2023

Williams, Claudia Acott, *Cecil Beaton, The Royal Portraits*, Thames & Hudson and the V&A, 2023

Williamson, David, *Kings & Queens*, National Portrait Gallery Publications, 2016

Wilson, A. N., *Victoria: A Life*, Atlantic Books, 2014

Windsor, Duke of, *A King's Story*, Pan Books, 1957

Windsor, Wallis, *The Heart has its Reasons*, Michael Joseph, 1956

Woolerton, June, *A History of British Royal Jubilees*, Pen & Sword Books Ltd, 2022

Worsley, Lucy, *Queen Victoria: Daughter, Wife, Mother, Widow*, Hodder & Stoughton, 2018

Young, G. M., *Portrait of an Age*, Phoenix Press, 1936

INDEX